Springer Texts in Business and Economics

For further volumes:
http://www.springer.com/series/10099

Sanjay Mohapatra

E-Commerce Strategy

Text and Cases

Springer

Sanjay Mohapatra
Xavier Institute of Management
Xavier Road
Bhubaneswar, Odisha 751013
India

ISSN 2192-4333 ISSN 2192-4341 (electronic)
ISBN 978-1-4614-4141-0 ISBN 978-1-4614-4142-7 (eBook)
DOI 10.1007/978-1-4614-4142-7
Springer New York Heidelberg Dordrecht London

Library of Congress Control Number: 2012939514

Printed on acid-free paper

Springer is part of Springer Science+Business Media (www.springer.com)

Dedicated to
Late Parmananda Mishra
Late Dr. Sushila Mishra
Dr. B. C. Mohapatra

Preface

This textbook is ideal for the E-Commerce class in an MBA program. It can also be used in senior undergraduate electives and for IT consultants and practitioners. The book has many strengths:

- Placing e-commerce in the historical context: a chronological events of evolution of e-commerce that provides the perspective on the rise and fall of dot-coms. The book analyzes the cause of the failures of dot-coms, provides a report card of the different sectors of e-commerce, and the challenges of the future.
- Unique topic coverage: the book covers topics not found in many competing books (e.g. open source, online research, m-commerce, peer-to-peer systems, socio-commerce, web 2.0). Some topics are also covered in much greater depth (e.g. e-channel adoption, factors affecting e-commerce adoption and strategy design, integration of e-commerce with social networking sites). New ideas are placed in the context of respected theories. Managerial frameworks are provided. The approach relies on information and theories from many disciplines. I have tried to integrate these different perspectives to create an integrative overview of the field.
- Case studies: this book presents both the positives and negatives of new ideas. In-depth case studies analyze well-known companies (i.e. Amazon.com, eBay). Rather than limiting the discussion to successes, cases also cover failures (e.g. Fabmall.com, Walmart.com). Unlike other books on the same topic, it illustrates cases from developing countries where e-commerce has strong potential.
- Learning objectives: Learning objectives appear at the beginning of each chapter and highlight the major goals to keep in mind while reading each chapter.
- Summaries: an executive summary is provided for each chapter. This is ideal for the busy student of today. Instructors can also peruse the summary to get a better idea of the contexts.
- Written with a practitioner's approach, this book can be utilized in a variety of courses in information systems, e-marketing, and management.

- The book is divided into two parts—Part I and Part II. Part I deals with fundamental concepts such as Web design technology, concepts of e-business, evolution of e-commerce, e-tailing, etc. which are part of the syllabi offered in most universities. Part II deals with e-commerce strategy, socio-commerce strategy, e-commerce distribution channel design strategy, role of stakeholders, adoption of e-commerce in small and medium enterprises. The chapters for Part I deal with fundamentals while the chapters for Part II deal with strategy.

Acknowledgments

The production of any book of this magnitude involves valued contributions from many persons. I would like to thank Amboy Matthew for providing us the editorial support and making this project a reality.

One chapter of the book has been contributed by Inma Rodríguez-Ardura, Antoni Meseguer-Artola, Jordi and Vilaseca-Requenaeed (Drivers of online-selling diffusion: a look at organizational and environmental factors through time). The undersigned acknowledges their contribution with gratitude as they took quite an effort to prepare the write-up for the book.

I would also like to thank Soumya Das from XIMB who has helped me in preparing contents on irctc.co.in. I would also like to place in records the help extended by Amrit Swain, Mani Tiwari, M Srikanth, Mainak Das, Nishith Sahu, and Piyush Panda while preparing the manuscript. I wish them fulfilling and rewarding careers. May God bless them all.

Asit Mahapatra, Commissioner of Income Tax has gone out of his way to provide a smooth passage for the contract with the publisher. The author acknowledges his efforts and wishes him Godspeed in all his endeavors.

Last but not the least, I would like to thank Dr. Bharati (my wife) for helping me in taking decisions at a critical stage of the manuscript.

Dr. Sanjay Mohapatra

Contents

Part I Fundamentals

Part I
Fundamentals

Chapter 1
Understanding E-Commerce

1.1 Learning Objectives

At the end of the chapter, the students would learn

Evolution of e-commerce
Role of technology in e-commerce
Internet and e-commerce

1.2 Introduction

Internet has changed the lifestyle. It has entrenched itself in every walk of life, be it sharing thoughts, social networking, playing online games, marketing and even buying and selling. Earlier consumers would consider going for window shopping; this was considered a recreation as well as a chance to meet with acquaintances. With virtual social networking available on mobiles, one of the most popular activities on the web is socializing and shopping. It has lots of attractions as we can shop at our leisure from the comfort of your home without the need to go through the traffic snarls.

History of e-commerce dates back to the year (1991) when the Internet was made available for commercial purposes. The start of the very old notion of "sell and buy", using computers, modems, and the Internet was the first step in evolution of e-commerce. E-commerce became possible in 1991 when the web sites were allowed to use Internet for business transactions. Since then thousands of businesses transactions have taken place through web sites. At first, the term e-commerce meant the process of execution of commercial transactions electronically with the help of the leading technologies such as electronic data

S. Mohapatra, *E-Commerce Strategy*, Springer Texts in Business and Economics,
DOI: 10.1007/978-1-4614-4142-7_1,

interchange (EDI) and electronic funds transfer (EFT). These technologies allowed users to exchange business information and carry out electronic transactions. Even though these technologies were made available in the late 1970s, still the commercial use for e-commerce happened quite late (in the 1990s). Initially, these technologies allowed companies to send and receive documents electronically.

As we go through the evolution of e-commerce, we find many factors that slowly started increasing confidence of consumers in using e-commerce. Initially, there was always fear of wrong usage of credit information. These fears were accentuated by the frauds that were detected when scores of online data were stolen. As a result, even though the Internet began to gain its popularity among the general public in 1994, it took quite some time to instill confidence among online users. After developing different security protocol such as HTTP, consumers started looking at online marketing option seriously. In addition to that, introduction of Digital Security through DSL allowed rapid access and a secured connection to the Internet. This additional security features in the Internet, which came into being around 1998, helped to increase traffic in the online marketing arena. Around the year 2000, a number of companies in the United States and Western Europe started their online marketing services through the World Wide Web. Because of introduction of new security features in the Internet, the meaning of the word e-commerce was changed. People began to define the term e-commerce as the process of purchasing of available goods and services over the Internet using secure connections and electronic payment services. This era came to be known as dot-com era.

1.3 The Dot-Com Era

With the dot-com collapse in 2000, the e-commerce world was shaken up. It led to the closure of many organizations that thrived on online business only. These unfortunate results saw many of e-commerce companies disappeared. But many traditional “brick and mortar” retailers recognized the advantages of electronic commerce and began to add such capabilities to their web sites. For example, Fabmart (www.fabmart.com, later on it was renamed as India Plaza) came into existence and became the first generation e-commerce portal to provide service. In spite of ‘dotcom’ burst, the e-commerce sales continued to grow in the next few years and, by the end of 2007, e-commerce sales accounted for 3.4 % of total sales.

E-commerce has a great deal of advantages over “brick and mortar” stores and customers prefer e-commerce over tele orders. While in e-commerce site, the consumers can easily search through a large database of products and services. They can see actual prices, build an order over several days and e-mail it as a “wish list” hoping that someone will pay for their selected goods. Customers can compare prices with a click of the mouse and buy the selected product at best prices. They can add to their cart and decide to come back later on to buy. Online vendors, in their turn, also get distinct advantages. The web and its search engines provide a way to be found by customers without expensive advertising campaign.

Even small online shops can reach global markets. Web technology also allows to track customer preferences and to deliver individually tailored marketing.

1.4 Amazon.Com: Synonymous with E-Commerce

History of e-commerce is unthinkable without Amazon and eBay which were among the first Internet companies to allow electronic transactions. Thanks to their founders we now have a handsome e-commerce sector and enjoy the buying and selling advantages of the Internet. Currently, the largest and most famous worldwide Internet retailers are Amazon, Dell, Staples, and Hewlett Packard. According to statistics, the most popular categories of products sold in the World Wide Web are music, books, computers, office supplies, and other consumer electronics. We have been using amazon.com for buying different goods as it is one of the early adopter of e-commerce and has become top of the mind recall. It is the most famous e-commerce companies and is located in Seattle, Washington (USA). It was founded in 1994 by Jeff Bezos and was one of the first American e-commerce companies to sell products over the Internet. After the dot-com collapse, there was a period where the business model which was only based on e-commerce, was questioned. It lost its reputation as a successful company, but within some time, it bounced back. In 2003, the company made its first annual profit which was the first step to the further development.

At the outset, Amazon.com started its operations with sale of books only. It was considered as an online bookstore, but as time passed by it increased the volume of operations and offered a variety of goods by adding electronics, software, DVDs, video games, music CDs, MP3 s, apparel, footwear, health products, etc. Amazon started its operations by the name Cadabra.com. It increased its volume and revenue in no time and became a popular web site for many. After it become popular in the e-commerce model with large volume of transactions, its founder Bezos rechristened it as "Amazon". The name was to signify the increase in transaction volume similar to that of world's most voluminous river. Time magazine even declared the founder Jeff Bezos as the Person of the Year in 1999. The company was registered in the USA and very soon it started its operations in other countries as well. For each country, to take care of logistics, Amazon set up separate web sites in other economically developed countries such as the United Kingdom, Canada, France, Germany, Japan, and China. During its expansion, it started special services that offered products and services from Marks & Spencer, Lacoste, the NBA, Bebe Stores, Target, etc.

Apart from offering products from Marks & Spencer etc., Amazon started relationship marketing with other business partners through affiliate marketing programs. Using these affiliate programs, Amazon displays goods from these affiliate partners, and sells them through designated logistics partners. This helped increase volume and revenue for Amazon, affiliate partners, and logistics partners. In 2011, the company gets about 40 % of its sales from affiliates and third-party sellers who list and sell goods on the web site. Apart from the affiliate partners, Amazon has started sponsoring cinema and partnering in their distribution.

According to the research conducted in 2010, the number of customers for Amazon.com has reached about 900 million customers. The web site allows its customers to write reviews about the products that they buy. The customers can write about the quality, price, delivery and then rate the product based on total buying experience. This review system has become the most popular feature of the web site as it enables the visitors to submit their reviews and rate any product on a rating scale from one to five. This increases transparency and has helped Amazon.com to be known for its clear and user-friendly features. It also allows advanced search facility which enables visitors to search for products using keywords.

1.5 Dell: An Evolutionary E-Commerce

One more company which has contributed much to the process of e-commerce development is Dell Inc. This is a company that changed the characteristics of personal computer (PC) industry. The company was incorporated in Texas, changed the way PCs were being sold earlier. The change was done through adoption of e-commerce business model.

The PC industry as seen today has changed over the years. These were the works of innovators who had radical thoughts. In the early 1980s, innovators such as Stephen Jobs of Apple Computer and Michael Dell of Dell Inc. changed the personal computer industry. Both had the same simple idea that PCs needed to be simpler. However, both had different approaches and went about the task in different ways. Stephen Jobs simplified the computer itself by inventing the Apple Macintosh with its easy point-and-click instructions. Dell did something different but equally interesting. He did not simplify the manufacturing process, but simplified the process of selling PCs. Stephen Jobs revolutionized the product and created a new model as to how PCs would be made in the future. Dell modified the distribution channel and influenced how PCs would be sold in the future.

Stephen Jobs and his friends built computers from scratch. On the other hand, Dell did not build computers; rather he assembled them from parts in his college dorm room. This perspective allowed him to come up with a new and powerful concept—*customized product configuration.* He had the idea that since the quality of different parts were basically the same, and there was hardly any differentiating factor, he thought that there would be value in buying a bunch of parts *and* then customize to suit the needs of an individual consumer.

As the business model of selling customized products slowly stabilized, customers thoroughly enjoyed the process as they were part of the customization process. The involvement ensured that these customers came back to Dell again and again and over a period of time, returning prospects navigated through thousands of possible PC system combinations available for sale. By applying this concept to the selling process, Dell understood customer needs, learned how to translate what the customer wanted, was able to offer better configuration by using customer designed PCs, and also developed search engines that allowed prospects to zero in products based on the price, RAM memory as well as based on usage. All these happened in plain English rather than technical language. The prospects as well as customers reveled at being able to own a product that they felt was best for them and it generated a lot of discussions among peer group and subsequent product recommendation to others for customized computer built just for them. Dell made it easier for the average person without a technical degree to select and buy personal computers. All these happened without a physical product sitting in a store, which reduced the administrative cost and without the help of an expensive channels and sales representatives. All these reduced the operating expenses for Dell.

In practice, this meant that Dell could sell PCs over the phone and Internet while other organizations were still using traditional channels such as expensive field salespeople and retail stores. To make this happen, they laid out options in a print catalog so customers could see the choices they had. They also used software to find the cost of the customization and add-ons on the fly while browsing. Finally, the representatives from call center would call the prospects and close the deal. And Dell used a new technology—the "fax back"—to immediately sends proposals back to the prospects at the push of a button. Soon, Dell's selling costs were at one-third of the cost of the competitors. This became a significant gap in a business where margins were shrinking, as the price of personal computers continued to drop in the wake of the low-cost Apple product line and Dell could transfer the margin to customers by reducing the price. This started a price war and the competitors had a tough time in maintaining their profitability.

Dell used new software called "product configuration software" that automated this process of product selection which helped to adapt the PC for sale through Internet. This new business enabling software allowed different combinations of parts which made thousands of customizations a possibility. This could not have been possible through manual process. It also calculates the money that the prospect has to pay for the customization that he has chosen and gives recommendation. This acts as an intelligent system using previous customization database as well as expert knowledge to suggest the best possible customization.

This phenomenon brought in factors such as integration of customers in the supply chain. Their needs were available in terms of customization, which helped Dell to reposition their products and also price them accordingly. Dell was the first PC manufacturer to classify their products such as products for home and personal division, office division, etc. This helped to develop products for each category separately and improve it further. The satisfied customers talked about their experience to others in their peer circle and created excitements among others. Not only these discussion forums became marketing platforms, the brand name also became top of the mind brand giving Dell the mileage. In traditional marketing approach, Dell would have spent thousands of dollars to achieve this top of the mind recall brand.

Armed with these tools, Dell began to sell computers over the Internet in 1996 and was soon averaging- over a million dollars in online sales a day. By the turn of the century they were doing over $13 billion in sales online a year—half of their total sales. This focus on making products ready for technology-enabled channels helped Dell to grow faster for less money. By automating marketing processes that were repetitive and involved manual intervention, Dell could sell its products through low-cost web channels. Within a period of 5 years, Dell was growing at twice the rate as the rest of the industry and became the number-one seller of PCs in the United States.

Launched in 1994 as a static page, Dell.com has made rapid strides, and by the end of 1997 was the first company to record a million dollars through e-commerce sales. The company's unique strategy of selling goods over the World Wide Web without using the standard supply chain partners, with no retail outlets and no middlemen has been accepted as a 'best practice' in the industry. The key factor of Dell's success is that Dell.com enables customers to configure a product based on their choice and budget. They can browse the site and assemble PCs piece by piece choosing each single component based on their budget and requirements. Fortune magazine has ranked Dell as the 34th largest company in the Fortune 500 list (year 2007). This shows that e-commerce business model could transform Dell as one of the most successful and admired companies in the USA in recognition of the company's business model.

As we progress to the next decade, we are sure to see many more organizations adopting the virtual world approach through e-commerce which will evolve according to customer demand. Evolution of e-commerce world will enable secure foundations for the future generations.

1.6 What is E-Commerce?

E-commerce is a short version of the term Electronic Commerce. It implies transactions related to online buying and selling of products or services. These transactions are done using electronic systems such as the Internet and other computer networks. The volume of these types of transactions (which have been conducted electronically) has grown exponentially. The penetration and spread of the Internet has fueled such expansion. Nowadays, a wide variety of business transactions are conducted in this way, such as electronic funds transfer, supply chain management, Internet marketing, online transaction processing, EDI, inventory management systems, and automated data collection systems. Thus, the definition of e-commerce in modern the modern times implies that a transaction is termed as electronic commerce if it typically uses the World Wide Web at least at any point in the transaction's lifecycle. This means e-commerce can encompass a wider range of technologies such as e-mail as well.

In web sites, such as Gartner.com and Forrester.com, make their basic contents available for free. However, for premium contents, they charge an amount and fee needs to be paid to download such premium contents. Such payments, which are made using one's credit or debit card, is also part of e-commerce definitions. Thus, in addition to transactions that involve transportation of physical items using logistics partners, any transaction that involves money transfer through online portals is called e-commerce. Online retailers are sometimes known as e-tailers and online retail is sometimes known as e-tail. In the present economy almost all big retailers have electronic commerce presence through Internet.

E-commerce that is conducted between businesses is referred to as Business-to-business or B2B. B2B can be of two types—(1) open to the entire public or (2) limited to a group of businesses who have been part of the specific group and are prequalified participants (private electronic market). Electronic commerce is generally considered to be the sales aspect of e-commerce. It also consists of the exchange of data to facilitate the financing and payment aspects of the business transactions. Traditional buying and selling processes require physical buying and selling of products and services. This means buyers have to be physically present in the store or at the selling point to buy the goods. However, with e-commerce the business model has changed. E-commerce can be classified according to the transaction partners and these can be business-to-consumer (B2C), business-to-business (B2B), business-to-government (B2G), consumer-to-consumer (C2C), and consumer-to-business (C2B). Within these broad categories, there are a number of variations in the way the models are implemented. Many traditional brick and mortar retailers such as Barnes & Noble are now e-tailers with a web storefront. These combined brick and mortar/online businesses are also known as *brick-and-click* companies.

Some B2C e-commercees provide high-value content to consumers for a subscription fee. Examples of e-commerce following this subscription model include the *Wall Street journal* (financial news and articles), *Consumer Reports* (product reviews and evaluations), and *eDiets.com* (nutritional counseling). B2C e-commerce models include virtual malls, which are Web sites that host many online merchants. Virtual malls typically charge online merchants setup, listing, or transaction fees and may include transaction handling services and marketing options. Examples of virtual malls include *excite.com, choiceMall.com, women.com, networkweb.com, amazon.com, Zshops.com,* and *yahoo.com*.

Today, B2B and B2C e-commerce models are being talked about which use electronic medium for transactions. Electronic markets are emerging in various fields. Different industries have markets with different characteristics. For example, an information B2C market differs in many respects from the automotive B2B market. The former represents companies that sell digital information goods, such as news, articles, music, books, or digital videos. In the information B2C market, the electronic infrastructure not only helps match customers and sellers, but also acts as the distribution channel, delivering products to customers. In this case, the infrastructure, such as servers and networks, must support the delivery of large files, streaming media, and other types of digital goods in an efficient way. This B2C market over the Internet can be viewed as an open system, where the number of participants is unknown. In the automotive B2B market, the products traded have a high degree of specificity, such as parts and components of cars. The market infrastructure used to be mainly based on EDI over expensive VAN services. EDI involves the exchange of standardized, structured information between organizations, permitting direct communication between computer systems. Now, the automotive B2B market is using the Internet for many of its activities.

At the heart of B2B applications is the strong integration of different applications. Servers, networks, and software should provide the infrastructure to integrate Web-based applications with mainframe and legacy systems. B2B is also a closed market in the sense that the number of participants involved in trading is limited and known a priori. Understanding the nature of the market's requirements is critical for creating the underlying e-commerce infrastructure. The relation between B2B and B2C models is clearly shown in Fig. 2. B2B covers business transactions along the various interactions existing in the value chain from producers of raw materials to retailers, including manufacturers and distributors. On the other hand, B2C reflects only the interactions between a customer and a retailer. Basically, B2C transactions include the following steps. (i) account acquisition, (ii) product discovery through search and browse, (iii) price negotiation, (iv) payment, and (v) product delivery. In some cases, dispute resolution and customer services may also exist.

1.7 The Changing Times in E-Commerce

The meaning of e-commerce has changed over the last three decades. Originally, e-commerce started with exchange of commercial transactions electronically, using technology such as EDI and Electronic Funds Transfer (EFT). These technologies, in 1970s, allowed businesses to share different documents like bill of materials, warehouse receipts, purchase orders or invoices electronically. In 1980s, the advent of technology in banking systems introduced new products such as Automated teller machines (ATMs). This along with growth and acceptance of credit cards, and telephone banking became part of e-commerce. From the next decade i.e., in 1990s all enterprise-wide systems added e-commerce capabilities. As a result 'Enterprise resource planning systems' (ERP), data mining, and data warehousing included e-commerce features in their portals.

1.7.1 Growth of Internet

With the growth Internet, role of e-commerce changed. In the early years, e-commerce was considered to be an aid to the business. Later on, it became a strategic tool for organizations. As Internet became more penetrative (meaning making its presence felt in all business processes), many experts, journalists, and pundits forecast that e-commerce would soon become a major economic sector.

However, it took about 4 years for security protocols (like HTTPS) to become sufficiently developed and widely deployed. Subsequently, between 1998 and 2000, a substantial number of businesses in the United States and Western Europe developed rudimentary web sites. In the dot-com era, electronic commerce came to include activities more precisely termed "Web commerce"—the purchase of goods and services over the World Wide Web, usually with secure connections with e-shopping carts and with electronic payment services such as credit card payment authorizations.

The emergence of electronic commerce also significantly lowered barriers to entry in the selling of many types of goods; many small home-based proprietors are able to use the Internet to sell goods. Often, small sellers use online auction sites such as eBay or sell via large corporate web sites like Travel agencies had to close their shops as their business models did not become profitable anymore. E-commerce based applications made travel easier as travelers could book through the comfort of their home without having to pay any commission to the agents. This reduced total cost of travel and in turn increased by almost 20 % in the year 2010 (Indian travel data).

1.7.2 Chronological Events

1990	First web browser introduced by Tim Berners-Lee
1994	Mozilla browser is launched by Netscape
	Pizza Hut enables pizza ordering through Internet
	Banks offered their services online
	Many web sites offered to accept orders and deliver flowers to the customers
	Magazine subscriptions were offered through online
	SSL encryptions were introduced that made transactions secure
1995	Amazon.com was fully operational through e-commerce model. Jeff Bezos was the founder
	Live streaming of radio stations were launched viz. Radio HK and NetRadio started broadcasting
	Dell and Cisco began to aggressively use Internet for commercial transactions
	eBay was founded by computer programmer Pierre Omidyar as a virtual auction site
1998	In the USA, electronic postal stamps can be purchased and downloaded for printing from the government site
1999	For the first time peer-to-peer file sharing software Napster was launched
2000	The (unfortunate) dot-com bust
2003	For the first time Amazon.com reported profit after breaking even

All these events increased the role of e-commerce. More and more business applications were involved in e-commerce. Business applications such as 'E-mail and messaging', 'Documents, spreadsheets', 'database', 'Accounting and finance systems', 'Orders and shipment information', 'Enterprise and client information reporting' and 'Domestic and international payment systems'.

1.7.2.1 Government Regulations

Internet Tax Freedom Act, instituted in 1998, helped to consolidate taxation burden on e-commerce companies. In the United States alone, some 30,000 taxing jurisdictions could otherwise have laid claim to taxes on a piece of the Internet. The law, however, did not affect sales taxes applied to online purchases. Even if the rates of taxations are different, the enactment of this legislation has coincided with the beginning of a period of spectacular Internet growth. Its proponents argue that the benefits of knowledge, trade, and communications that the Internet is bringing to more people in more ways than ever before are worth the tax revenue losses, if any, and that the economic and productivity growth attributable to the Internet may well have contributed more revenues to various governments than would otherwise have been received. Opponents, on the other hand, have argued that the Internet would continue to prosper even if taxed, and that the current federal ban on Internet-specific levies denies government at all levels a much needed source of revenue.

With increase in the volume and closure of many organizations because of Dot-com burst, the Government decided to put regulations in place so as to avoid a similar situation later on. With the impact of Dotcom burst being the maximum in the United States, the federal government decided to regulate electronic commerce activities. A commission was instituted named as Federal Trade Commission (FTC). The scope of their jurisdiction included activities such as the use of commercial e-mails, online advertising, and consumer privacy. An act named 'The CAN-SPAM Act' of 2003 was established to develop national standards for using e-mails for direct marketing. The Act had the intentions to regulate all forms of online advertising, including e-mail promotions so that advertising must be truthful and non-deceptive. Using its authority under Section 5 of the FTC Act, which prohibits unfair or deceptive practices, the FTC has been successful in preventing unlawful advertisement practices. It has been able to make different companies to change the corporate privacy statements such that the end-consumers could get a real picture of the company's intentions and involvements in different matters. These statements also provided degree of liability of the companies in maintaining confidentiality of customers' information. At present, any corporate privacy policy related to e-commerce activity may be subject to enforcement by the FTC.

1.8 Present Scenario

Online marketing has become a craze as well as necessity. It has given convenience in marketing and has been a remarkable experience. It has increased market potential of products and services tat could not have been achieved through traditional shopping. It is so much better than any other way of shopping that it has already attracted many users. Initially, it was a buzz word, now it has become the order of the day. People seem to shop literally everywhere—at their workplaces during lunch times, in rush hour when there is nothing else to do but switch on their laptops and start buying. E-commerce today gained so much popularity because technologies being used are user-friendly and customer oriented. With time, the technologies are evolving at giant steps. We are even offered to "feel" the product with a 3D technology so that we can better understand its shape, size, and texture. This new technology will make the experience of online still better. In fact, it will address the challenge that e-commerce faces today that customers can not 'feel' the products before buying. This will increase the customer base, because there will be no need to go to the physical stores and waste time in traffic, waiting in the queue at the payment counters. Even stocks that may not be available physically can be purchased online. All the online orders will be delivered at your door step.

1.9 Future of E-Commerce

E-commerce today offers so much luxury that growth of sales through physical stores has declined compared to that of online marketplace. Although, it will be a long way for an e-commerce to replace "brick-and-mortar" stores, still it has every chance to happen in the future. E-commerce which we are witnessing today brings in so much adventure into our lives that it is enjoyed by the whole online community. However, there are challenges that e-commerce needs to overcome. Different researchers predict a promising and glorious future of e-commerce in the coming years. In the foreseeable future, e-commerce will establish itself as a major tool of sale. With investment in Internet, success of e-commerce will depend on the ability to provide uninterrupted, secured Internet connections to the larger population. This will make e-shopping more and more popular and natural. At the same time severe rivalry in the sphere of e-commerce services will intensify their development. Thus, prevailing future trends of e-commerce will be the growth of Internet sales and evolution.

Each year number of e-commerce deals has grown substantially. Sales volumes of online stores are more than comparable with those of "brick-and-mortar" ones. Marketing through Internet saves a lot of time and gives opportunity to choose goods at the best prices. Present day Internet sales boom is the foundation for magnificent e-commerce future. The "quantity to quality" perception of e-commerce attracts more and more buyers. While the sites that offer guaranteed quality will attract more buyers, other sites which do not provide such assurance may have less consumer base. For example, www.valyoo.in site offers 'fourteen days no question asked' policy for the products purchased through online marketplace from its site. This instills confidence that if the product is not liked by the consumers, he can return the same without any hassles. With better quality assurance, and as the Internet has excluded geographic factor from the sale, e-commerce will increase the customer base. So, it does not matter if the store is situated in New Delhi or Lucknow or in a small town, customers can access the required information anywhere. To survive, merchants will have to adapt rapidly to the new conditions. To attract more customers, e-store owners will have not only to increase the number of available services, but to pay more attention to such elements like attractive design, user-friendliness, appealing goods presentation, and provide assurance on products. They will also have to employ modern technologies for their businesses to become successful in e-commerce on the long run.

To become successful in the future, many factors decide the sustainability in e-commerce. As we will see in the case of Wal-mart, previous experience in physical store does not guarantee anything. Only an appropriate e-commerce solution in combination with thorough e-marketing and advertising can buy you business insurance.

1.10 Constituents of E-Commerce

The most important component of e-commerce based firm is the web site. The web site should have technology that will make it easier for its customers to navigate and find the merchandize that they are looking for. The site should offer every single feature necessary to run a fully functional and successful e-commerce web site. The site should have a good web site, stable server for hosting it and provide customer specific services. The firm also should have technology partners who constantly upgrade the features as well as technology. The up gradation will help business partners such as logistics partners and suppliers to share and exchange business data with each other seemingly.

There are many organizations who offer these components as services who want to run e-commerce business. The following sections illustrate the services provided by these consultants

1.10.1 E-Commerce Design Services

Look and feel of a web site is quite important. Many times the customers get attracted to web site because of graphical user interface (GUI). They judge a web site by its appearances, the way information have been arranged and presented.

The web site should have the appeal as well as the information required for the customers based on their past purchasing history, desires and preferences.

1.10.1.1 E-Commerce Hosting

With the rising growth of the Internet, businesses are using e-commerce models to widen their horizons into new markets, to create new opportunities, and new challenges. The Internet raises a multitude of opportunities for online businesses to succeed. However, setting up and hosting a web site is not as simple as it seems. It is imperative that the sites are focused and functional, easy to use and deliver quality information.

The Internet is powerful and ubiquitous enough to allow the smallest of businesses to access markets. It helps to develop a presence that allows them to compete against the giants in the industry. Moreover, the hosting site should offer reliability, availability, and scalability along with information security so that the buyers do not hesitate to share their financial information.

A firm has two options while deciding for hosting. It can have the server placed in its own premises or have the server hosted at an outside location. In the first option, it needs to have its team of technicians who will have to manage the technicalities of hosting a server. Of late the second option has been used considerably as firms want to focus on their core business rather than wasting time on technicalities. They would like to outsource the same to third party. Small business and start ups usually take this approach. Most small and mid-size online businesses are not capable of hosting their own sites in-house. The cost of running an in-house development department and data center is too expensive. That is why these small companies look to companies specializing in web hosting. There are many e-commerce hosting companies who offer their clients 'customized and quality services enabling' by providing different services. This allows a startup to gain an online web presence quickly and inexpensively. These professional web hosting providers allow many customers to take advantage of economies of scale: operation of large data centers. Cost savings are passed along on everything from hardware, software licenses, bandwidth, backup systems, and environmental control systems. The web site hosting should have guaranteed 99 % uptime, e-mail accounts, reliability and support for providing integration with other technologies.

1.11 E-Commerce Web Design

It is of great importance that an e-commerce web site design produces a favorable impression on potential clients and existing customers and helps to generate actual sales. The web designers should make sure that the web e-commerce design is of an outstanding quality, has commercial appeal and every expectation of your target audience. There are so many ways to portray an e-commerce design. Someone likes it simple, while others—sophisticated. Some prefer an adventurous design, while others—conventional. However, despite this, the e-commerce web site design should be charismatic, customer winning and captivating in look and feel in order to be up to and above par. The design professionals should provide good artistic creativity, vivid imagination and perfect understanding of the needs to produce a web site, which is loved both by all.

1.11.1 E-Commerce Development

The Internet has a great deal to offer to any business be it small, medium or large. It provides a flexible and dynamic marketplace for exchanging products, services, and information. It creates plenty of opportunity to reach local and global markets and gain worldwide brand recognition. The Internet is also a powerful tool which can bring revenues if used wisely. E-commerce development is an efficient way of promoting businesses, bringing in handsome profits and delivering better services. Web site development is the core of the entire e-commerce development process and requires team efforts, considerable knowledge and skills.

For developing e-commerce web site, a firm can use its in-house resources or outsource the activities to another organization. The development should have experience and expertise to develop professional and state-of-the-art e-commerce web sites. They should follow all new development methodology and trends in the e-commerce development field and build the web site utilizing the latest methods and techniques. In addition to developing the e-commerce web site, they should provide innovative solutions to meet customer needs. The site developed should provide low entry cost and provide 'ease of use' to its customers.

1.11.2 Marketing E-Commerce Portal

Many people believe that an eye-catching e-commerce design and a professional backend programing is more than enough. However, this is a fundamental error committed by many "fresh" web site owners. E-commerce marketing involves writing a piece of code that will help it in obtaining high rankings on the major search engines, attract customers, and be able to make sales. At first, some web site owners may ignore the importance of an e-commerce marketing campaign. However, sooner or later they do realize that it is an intrinsic factor of the e-commerce web site development process.

1.12 E-Commerce Portal and Web 2.0—Future Trend

Web 2.0 has been a revolution in the present times and has opened up many avenues. All forms of business activities have been impacted by web 2.0. For e-commerce, anyone doing business online requires that the executives understand the power of web 2.0 and collaborate with that. The collaboration becomes a mutual touch point for all the stakeholders such as executives, its business partners and customers. This helps in aggregating information about people, products, and services and can be used for designing new products and services. It also reduces time spent searching resources for information, eliminates redundant data thus reducing the overload of information. Information thus available has increased relevance, delivering key information to places where it can be used effectively, and alerting recipients to its presence and availability.

1.12.1 Web 2.0

Web 2.0 refers primarily to the way people use the Internet—using thin client for connecting to the Internet (this process is also known as computing) and peer-to-peer user-generated and shared contents. The web portal, which uses web 2.0 techniques, plays a pivotal role in gathering, storing and sharing the information. Web 2.0 uses thin clients so that data and applications are stored on web server. A user has to have access to these data (usually a user has to go through a registration process); he can access these data and information from any computer by using a web browser. All the applications to store the data and then retrieve it from the database are executed in the server, thus, turning the web into a gigantic application server.

As an example, Google Apps is a collection of Google applications and utilities offered as a package. Some of these applications are free while others are used after paying for the applications. In 2007, Google combined its e-mail, instant messaging, calendar, word processing, spreadsheet, and web authoring applications along with administration utilities into Standard and Premier Editions. These editions were made available either as free or premium editions. The popularity of these editions came from the fact that these were developed and modified by persons using them. Google used this concept of offering web based applications (with technical support) to improve networking, storing, sharing and simultaneous updating by several users at a time. Google used the 'thin client computing concept' to compete with the office software arena from Microsoft's Office suites. The significant difference is that Google Applications are web-based. Without installing this software on their local notebook, the users can access these office applications (such as word processor, spreadsheet, etc.) through the Google portal.

Web 2.0 also stores and shares user-generated contents (UGC). These contents can vary from digital video, blogging, podcasting, news, gossip, research, mobile phone photography and experience. These are uploaded to social networking sites like MySpace, Facebook and Flickr. UGC lets everyone have their say on anything and publish it to the world at large. This is made possible through Web application services, a standardized way of integrating Web-based applications using the XML (Extensible Markup Language), SOAP, WSDL (Web Services Description Language) and UDDI (Universal Description Discovery and Integration) open standards. These are then published over an Internet protocol backbone. XML is used to tag the data, SOAP is used to transfer the data, WSDL is used for describing the services available, and UDDI is used for listing what services are available.

Internet application techniques such as Ajax, Adobe Flash, Flex, Java, and Silverlight have the potential to improve the user experience in browser-based applications. These technologies allow a web page to request an update for some part of its content, and to alter that part in the browser, without needing to refresh the whole page at the same time. This allows simultaneous update from different users at different sections without the need to shut down the page for updating. Ajax (Asynchronous JavaScript and XML) is a group of interrelated Web development techniques used for creating interactive Web applications. A primary Ajax characteristic is the increased responsiveness and interactivity of Web pages achieved by exchanging small amounts of data with the server "behind the scenes" so that the entire Web page does not have to be reloaded each time the user performs an action. This increases the Web page's interactivity, speed, functionality and usability. Portlets ("gadgets," "widgets," "Web parts," "mini-apps," etc.) are specialized content areas that occupy small windows on portal pages—e.g., weather info, news flashes, stock tickers, etc. Java Specification Request (JSR) 168 standards enable portal developers, administrators and consumers to integrate standards-based portals and portlets across a variety of vendor solutions. As Web applications within a browser window, displayed in an effective layout, portlets are aggregated by the portal page.

1.12.2 Changing Role of Web 2.0

Web 2.0 has two main components (i) thin client computing and (ii) user-generated content. The web portal plays a pivotal role in both the areas. In thin client computing, data and applications are stored on Web servers, and a user has access from any computer via a Web browser. This implies that the server becomes a gigantic web application server and all the transactions happen at one place. This helps in accumulation of data related to interactions, preferences and social network. Good e-commerce portals usually have all of the characteristics and capabilities of consumer Web 2.0 techniques, such as dynamic usability (Ajax, drag-and-drop, simultaneous updating), tagging, simpler user experiences and tools, peer-to-peer user driven capabilities and experiences.

According to University of Washington's School of Business, portals come in three basic varieties,

1.12.2.1 Horizontal Portals

Google (www.google.com), Yahoo (www.yahoo.com), MSN(msn.com), and AOL (aol.com) are known as horizontal portals. These sites provide gateway access to the Internet's other sites which supply vast store of content and services. They also provide tool bars that help in locating information in different web sites. These tool bars communicate with other similar tools and exchange information. These portals also help develop online communities which have similar interest. They make money through advertising and transaction fees from multiple vertical solutions channels.

1.12.2.2 Vertical Portals

Different portals like justdial.com and sulekha.com provide detailed content and information on different areas. They provide information related to conducting business while providing entertainment, shopping opportunities and developing online communities. These portals are often composed of a variety of business models, all of which generate separate revenue streams. They also generate advertising and referral fees. If transactions are not completed online, then these portals generate referral fees and if transactions are completed online, then they earn commission on these business transactions. The users get benefited as they get to know information at one place.

1.12.2.3 Affinity Portals

Portals are known as affinity portals if they provide specific contents for their target group. Web sites such as pantaloon.com, futurebazaar.com provide specific information to their customers. Similarly, carwale.com and cardekho.com provide information related to its products and can be termed as affinity portals. These portals usually provide required information related to its products, cost and other financial terms and conditions and community features but these offerings are targeted toward a specific market segment or even a specific gender. The revenue model is similar to vertical portals, with cost and asset models based on the business model adopted by the portal.

It is predicted that more than 80 % of the households will be using Internet in India by the year 2014. As a result, portals and content sites will be forced to compete for market share and attracting customers by experimenting with broadband-oriented technologies such as Flash-based home pages and customized really simple syndication (RSS) feeds.

1.13 E-Business and E-Commerce Web Portals

Nowadays, it has been a practice to offer all the information related to an organization through web portals. E-business refers to web portals used for providing information on the organization and also it may cover internal business systems such as CRM, ERP, HR, etc. These systems can be integrated with e-mail, voice mail, VoIP, content management, business process management, and e-commerce. This integration can be used for transmitting funds, goods, services and/or data between businesses (B2B) or between the business and its retail customers (B2C).

Web 2.0 technologies have gone one step further and have been used for increasing the depth of business offered by these sites. The technology (web 2.0) helps to create web based communities, and services such as social networking capabilities, wikis, blogs, etc. These are aimed at facilitating creativity, collaboration, and peer-to-peer sharing among users. Using new technologies such as Ajax, Adobe, Flash, Flex, and Java, the organizations have been able to improve the user experience through web based applications. RSS feeds from news sites, blogs, wikis, and enterprise applications send information to the recipients' mobile devices, e-mail clients and desktops.

Web 2.0 has greatly impacted the e-business role of e-commerce. With this technology, sales of goods and services through online transactions have satisfying experiences. Through this technology, when before an order is placed by the buyer online, price and terms of sale are negotiated over the Internet. During these online transactions, data are passed onto relevant players such as supplier, bankers that have issued credit cards and logistics partners. These data transfer are usually done through EDI network, electronic mail or other online integrated systems. These web sites aggregate data from a large number of players and store this information for future decision making process. Using these stored data, these sites can even suggest what customers should buy.

"The portal (now) becomes a composite front end that integrates disaggregated services into a coherent, fluid user experience," wrote Simeon Simeonov in *E-Commerce 2.0—The Velvet Revolution.*

1.13.1 Variety of Portals

The world of consumer e-commerce provides a range of e-commerce portals. Some of the well known portals are: merchandise retailers like shoebazaar.com, indiatimes.com, ndtvshopping.com, sifyonline.com, Wal-Mart, HomeDepot, Kroger, Costco, and Target, with their extensive logistics and supply chains, all have brick-n-click, dot-com online presences. Vertical affinity service providers like iVillage and WebMD offer a shopping component on their Web sites. The big Web-only shopping portalsinclude eBay, Amazon.com, BizRate.com, MySimon.com, yahoo.com, Shopping, NexTag.com, Overstock.com, Shopping.com, Pricerunner.com, PricingCentral.com, MSNShopping, Shop.com, and Shopzilla.

All these portals have adopted Web 2.0 technologies. For example, APIs from eBay facilitate buyer to seller auction management; Amazon provides a set of retail APIs that allow developers to create computer programs that make use of Amazon's online retail infrastructure. Third-party software developers have used this to create customized applications for their own use. The eBay portal has offered the eBay API through open source. This will enable developers to communicate directly with the eBay database in XML (extensible markup language) format. eBay gets benefits as it does not have to develop separate software for integration with these web sites. The eBay also uses web 2.0 for creating feedback forums, chat rooms, discussion boards, and sharing news related to products and services. It allows members to offer their own expertise on different topics. The eBay Blogs lets members create their own blogs to promote their businesses, discuss favorite topics, products, and provide constructive feedback to improve quality of services.

Amazon launched Amazon Web Services (AWS) in 2002. The service provides access to source code, backend software development processes. By getting access to these services, software developers, Web site owners and merchants have collectively developed many applications that have made eBay improve its site with rich features. These collectively developed features have made online auction at eBay a memorable one. Using these approaches, in 2008, AWS also teamed up with Facebook to form teams of developers, who would build customized applications. These customized applications would help in scaling up the operations for Facebook as well as Amazon. Using these applications, customers in Amazon's online community can personalize web pages, provide product reviews, online recommendation lists, create wish lists, can upload images, provide buying guides and can initiate discussions on different topics. Amazon describes Amapedia, its lightly promoted Wikipedia clone, as "a community for sharing information about popular products." The Amazon Daily blog (formerly known as "Plogs") contains posts from throughout the Amazon site.

1.13.2 E-Commerce and Social Networking Portals

E-commerce in social networking involves customer driven online transactions. Usually, these social networking sites integrate across a number of online portals to promote sales. The need for the integration of several portals is to connect customers to one another such that they can share, recommend products and services which will improve company's business. Social commerce sites like mouthshut.com, cardekho.com, etc. engage in users in sharing, recommending and chatting on similar products and services and then using this knowledge to help them buy products and services. For example, if a user wants to watch a movie, mouthshut.com lists all the reviews of the customers who have seen that movie. After watching the reviews, mouthshut.com has links to movie ticket booking sites. Similarly, cardekho.com encourages its users to write their experience about different models of car manufacturers and share them with prospective buyers. The prospective buyers can go through these comments and decide the model they would like to buy. The web site, then has integrated with car financing companies and car manufacturers so that the prospective buyers can use correct finance options. The sites don't directly sell things, but they encourage users to share links to good bargains, and discuss qualities of products.

Social commerce also uses user-generated contents that help in trust and reputation building as well as information sharing. Indiatimes.com and NDTVshopping.com are e-commerce sites that use social commerce sites and are based on information sharing after actual purchase. The sites have features that are designed to put its community members in touch with other shoppers who have similar interests in products. As memberships grow, the users come to know the community and share their reviews. Their product reviews become more relevant based on recognition of some of the reviewers. Similarly, Flipkart.com is an online media and social-shopping portal where people find reviews about the seller, quality of products that these sellers offer before they buy. After purchase, they recommend and share their experience about products for others to discover and purchase online. Instead of traditional word-of-mouth recommendations from trusted sources called 'opinion leaders', we have well thought of intellectually stimulating experience sharing by actual users (unlike opinion leaders who would have used their wisdom to suggest a product 'without using them').

1.13.3 Business to Business

Business to Business portals deal with transactions between a business house with another business house. The transactions can be between a supplier and purchaser, manufacturer with retailer (or warehouse or between two business houses who have collaborated with each other. B2B Web sites can generally be sorted into company sites, product supplier sites and online procurement exchanges sites (e-auction sites such as metalexchange.com), brokering sites that act as intermediaries between buyers desirous of products or services and suppliers (e.g., equipment leasing, information sites, sometimes known as "infomediaries"). B2B can also have specialized or vertical industry portals that provide information, product listings, discussion groups and other features in a particular industry. These domain portal sites thus have roles that will include buying and selling, providing information to all the players and acting as guardian of the industry.

There is another variation of B2B service offering using e-commerce. In creating new venues for the social scene, social networking sites like MySpace, Facebook, Friendster, etc. have helped open the way for business users to adopt similar techniques to network and generate new business leads. The efficiency of online communities at sharing and prioritizing information are transforming enterprise business processes. Business networking services such as LinkedIn and academia.edu bring Web 2.0 social networking techniques to business users. Linkedin.com has started providing background information to recruiters and also validates information provided by the members. Many business houses have used these sites to find potential target groups for their service offerings. Campusnet.com used linkedin.com members profile to offer training programs in testing services. These offerings are another variation of B2B service model.

Two other examples of B2B e-commerce portals are Globaby.com and Alibaba.com. Globaby.com calls itself a "B2B 2.0 portal". This site is specially designed for providing professional help for online shopping so that the buyers get cost-effective products. In Globaby.com, it provides locations called "MyHouse" which allows buyers to register their suppliers and manage orders on the site. This can be construed as similar to 'cloud computing' hosting, where the site (Globaby) will manage suppliers and their delivery schedule. These deliver schedules would be based on Service Level Agreements (SLAs) that 'Myhouse' owners would have provided. Buyers can leave messages for suppliers for further communication and invite suppliers to bid for the products that the buyers would have put in 'Myhouse'.

Alibaba.com claims to be well frequented 'international B2B trade portal'. The web site uses English language and specializes in providing business leads for Chinese suppliers. Alibaba.com is designed specifically for international buyers trying to get into contact with Chinese sellers. The MyAlibaba Community function allows members to add and update products, check messages, post trade leads and more.

1.13.4 Future Trend in Web 2.0 and B2b E-Commerce

Web 2.0 and social networks are being seen as catalysts in B2B models in changing into market places. Most consumer-facing companies and brands will have to develop robust social network offerings to remain relevant, and B2B executives should create and execute strategies in line with the new trend. The way, many organizations have used LinkedIn and Facebook means that they are getting experience with these spaces and tools, which will change their expectations and drive further adoption in the near future.

1.14 Case: Sullekha.com

Sulekha.com was born on Feb 25, 1998 and was owned by Satya Prabhakar. Initially it was projected as the Web Magazine for the Indian Sub Continent. Sulekha.com was started as collaborative article writing where, different articles were complied for online publishing. Many people used to voluntarily submit articles to be published onto sulekha.com for free. They also organized the web site into separate columns or headings such as Articles, Columns, Coffee House Discussions, Cool Tools, and Movie Reviews/ratings, etc. They projected the site as smart information provider to anyone who wants it. In order to generate revenue they also joined with e-commerce partners (or affiliate marketing) with amazon.com, commissionjunction.com, expedia.com, etc. They updated information for different categories periodically so that the users get the latest information. It also provides local e-commerce services through its classified and yellow pages sections, which allow its members to post ads to buy or sell items such as cars, flats, furniture, vehicles, and also search for jobs.

In 2000 sulekha.com offered free e-mail accounts and online advertisement to those who might be interested in publicizing their web site onto sulekha.com. The advertisers could place their banner advertisements on sulekha.com. They also started to offer sale of tickets for movies and transport (buses plying between Chennai and Bangalore and also between Chennai and Coimbatore). Banner advertisements in India were rare and soon it caught attention of users. Banner advertisements for dish network, movies, India calling cards (these are cheap way of calling to India from outside India), kbs-tv.com, sendwise.com, etc. were prominent and attracted users as well as buyers to the site. With addition of new advertisers such as Western Union, Relax Herbals, razacomm.com for phone calling to India, etc., the e-commerce web site was gaining attention from all the quarters.

With the passage of years, more and more advertisers were attracted to the sites. The banner advertisements clearly showed that sulekha.com was becoming popular in providing users the information that they wanted. The traffic of users increased and so also the popularity of the e-commerce site. Even if there were no sales through the web site, it still was the hub for all to visit. In 2005, the site was redesigned so that the users could select his/her location in multiple US/Canada states such as Atlanta, Austin, Bay Area, Boston, New York, Toronto, Dubai, London, Singapore, etc. Also, apart from Chennai, information for few Indian cities was added such as Banglore, Chennai, Delhi, Hyderabad, Kolkata and Mumbai. Sulekha.com also published list of service providers under the name Sulekha Media Kit to further attract advertisers and users.

Sulekha.com has won the award for the 'Best Multi Utility Website' at IAMAI's 2nd India Digital Awards. Sulekha.com has been recognized for innovatively integrating multiple mechanisms such as business listings, classifieds, deals, e-commerce and reviews/ratings—through which users get their local needs across multiple domains. Sulekha.com covers over 2500 categories in terms of local information needs of visitors.

The Internet & Mobile Association of India (IAMAI) represents the interests of the online and mobile value added services industry, and presents the coveted India Digital Awards to recognize and celebrate the achievements and efforts of all those individuals and companies who have contributed toward the development and enhancement of online and mobile value added services in India. The award for Sulekha.com metamorphosed the company into a well recognized e-commerce company. The site (which uses both B2B and B2C models) has integrated classified information, yellow pages and search facilities with new offerings like deals and social media properties.

Internet portal Sulekha.com, which revamped its site in 2009 few weeks ago, is now embarking on a brand-building campaign across media. As per Satya Prabhakar, CEO of Sulekha, said, "We have earmarked a budget of Rs 10 crore for brand-building exercise in the next 1 year. Out of which we will spend Rs 4 crore on TV, print, radio and outdoor campaigns in the next 3–4 months with 75 % of the total ad spend going into TV advertising".

Apart from the campaign which promotes the e-commerce features on the site, Sulekha has also made some changes to the way transactions are made on its classifieds and yellow pages. It has introduced 'Pay per Response' for classifieds users and 'Pay per Lead' for yellow pages users. In 'Pay per Response', a user who posts ads in the classifieds section has to pay money only when he gets a response to his post. In 'Pay per Lead', a user who has put a listing in the yellow pages section only has to pay for the listing if he gets some business inquiry or proposition out of it. Sulekha.com also launched a mobile site which will allow its members to post ads via their mobiles. It already allows Reliance Mobile, Vodafone, and Airtel subscribers to search for information on its classifieds and yellow pages on mobiles.

1.15 Summary

E-commerce strives to share a commitment to provide a greater customer experience throughout the world. Industries using e-commerce solutions and services address the need to increase revenue, enter new markets, improve service level agreements and improve profit margin. With e-commerce solutions, companies get competitive advantage, predictable performance and speedy fulfillment of complex multichannel, multilocation order cycles. This will enable transformation of customer's business processes to improve flexibility and effectiveness. The approach can be summarized as follows

Revenue needs	Increased reach	Control and agility	Operational efficiencies	Speed of execution
Service needs	Predictable performance	Efficiency in delivery	Fulfillment of orders	Ability to manage multichannel, multilocation order cycle
Operation needs	Increasing revenue from customers through B2B and B2C channels	Consolidated view of demand, inventory and supply	Reduce order processing costs	Faster decision making cycles
Customer needs	Information available	Transparency in pricing	Able to compare among different suppliers	Complete purchase cycle faster

1.16 Review Questions

1. What is e-commerce? How is it different from traditional business models?
2. What are different business models available for e-commerce?
3. Explain differences between B2B and B2C in terms of serviceability, control and order completion cycle.
4. How do you ensure transparency in B2B models?
5. How customers are benefitted from e-commerce?

Chapter 2
Technologies for E-Commerce

2.1 Learning Objectives

At the end of the chapter, the students would understand

- Role of technologies in e-commerce
- Web architecture
- Hypertext transfer protocol (HTTP)
- Web pages (static and dynamic)
- Cookies

2.2 Introduction

E-commerce has a three-tier system model. These three tiers refer to three main components viz. Client side, server side and the connecting bridge which is known as internet. These three make an e-commerce system model. However, for fulfilling any order, we need to integrate other systems as well such as supplier system, warehouse system, logistics system, etc. In such a scenario, the web browser is the interfacing page which is the client interfacing page. This also called the graphic user interface (GUI). The back end tier is the combination of data and application server, where all business logic and database are stored. To connect these two tiers, internet becomes the middle tier that allows the users to connect through the internet, which acts as a medium. As the clients and application servers are connected to the internet, there is a need to arrange a rule-based system that will allow each of these tiers to 'talk' to each other. These rules are 'protocols' that allow these talks to happen through certain processes. This protocol is called the HTTP. The internet and application server form the basic infrastructure for the e-commerce system.

S. Mohapatra, *E-Commerce Strategy*, Springer Texts in Business and Economics,
DOI: 10.1007/978-1-4614-4142-7_2,

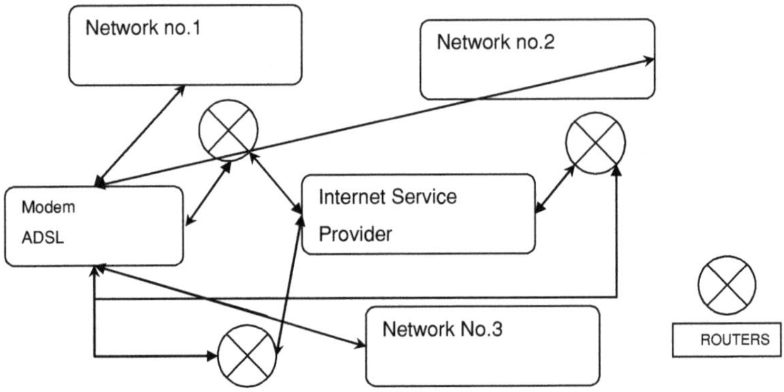

Fig. 2.1 Basic network architecture of the internet connections

2.3 Basic Architecture of Internet

The term internet implies that it is a combination several networks. These networks are connected to each other terminal devices known as routers. These routers are actually nodes that start as well as end several connecting networks. These routers are connected to each other through service providers known as internet service providers (ISP). Unlike other network connections, these connections transfer information through packets. A packet looks like a parcel, which carries an address to which the packet needs to be sent. The ISP uses this address and sends the packet to the final address. The catch is that the ISP only tries to provide its best effort to send the packets. Depending on the network bandwidth, traffic volume, the delivery may be delayed or lost (which happens in rare events). Please refer to Fig. 2.1 which explains the network connection.

2.4 TCP/IP

The internet is based on a layered model called transmission control protocol/ internet protocol (TCP/IP). The layering implies that the complex process of transferring packets from one computer to another computer across the internet can be broken into small tasks. This creates modularity among different layers, which are nothing but different network connections. These layers are connected through different rules and definitions. As a result each layer has independence to be connected to another one. There are four layers such as application layer, transport layer, network layer, and link layer. The link layer is meant for providing access to internet. The network layer helps in forwarding packets to different layers depending on the address on the packet. These forwarding takes place through transport layer which provides end-to-end transport service between two layers.

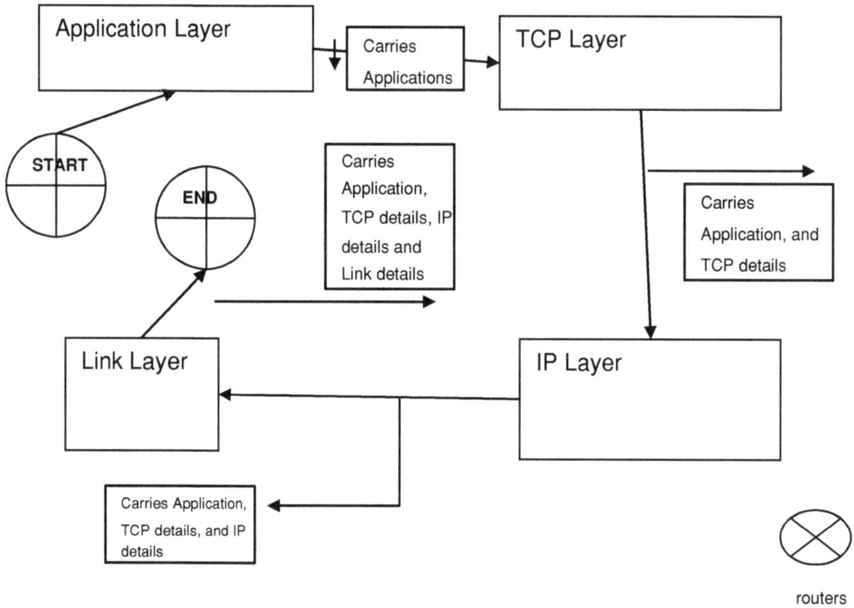

Fig. 2.2 Arrangements of layers

The application layer supports transport of each and every application across networks. All these functionalities of different layers are systematically managed through a rule-based protocol called TCP/IP. Total arrangement of these layers is shown in Fig. 2.2.

It would be good to explain roles and functionalities of each layer in details. Link layer is the starting point for the network. This provides access to the network. This layer deals with physical and medium of access. For example, for home users, the most common way to access internet is either through mobile or broadband internet connections. Using modems, digital data can be turned to analog signals. These signals then can be transferred through public network. As we progress on 3G spectrum, the network bandwidth (meaning the maximum rate of data transfer) is increasing. In commercial transactions, such as offices, LAN and WAN are used for data transfer. Ethernet is the most popular LAN protocol and carrier sense multiple access with collision detection (CSMA/CD) defines the access control for this medium. The advantage of CSMA/CD is that the computer can transmit data at any point of time if it detects that the channel is free. In case more than one computer want to send the signal at the same time, then the signals will be transmitted after queuing it for an amount of time.

The main purpose of network layer is to forward packets to their destinations. In our postal network, this is similar to forwarding a courier through the postal network. This layer considers two parameters, such as the address of the destination and how to forward or the mode of routing the packet. These two are addressed before the IP layer takes control of the protocol.

Table 2.1 Intended uses of IP addresses

IP class	The number starts with	Number of bits	Range of IP address	Possible number of networks	Intended use
A	0	First 8 bits	0.0.0.0–127.255.255.255	2^7	Many can share the network
B	10	First 16 bits	128.0.0.0–191.255.255.255	2^{14}	The network access is limited to some
C	110	First 24 bits	192.0.0.0–223.255.255.255	2^{21}	Few have access to the same network
D	111	Not applicable	224.0.0.0–239.255.255.255	Not applicable	Dedicated users (securitized)
E	1111	Not applicable	240.0.0.0–247.255.255.255	Not applicable	Experimental users only

The next layer that comes into play is IP address layer. Each packet has an IP address. Each IP address has 32 bits. However, since it is too long, the address is expressed in the dot decimal format e.g., 120.02.227.301. If the binary form would have been displayed, then it would have been a long number with combinations of 1 and 0. Each IP address has two parts: the network number and the host number. Within the same network, all hosts have same network number. Routers forward packets based on the network number rather than the host number so that they only need to know the network numbers. The IP addresses are classified as from A to E, which will indicate different types of uses. Table 2.1 indicates the class of IP address and their intended use.

To explain this further let us consider an IP address say 128.0.0.1. As is evident from Table 2.1, this is a class B address. In binary notation, it is 10000000.00000000.00000000.00000001. The first 16 bits represent the network number and hence the network number is 128.0.0.0. Hence, the possible host number (as per the Table 2.1) are from 128.0.0.01 to 128.0.255.254. This type of numbering has one drawback. If the network does not have sufficient number of hosts to cover the available IP addresses, then only few IPs are only utilized. To address this, internet engineering task force (IETF) has come up with internet standards called 'Request For Comments' (RFC 950*). In this method, subnetting method is used to divide class A, B, and C to subnetworks so that all the IPs can be efficiently utilized. In this method, a part of host numbers becomes subnet numbers as specified by a subnet mask. This mask is used to indicate IP address. With subnetting, the standard network prefix together with the subnet number identifies the effective network number.

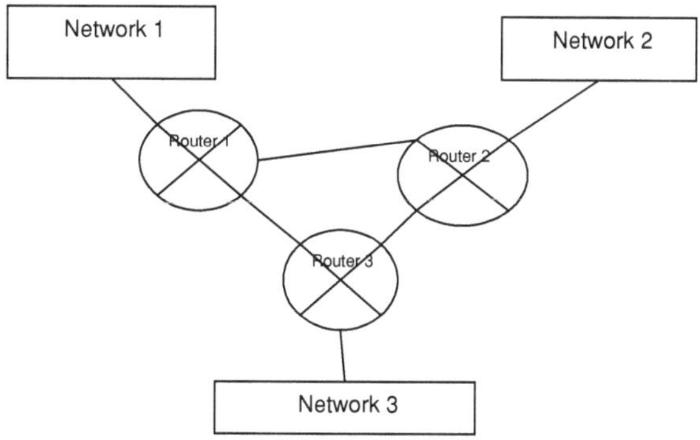

Fig. 2.3 Routing connections for packet transmission

Routing helps in forwarding the packets to and from internet. Each routing has rules in the form of table which directs where a packet should be forwarded. Each network is connected a router which is specific to a network. At the end of each transfer, a router directs the packet to the next hop router. Please refer to Fig. 2.3. A packet from network 1 destined for network 3 will go through router no. 1 and then to router no. 3 before being delivered to the network.

The Fig. 2.3 shows the basic principles in intradomain (intranetwork) routing protocol. All the networks shown here are in the same autonomous system. This means that each router contains the routing information to reach other networks in the same domain. In practice there are two different types of intradomain routing protocols based on two different working principles. The first one, known as routing information protocol (RIP), distance vector routing protocol is used. The principle used is that each router forwards its routing table to the adjacent routers so as to continuously update router tables in each router. This is quite dynamic in nature. The second principle, compared to the first one, broadcasts its link status to each router. This is why it is called link status routing protocol. Here, the traffic loading (link sates) are broadcast to other routers. As the link status has been broadcast and made known to all routers, each router can then build an image of the network and use this image to construct the routing table. Compared to the first principle, less routing information is exchanged but more processing is required to create and update the routing table in each router.

Finally, the transport layer comes to picture for packet broadcasting. The IP provides the best effort service to deliver packets. For this to happen, a transport layer is needed on top of IP layer to provide end-to-end delivery of packets. There are two types of transport protocols that used, the user diagram protocol (UDP) and TCPAs per the IETF standard RFC768, UDP is connectionless whose main function is to pass data through different 'ports'. As a computer can execute several applications at the same time, ports are used to identify execution of an application. The connection between two computers is identified through IP address, port number, second computer IP address and second port number (destination computer's port number). As specified by IETF vide RFC 1700, certain port numbers (such as 8000) is standardized for HTTP, which is used for internet applications.

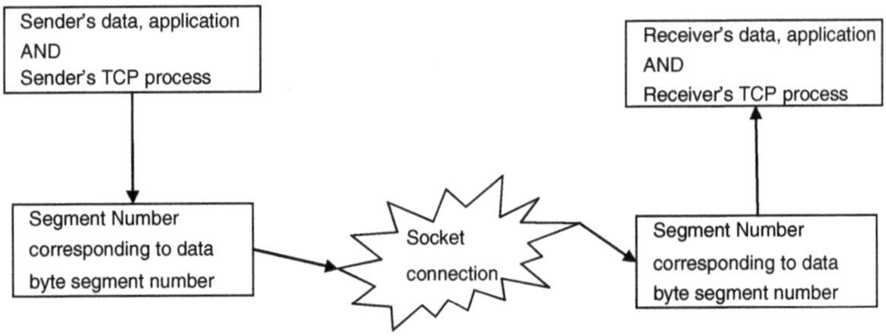

Fig. 2.4 TCP layer process

TCP is a connection oriented protocol for providing reliable data transport service between two computers (hosts) over internet. To create a communication link through TCP, both sending and receiving computers set up a socket and a port number. The socket is represented by its IP address. The TCP connection is set up between two sockets through a three way hand shaking process, which means the sender initiates the communication link, the receiver acknowledges the request for connection and the sender again acknowledges the receiver's acknowledgment. After the connection is established, the sending TCP process divides the application data into segments and sends them via IP to the receiving TCP process. Each segment is identified by a sequence number which is also the sequence number of the data byte that is being transmitted. Based on this transmitting sequence number of the data byte, the receiving TCP can rearrange segments and then send acknowledgment to the sending TCP process (which is at the sender's side). If there is a problem, then the sending computer does not receive the acknowledgement from the receiving TCP process; this results in 'time out'. After time out period, the segment will be retransmitted. Sometimes, to prevent the sender from sending many requests simultaneously and thus overload the system, the sending TCP process limits the number of bytes that can be sent to the receiver (this is usually done through sliding window mechanism). The entire transport process is shown in Fig. 2.4.

Application layer is meant for providing a particular application. There are varieties of application layer protocols which have different purposes. A simple mail transfer protocol is used for supporting email services. Similarly, file transfer protocol (FTP) is used for supporting file transfer services and HTTP is used for communication between a web client and web server. Telnet is another protocol is used for allowing users to log into remote computers. For e-commerce purpose, HTTP is used. HTTP relies on domain name system (DNS) for its operations. As defined in RFC1034 and RFC1035, DNS helps in providing a meaningful name to each and every IP address. An example is given here to make this clear. The network uses IP addresses for transmitting which are in the form of binary numbers. These binary numbers are transmitted from one computer to another. While sending as well as receiving an operator would like to receive meaningful names rather than large binary numbers. For example, instead of the receiver receiving a number like 100.112.234.43, he would like to receive it as meaningful name such as http://www.Indiaplaza.com. To translate these binary numbers onto scriptable domain name, DNS is used. DNS translates the IP address to a domain name, also provides a hierarchical naming system so that we can arrange the information. The DNS also consists of a distributed database system for storing domain names. As a result it uses the index mechanism for searching the corresponding IP address when someone searches a domain name. Some examples are com (for company), edu (education), gov (government), mil (military), net (network provider), org (usually non-commercial organizations), hk (for Hong Kong), uk (united Kingdom), in (India), etc.

Each domain name consists of a sequence of terms divided by periods. The first sequence is known as leaf node and the subsequent ones are known as the successive parent nodes till the root. Thus, in www.infosys.com, www is the leaf node, Infosys is the parent node and com is the parent node of Infosys. When someone searches for Infosys, DNS helps to find the IP address of Infosys website. DNS servers are responsible for handling queries or searches. These DNS servers use distributed servers for storing these IP addresses. When someone searches for a domain name (such as Infosys), a program known as Resolver is invoked. The Resolver then makes a query to the associated DNS server. If the associated DNS server has the mapping of IP address and the domain name, then the IP address will be returned to the search engine. If it does not have the mapping of the IP address and domain name, then the search may have to go through a series of DNS servers before the IP address is returned to the search engine.

2.5 IPv4 Versus IPv6

The current IP is called IPv4, where 4 stands for version number. New version of IP called IPv6 has been developed for the next generation internet. IPv6 uses 128-bit addresses. IPv4 uses 32-bit address as a result of which the number of hosts or computers that can be part of the network is not sufficient. In IPv4, if a packet is to be transmitted, then it has to be multiplicated and then sent to different locations. This results in clogging the network bandwidth and wastages of the network. However, in IPv6, multicast is used by which a single packet can be transmitted to multiple locations. The most important development in IPv6 has been security control. An IP Security protocol named IPSec has been developed. This protocol is used to set up virtual networks over internet thus allowing business partners to communicate with each other securely over internet. Table 2.2 shows difference between IPv4 and IPv6.

Table 2.2 IPv4 versus IPv6

IPv4	IPv6
Addresses are 32 bits (4 bytes) in length	Addresses are 128 bits (16 bytes) in length
Address (A) resource records in DNS to map host names to IPv4 addresses	Address (AAAA) resource records in DNS to map host names to IPv6 addresses
Pointer (PTR) resource records in the IN-ADDR.ARPA DNS domain to map IPv4 addresses to host names	Pointer (PTR) resource records in the IP6.ARPA DNS domain to map IPv6 addresses to host names
IPSec is optional and should be supported externally	IPSec support is not optional
Header does not identify packet flow for QoS handling by routers	Header contains flow label field, which identifies packet flow for QoS handling by router
Both routers and the sending host fragment packets	Routers do not support packet fragmentation. Sending host fragments packets
Header includes a checksum	Header does not include a checksum
Header includes options	Optional data is supported as extension headers
ARP uses broadcast ARP request to resolve IP to MAC/hardware address	Multicast neighbor solicitation messages resolve IP addresses to MAC addresses
Internet group management protocol (IGMP) manages membership in local subnet groups	Multicast listener discovery (MLD) messages manage membership in local subnet groups
Broadcast addresses are used to send traffic to all nodes on a subnet	IPv6 uses a link-local scope all nodes multicast address
Configured either manually or through DHCP	Does not require manual configuration or DHCP
Must support a 576-byte packet size (possibly fragmented)	Must support a 1280-byte packet size (without fragmentation)

2.6 Evolution of Internet

E-commerce cannot exist without internet. But evolution of internet was not related to e-commerce. Internet birth dates back to European particle physics laboratory called CERN, where in the year 1989, physicists stated heir experimentation on nuclear physics. During this research work, there were several documents that needed to be exchanged among participating scientists. Tim Berners–Lee proposed and demonstrated a concept of hypertext for linking text based documents over computer networks. To achieve this linking he developed a text based browser. This was the birth for future research on web based browsers. In 1993, Mark Anderson (university of Illinois) developed fist graphical user based web browser called Mosaic. Based on this invention, he started a new enterprise called Netscape Communications Corporation (popularly known browser Netscape was launched here). Netscape became hugely successful and the company was listed in NASDAQ in 1995. The product of this company, the Netscape provided web browser to the entire world. Subsequently, in 1995, World Wide Web consortium was formed (http://www.ww3.org) which helped in standardizing web browser technologies.

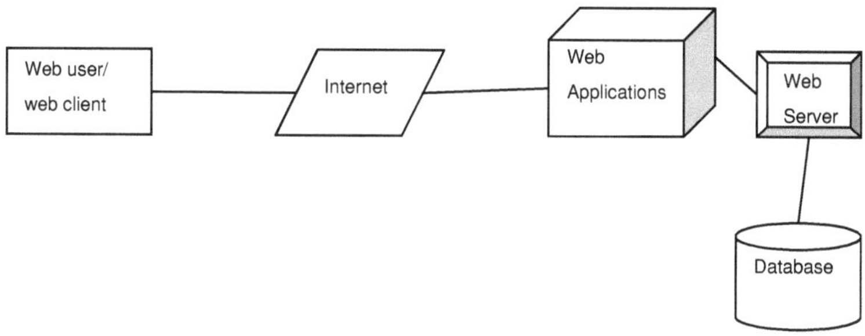

Fig. 2.5 Web components

The web based technologies had basically three components—web browser, web server, and web application server. The forum standardized the technologies related to these three components. Let us discuss further on these three components of web technologies.

Web browser. This is the interface with the end user or client. This is used for displaying information to the user; this is also used to collect information from the user which goes in the form of input to the system. These information is then shared or transferred to the web server using HTTP.

Web server. It is the main component of the web architecture. It interacts with the web browser (known as web client) and also with the back end system (web application server).

Web application server. This hosts the e-commerce applications, including business rules, business logic and transaction data (sometimes the transaction data can reside in another server). Figure 2.5 shows pictorial relation between the three components.

Database management. This component fulfills requests for storing and retrieving data from different e-commerce transactions. Efficiency of database will help improve the experience at the end user level.

Internet. This is a medium to transfer and exchange information between web servers and web clients. For the communication to happen between all the components, there is a need to have protocol which will allow hem to 'talk' to each other over internet. This process is called HTTP.

2.7 Uniform Resource Locator

Uniform resource locator (URL) is used for providing unique address for a web page. To identify a web page, an addressing system or scheme is provided. Basically, a web page is given an address which is known as URL, which can be treated as an internet resource. For each application, there will be a unique address. General representation of any URL is as follows:

Protocol://domain_name/directory/resource

where protocol represents definition of protocols, e.g., http stands for hypertext transfer protocol; https represent secure hypertext transfer protocol, ftp represents file transfer protocol and telnet represents protocol for accessing a remote computer. For website, http://www.xyz.com/welcome/main.html is the URL for a particular page. In this example, the protocol is http, the domain name is www.xyz.com, the directory is welcome and the file main.html is stored under the directory welcome.

2.8 Hypertext Transfer Protocol

HTTP is used for communicating between web client and web server. When we click on the URL of http://www.xyz.com, the browser obtains the IP address of the domain XYZ through DNS. After receiving the reply, the web client establishes a TCP connection to port 80 of the web server. As we know port number 80 is the default port for HTTP. Then it issues a command which contains GET/welcome/main.html to retrieve the web page main.html from the web server. The request is specified in ASCII text format. The web server then returns the corresponding file to the browser. The response is specified in multipurpose internet mail extension (MIME) format such as text, image and audio. The common types of server responses are text/html, image/JPEG, image/GIF, image/BMP, etc.

If there are multiple requests from the same browser, then all the corresponding IP addresses are obtained in the similar fashion. In many companies, they install a proxy server for security and other administrative reasons. In these cases, we need to access other domain (web) servers through proxy servers. The process in this case is that a user's browser issues a request to the proxy server first and then the proxy web server retrieves the specific web pages. Having retrieved the web pages, they are displayed on the user's computers. The proxy servers are used to stop any unauthorized access to the web servers, but it might slow down the performance. To overcome the performance issues, cached copies of different web pages can be stored such that they can be returned to the users immediately. This increases the response time immensely.

2.9 Cookies

HTTP does not keep any information related to users. For example, when a web server receives a HTTP request for any information, the server does not know whether their request is fro anew client or an extended session from the previous clients. This means HTTP will not have knowledge about the request being made—whether the request is related to previous request. In e-commerce business knowing about the users' state and requests are important as that can be used to develop business analytics so that customers can be understood better. For example, while logging in the server should know details of the previous transactions that have been made in the same account. To address these issues, a method called 'cookies' were developed by which a web server would save data at the web client. The method was used by Netscape first and these details can be found at http://www.netscape.com/newsref/std/cookie.spec.html, and has been standardized in RFC2109. There are limitations to number of days that a cookie can be stored. Similarly, there are restrictions on number of cookies that can be stored, and the size of each cookie that can be stored.

Let us look at the usefulness of cookies in e-commerce business applications. Let us say someone has purchased items in indiaplaza (an e-commerce website) and there are already three items in the shopping car. The first one has a product code (say 111), the second item has a product code 222 and the third one has 333 as product code. If there is a request to put the fourth item with product code 444 into the basket, the server will set a cookie by including the following cookie header:

Se-Cookie: Item=444. At the end the next HTTP request to the web server will be

Cookie:Item1=111
Cookie:Item2=222
Cookie:Item3=333
Cookies:Item4=444

By reading the cookies, the server knows the contents of the shopping cart so that it can be displayed at the web client.

HTTP has been enhanced to HTTP/1.1 where many enhancements have been included so that the performance, functionalities have been improved. Many of the limitations of HTTP have also been removed. In the improved version, many additional headers have been added so that the improved enhancements can be performed. Some of the enhanced performances are noted below:

Simultaneous requests. In the earlier version (HTTP/1.0), a connection is released after the request was received. As a result if a web client waned to retrieve other pages from the web server, will not be able to do so and have to wait for sometime till the previous request has been closed. However, in HTTP/1.1, a connection is kept open such that the web client can send multiple requests over the same connection. For example, a user can read about profile of the directors and can still request for the page that contain information related to products and services. So a web client sends a request for another page without waiting for the previous page. This is known as pipelining of requests and responses.

Efficient use of IP addresses. In HTTP/1.1, a host header must be included in the HTTP request message to specify the name of the host in the web server. This enables different organizations to share the same IP address of the web server thus allowing efficient use of IP addresses.

Break point request. During a request, there could be chances that the collection is lost or broken when a large file is being retrieved. In HTTP/1.1, the web client can request web server to send the file from the point where the link was broken. This makes it faster to receive the file as well as makes it productive.

Cache control. The purpose of the cache control is to reduce the time to retrieve time of pages. Many of the web pages are static and the information may not be required to be updated dynamically. In such situations, a cache copy can be maintained of the previous responses in the web browser or the proxy server so that future requests can be served by the cache copies rather than by the original servers. The new protocol also has provision for updating the cache copy. For example, the original server can tell the proxy server when the cache copy can be updated. Even the web server can also instruct the proxy server not to maintain a cache copy by using syntax such as "Pragma: No cache header".

Security features. Another feature from HTTP/1.1 is that the proxy-authentication can be done through HTTP header commands (such as proxy-authorization and proxy-authentication). This helps in discouraging unauthorized entry.

Data compression, content integrity. The new HTTP/1.1 allows data to be compressed meaning it would take less space and consequently less time to execute. Similarly, using content header HTTP/1.1 provides trustworthy data to the end users.

2.10 Client Side or Web Programing

There are several ways of carrying out client side programing. The programing can be done in HTML, JavaScript, Java Applets, ActiveX controls, etc. Also, plug-ins can be used which are small applications that are embedded in a web page for performing special functions (such as animations). While there are many client side programing techniques are available, HTML and JavaScript are most commonly used for building the user interface at the client side. The choice of the programing technique depends upon the time it takes to download pages and data. This download time includes time required to download a web page and associated elements from the server side to the client side over the internet. The download time also depends on quality of the network, and the type f connections to the network. For B2C applications, many end users would be using slow version of the internet connection (such as mobile internet, etc.) and this connection would determine the download time.

The programing techniques take car of these factors and try to reduce download time to acceptable limit (7 s for downloading a page). It has been observed that downloading time for Java Applets is much more than that of HTML or JavaScript. Most of e-commerce web sites use JavaScript for programing client side pages. Authentication and data validation are other things that need to be considered while developing user interface. For data validation, the web client can check if the type (e.g. Integer) has been entered, range (between two numbers), sequence (chronological events) and business requirements are correctly entered. Type, range and sequence checking can be done at the web client side through programing techniques such as JavaScript and HTML documents. However, to check business logic, the server side will have database to check the logic.

In e-commerce transactions, a client is likely to be at a physically different location from the application server and thus the client should be able to respond to the requests faster. The response time is understood as the ease with which the end users use the application and get the desired web pages and data from the web servers. This implies that the usability of the web clients can increase if the response time is fast enough for the end users. Apart from the response time, the usability of the client also increases with consistency in performance, preventing error, improving performance and efficiency; user likes and dislikes system recovery etc. For these reasons, before a web page is designed, the following steps must be followed to get a good end result:

1. Understand the target audience
2. Define the information requirement for the end users
3. Develop logical design of he web site
4. Create the content and make it attractive with multimedia contents
5. Use the programing techniques such as HTML and JavaScript
6. Decide the server where it can be hosted

2.11 HTML Programing Techniques

HTML is a technique that would instruct the web browser as to how to format and display a web page. Predefined tags can be used to describe the format of a document. For example, by putting a tag pair <I>Name<I>, he word Name will appear in italics format in the web page. Most of these tags have a start and end tag and the content is embedded in between these tags. <HR> tag inserts a horizontal line in the web page. Basic structure of an HTML document is as follows:

```
<!DOCTYPE HTML PUBLIC '-//W3C//DTD HTML Final//EN'>
<HTML>
<HEAD>
<! Indiatimes Shopping welcomes you>
<TITLE>
</HEAD>
<BODY>
<HTML>
```

<!DOCTYPE> specifies the version of the HTML document and other related information. <HTML> and </HTML> tags indicate start and end of an HTML documents, respectively. With <HTML> tag, there are two main sections namely the HEAD section as included inside the <HEAD></HEAD> tag pair and the BODY section as included inside the <BODY> tag pair. Information related to

document title is provided in the HEAD section which is not shown to the end users. But whatever is written within <BODY> tag pair, is shown on the web page. Also, he information shown in the comment tag pair are used by programmers for future maintenance. These comments are displayed on he web page, but is quite helpful to the technical team that is involved in programing the web pages. Some of the common attributes are (BACKGROUND—specifies the URL of the background image, BGCOLOR—background color to be used, TEXT—color of the text in the web page, LINK—hyperlinks that are inactive, ALINK—active hyperlinks, VLINK—visited links).

2.12 Links

Links, as the name suggests, are used to link web pages. For example, two web pages that are situated in two different servers can be linked to each other through links (or hyperlinks). These links are defined by the anchor tag pair <A> and </A>. Basic hyperlink is defined through the statement as follows:

<A HREF=http://www.snapdeal.com/mobiles/nokia.html>Art</A>

Here Art is clicked, the browser links and opens the page nokia.html in the website snapdeal.com/mobiles. The link attributes are specified by the HREF attribute. As we know http stands for the HTTP, where the server name is snapdeal.com, mobiles is the directory and nokia.html is the file. In addition, we can add an email link to the page by using <A> tag. This is useful when we want that our customers should be able to write to the webmaster. This can be done as follows:

<A HREF=mailto:webmaster@snapdeal.com>Please give your feedback</A>. These links can be absolute or relative In absolute links, the web page opens with full address of the page (the URL will contain the full details here). But in relative links, the web page opens after the parent directory has opened.

2.13 Images

There are several image formats for the web viz. joint photographic experts group (JPEG), graphics interchange format (GIF), etc. These formats have been designed such a way that they store images in a compressed format. By compressing these images, the space required to store these images, without damaging the quality, is the least. Each format has specific characteristics, such as GIF works well when the details in an image are not high (GIF only provides 256 colors, hence intricate color details as well as contrasting colors can be missing). In JPEG format, which employs a lossy compression method, which allows to compress the size further with better graphic resolution. For including images, <IMG> tag is used. We can align the images by using different attributes (For example, ALIGN will define left, right, top, middle or bottom alignment, ALT describes the image, BORDER sets the border size, HEIGHT fixes the height of the image, HSPACE specifies the additional horizontal space to be added, SRC specifies where the image will be loaded, VSPACE marks the additional vertical space, WIDTH fixes the width of the image). <IMG SRC="snapdeal.jpeg" HEIGHT="50" WIDTH="150" ALIGN="CENTRE" BORDER="3" ALT="snapdeal" will insert an image in the web page as per the attributes explained above.

We can also create an image map for linking different URLs. These image maps can be server or client side image maps respectively. To specify image maps, <MAP> is used. For example,

<MAP NAME="map_id">

AREA SHAPE="RECT?CIRCLE" COORDS="40,30" HREF="URL"> will define area coordinates as well as the shape of the areas.

2.14 Tables

Tables arrange information in a structured manner for ease of reading. They also facilitate the layout of web page components. They are also used for describing the layout of web page components. For creating a table the following tag can be used:

```
<TABLE>
  <TR>
      <TH>Heading cell</TH>
      <TH>Heading cell</TH>
  </TR>
  <TR>
      <TD>Data cell</TD>
      <TD>Data ccell</TD>
  </TR>
</TABLE>
```

For starting and ending the table, <TABLE> and </TABLE> are used respectively. <TR> and </TR> specifies table row <TD> and </TD> defines data cell. There are other common attributes that can be used for table (such as ALIGN defines the alignment of the document, BGCOLOR specifies the back ground color, BORDER sets the border dimensions, COLS specifies the number of columns, WIDTH specifies the table width).

2.15 Frames

These are to display multiple pages in a browser. A web page can be divided into left frame and right frame; while the left frame can be used for providing links to different products, the right frame can provide navigation buttons for displaying other contents. These two contents can be written separately and displayed in the frames in the main browser. <FRAME> tag can be used to set up frames. Using frames, number of columns and number of rows can be defined (COLS="c1,c2,....cp"). The tag * is used to design the allocation of available space. Different attributes of frame are FRAMEBORDER (to indicate the usage of a frame boarder), HEIGHT (sets the frame height), NAME (specifies a name for identification purpose), WIDTH (sets the width of the frame).

2.16 Form

These are used to transfer data from clients to the server. After data is entered in the client through GUI, a program is used to invoke this data from the client. Using a background system, an HTML file is created which is responded back to the users. The response to the users will be done through HTTP. The FORM is written in the following way:

```
<FORM ACTION="User_data" METHOD="GET">
</FORM>
```

User_data is the program name that processes the form data and the METHOD describes the way data can be passed to the server. The other ways of passing the data are GET or POST. For taking inputs, textbox, password textbox, checkbox, radio button, submit button, file input field, hidden form field, comment box, select menu can be used.

2.17 Style Sheets

A web page has three main components, presentation structure, style, and content. In the early HTML, style and structure were integrated, but now they are separated by <P> tag. Using cascading style sheets, style is separated from structure. This gives flexibility to the web designers. The designer can use external style sheet, embedded style sheet, and inline style sheet.

2.18 JavaScript

JavaScript is a scripting language provided by Netscape for programing HTML. This is used to make the web page look more interactive and dynamic. Internet Explorer supports this programing technique and the programing is executed in the client side.

2.19 Summary

In this chapter, an overview of HTML and web page design processes has been explained. HTML makes use of tags to format documents, text. HTML can also be used to link documents, add images and to construct tables. Frames are also used to display multiple web pages in the same window. Using cascading style sheets, styles can be controlled. JavaScript can be used for making the web page more dynamic and interactive.

2.20 Review Questions

1. What is HTML and why do we need it in e-commerce applications?
2. Why do we need JavaScript?
3. How do you transfer data from client to the server and fetch it back to the end user?
4. What is the difference between HTML and JavaScript?
5. Explain the need to have frames in e-commerce web pages.

Chapter 3
Web Page Hosting

3.1 Learning Objectives

At the end of this chapter the student will learn:

- How to design web pages,
- The steps required to make thc dcsign error free,
- Process for publishing web page,
- Process for hosting web page,

3.2 Introduction

Every web page that needs to be developed has to keep three things in mind. It has to have a good content, should be convenient for the readers, and should be presentable. Before starting to design the web page, please check the facts that need to be published. Also, cite sources when required so that a creditable document can be prepared. Considering the visitors or readers of the document, the web page needs to have information which can be easily found by them. The visitors also should be able to navigate from one section to another, without any hassles. Once these two elements are taken care of, the web page designer should consider putting esthetic part into place. The look and feel of the web page will be appreciated only when the two concerns are met.

Some of the important points that need to be kept in mind while designing web pages are: (1) avoiding common mistakes such as inscrutable text, difficult to understand text should be avoided. Also, hyperlinks should be well understood and self explanatory. (2) Review the pages before installing them. These pages should be well written, viewed, and tested before being installed on a web server. It is advisable to develop the web pages at home computer before sending it to public

S. Mohapatra, *E-Commerce Strategy*, Springer Texts in Business and Economics,
DOI: 10.1007/978-1-4614-4142-7_3,

domain server. (3) The web page titles should be effective and meaningful. These web page titles also appear in bookmark bar when someone tries to save these files. (4) The download time should be short as otherwise the viewer will get bored and will get distracted. For this to happen, the amount of graphic contents should be optimal (so that the viewer is attracted and it does not take time to download). While designing the web page, consider the slowest speed that a viewer can have. This will determine ease of access of the web page. (5) Design the web pages for portability. For example, if the web pages are designed on a UNIX platform, then case sensitivity needs to be taken care of. Filenames need to be correctly remembered as they are case sensitive and this needs to be correctly recorded on the web page as well. If we create directories of web pages, then plan to use the same directory structure in the web page itself. In this context, we must use relative URLs rather than absolute URLs as relative URLs are better portable than the absolute URLs. This will make the links and directory structure stable when the files are used in multiple file directories.

3.3 Web Page Elements

A web browser is designed to display any ASCII text file that has a file name with extension .htm or .html. To experiment, find a file that has .txt extension in your computer, change the extension to .htm. Open Internet Explorer (IE), use the File - > Open menu; browse and open that file. You will be able to open the file and see the contents. Learning how to load a local file to load the browser is the first step in web design. We can open any text file with web browser, but if a file is written with web designing in mind, then the look and feel of the file will be vastly different than that of a normal text file. This file is different as it needs to be hosted in a web page for public view and it better be good so that it can be appreciated by its viewers.

3.3.1 Offline Web Pages

During the web design stage, first the offline web page needs to be prepared. A web server and Internet connection may not be required immediately. The offline web page can be viewed normally by any browser. In the offline web page, when opened with a browser, the entire text has been faithfully preserved; but the original formatting is not seen, for example, if there were headlines and sub-headlines, and text body, then the entire writings appear as one text body as all of them run together. The line breaks and page breaks do not appear at the same place. The display of final web page is done in such a way that end-users using laptops, desktops with different screen sizes and resolutions can be able to see all the web pages without any problem. This is a characteristic that offline web page design needs to take care of. This means, if the window is resized, then the web browser increases the width of each text line to fill as much of the horizontal web space as possible. Similarly, if the browser's window is decreased, the text lines are shortened accordingly. This is the reason the original page breaks and line breaks are not preserved by the web page while displaying it in the browser. The web browser dynamically reworks the window to display the entire contents suiting the screen size and resolutions available.

Web page publication will make sure that the same page is displayed in different ways for different readers (depending on the hardware that is being used). This is possible because of certain characteristics that Hypertext Markup Language (HTML) provides. As seen in Chap. 2, HTML is a markup language that gives control to web browsers for displaying the contents. The language helps to provide the users to see the desired formatting that were made during offline web page design. By inserting HTML tags, the required formatting is preserved and is adjusted at the user side. HTML is used to add a style, content, and graphical elements. In web pages, links are also provided. There are different types of links (absolute, relative) that can be provided in a web page.

There are four basic elements that should be presented in any web page. All web pages should contain HTML, HEAD, TITLE and BODY. All web pages should start with a template having all these four elements. HTML tags can be added to a text file by using any of the text editors such as word, text file, notepad, etc. However, with notepad the problem is when we try to open an existing .htm or .html file by using notepad directory dialog box, we must change the default setting file type from Text document to All Files. This is because, if we keep the default value for opening, no HTML file will appear in the directory window. Similarly, while using Microsoft editor, save the text file by using File - > Save As command; then save it as HTML file. Also, while saving in word editor, save it as .txt file format, without this option the word will not save it as plain text file.

To a text file, we can add HTML tags or pair of tags, such as <HTML> and </HTML>. The first tag marks the beginning of the HTML document and (/) marks the end of the HTML element. HTML tags will tell a web browser how to make a web page. HTML elements are used to divide a web page into segments where different kinds of information are displayed. Tag pairs can be used to provide nested tag pairs so that a hierarchical structure can be obtained. In the hierarchical structure, we have an HTML element, inside which we have HEAD and BODY elements. All web pages should contain these elements and arranged in a hierarchical manner. The HEAD contains information that is useful behind the scenes, but which is not displayed as part of the web page display. Figure 2.1 shows the hierarchical structure. At the top level, we have HTML and then inside are HEAD and BODY elements. All web pages should arrange these elements in this manner. HEAD contains information that is useful behind the scene but not part of web page display. TITLE element controls the title bar of the browser window. TITLE element belongs to HEAD element as well and is required for the browser to recognize the title bar (Fig. 3.1).

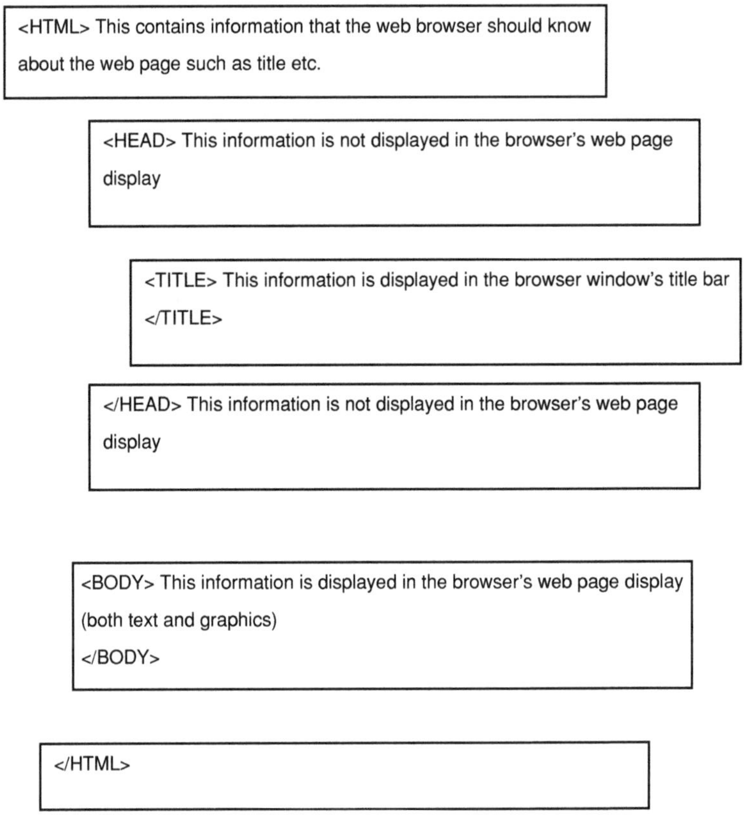

Fig. 3.1 Hierarchical structure in HTML programming technique

3.4 Web Page Development Life Cycle

The web page development cycle can be broadly categorized to four stages: (1) Prepare a file with .HTM or >HTML extension and save it to your hard disk. (2) Open the file through browser. (3) Review the web page and, (4) Rework on the page using a text editor or HTML editor. However, there are HTML editors who can provide a preview of the new web page so that the designer does not have to use the browser to open the same for viewing. This increases productivity and makes experimentation with HTML elements easier.

3.4.1 Formatting

The elements of a web page that are visible are in the section <BODY>. This is where the look and feel of the web page is controlled. To start formatting process, it might be a good idea to tell the users about what the document is all about. A title, if provided, will understand this fact. This can be done by using an element known as 'heading element' (this quite different from head element). There are six different sizes of heading elements, very large to very small. These are denoted as <H1> Very large </H1> , <H2> Large </H2> .....till <H6> Very small </H6> . The heading can be inserted at anywhere in the <BODY> of a web page. Sometimes, it is useful to fine-tune an HTML element by adding specific attributes to the element. For example, 'HTML attribute' will consist of an HTML attribute name and value. We can design the heading by using this attribute to either 'left justify' or 'center justify', etc.

3.4.2 Troubleshooting

After finishing the design in offline mode, we can open the file in the browser and see if the page opens properly. Chances are there that the web page may not open properly. These could be some of the reasons mentioned below:

- There could be typological error and starting end tags may not be present.
- The angle brackets should be exactly the way it should be.
- Quotations should be closed within the same tag.

It might be a good idea to periodically check the problems associated with the design by opening the offline file with the browser and checking the results. This will help in pinpointing the errors easily.

3.4.3 Publish the Web Page

After checking the web page for its correctness, choose an ISP and connect the web page to the server. This will allow others to see the page. However, the computer where the file has been stored will publish it to the public as long as the computer is switched on. Once the file is made unavailable by switching off the computer, the web page stops being available to the public.

3.5 Installing Web Pages on a Web Server

Once the web pages have been designed, they are ready to be published for public access. There are many ways to install the web pages or better known as publishing the web pages. While publishing, there are certain informations that are required to be known such as the designer web server details, personal account in that server, etc. To publish the pages, the HTML files that have been designed offline need to be installed. Some commercial sites offer free web space for hosting such as Yahoo, Google, Yola, etc. For this free hosting, the conditions that are put in is that your web page should allow free banner advertisements to appear in the browser window, each time someone visits the web page. The only need is to register in the web site and then publish the page. However, if it is not free service that one goes for, then by subscribing to a commercial ISP, we can publish the web pages without the advertisements. In this way, one can have complete control on one's web page.

To install the web pages, we need to copy the files onto the server and make sure that they go to the right place in the server. Some designers run into problem, because they know the name of the web server but are not clear where the web pages will go on the server. As a result, ultimately they fail to publish the web pages. Locations for files are specified by the directory paths. However, there can be more than one directory path. The path that we see in the URL may not be the directory path that we need to use while uploading the files to the server.

Once the web page has been uploaded to the server, the page is ready to be published to the entire world. Still, there could be minor problems. First, we must know the URL that will allow us to view our web pages with a web browser. If this URL is not known, then we can forward the same information to others for helping them to view the pages. In addition to this, we might have to make the properties such that protection codes are removed for viewing by others. Usually commercial sites allow the codes to be removed before publishing, but taking extra precaution will avoid extra effort required for reworks later on.

3.5.1 Steps for Web Page Publishing

There are steps that need to be adhered to for publishing web page. With experience, this will become a streamlined process, but for beginners, this will require extra initial efforts so that many hot and trials can be reduced.

3.5.1.1 Decide the Mode of Access to Web Page

After the web page has been made ready in offline manner, we need to follow this step. We need to know the access code (usually user id and password) for our account in the web server. This gives us access to the server. The server can be a free account or a paid account from one of the service providers.

3.5.1.2 Note the DNS Address

Once we have the account details known to use, we can find the web server's DNS address in online documentation for our account. The address is usually provided by the system administrator or in the frequently asked questions document. The DNS address usually has prefixes such as ftp://or http://. These prefixes represent the two different protocols that the web server might be supporting. Still, if we have problem in locating our DNS address, then help desk or customer service can be approached to resolve the issue.

3.5.1.3 Path Name

At this point of time, we should have the path name for uploading the files. The path name is the directory where we need to copy the files. The web administrator will be able to help us for the same.

3.5.1.4 Uploading the Files

For uploading the files, we can use a FTP client or web page construction tool such as Microsoft FrontPage 2003, etc. If we are using HTML construction kit, it needs to be checked to see if it has publishing features. This can be found by making a search with the keyword ‘publish’ and the returning results can indicate if the feature is enabled in the tool. This feature allows the designer to upload the web pages for publishing. We can also upload the files using web browsers such as Internet Explorer or Google Chrome as these browsers have the features enabled for uploading. Also, using an FTP client, we can upload the files. While uploading the files from web browsers, we can follow the steps as follows: (1) From the File menu, select Open Page and then use the directory dialog box to locate the HTML file in the hard disk. (2) From the File menu, select Publish. Fill in all other details for the popped up window at this stage. In the popped up window, there will be a field with phrase ‘HTTP or FTP Location to publish to:’ enter the DNS address and the directory path with a prefix ftp://or http://. Either of the two prefixes will work. This information is stored in the browser tool for uploading and next time, the browser will fill this information for us automatically. After that, user id and password need to be entered into so that the server can accept the web pages for publishing. We can have the option of saving the password so that we don’t have to enter every time for our account.

The browsers have good features that will allow us to upload groups of web pages that are related to each other in one screen. This means, if there are other files in the same directory as the current page, we can upload all the files along with the present file. Hence, if the whole web site is in one web sub directory, then we can upload the entire site by clicking the radio button “All files in the folder” and then clicking OK.

Care should be taken that once uploaded the file uploading cannot be undone. If the web server contains the same file name as one of the files that are being uploaded, then the second file will override the initial file in the server. There may not be any warning message and once the original file has been uploaded we will not be able to retrieve the same. Hence, we need to control the version of the file to be uploaded and proper back up mechanisms should be at place so that we can retrieve the same later on, if required.

File uploading can also be done through FTP clients such as WS_FTP or by simply typing the ftp web site address in the browsers. Just by clicking the correct web page directory, we can copy all the files in the same directory to the web server. But if the web server has too many files or many user accounts, then uploading by FTP might become slower. Also, if the bandwidth of the connection is less and the connection is slow, even then the uploading will be time consuming. Some of the FTP sites have settings to accept different files in a different manner. Hence, we need to check the settings of the FTP site before uploading the files. Sometimes, the web server (FTP site) may have automated settings; this will allow the site to figure out the file that is to be uploaded based on the extension and take actions accordingly.

All FTP servers can recognize the most common file types used for web pages. For example, if the files have .htm or .html extensions, then the server understands them to be text files and accordingly move them to different upload group. Similarly, for files with .jpg and .gif files, the server recognizes them to be binary files and upload them into another group. If we have wrong file extensions, then the files will be transferred to the wrong group and no error message will be flashed. The resulting wrong transfer will be jumbled up and not useable. In such cases, we need to transfer the files again.

3.5.1.5 Find the URL

After the transfer of files, find out the URL of the web page where your home page is hosted. Please note it down for future work and also for informing others.

3.5.1.6 Final Touch

This is required, if after going through all the steps; the web page is still not visible. There could be two types of errors displayed now—1. The error message could state that 'you are not authorized to view the page', then it implies that there is a need to make some adjustments to settings about access permission. Also, we may have to look at the properties of the files that have been uploaded and check if the files have been allowed for public viewing. If, however, the web page states that 404-Not found error message is flashed, then the web page has not been installed properly. To fix the problem, we may have to upload the files once again. We can also check the source information by right clicking on the web page and correcting on the web page itself (provided we have administrator rights).

An example is given here which has been found by right clicking on a published web page:

<!DOCTYPE HTML PUBLIC "-//W3C//DTD HTML 4.01//EN" "http:// www.w3.org/TR/html4/strict.dtd"><htmlxmlns:fb="http://www.facebook.com/

2008/fbml”><head><META http-equiv=“Content-Type” content=“text/html; charset=UTF-8”><link href=“http://economictimes.indiatimes.com/icons/etfav-icon.ico” rel=“shortcut icon”><meta http-equiv=“Content-Type” content=“text/html; charset=UTF-8”><meta content=“600” http-equiv=“refresh”><title>The Economic Times: Business News, Personal Finance, Financial News, India Stock Market Investing, Economy News, SENSEX, NIFTY, NSE, BSE Live, IPO News</title><meta content=“Economic Times India's Leading Business Newspaper offers Business News, Financial news, Stock/Share Market News, Economy News, Loans & Banking News, Live Stocks and News & Investment analysis on Mutual Funds, Gold, Forex and Real Estate.” name=“description”><meta content=“business news,personal finance,financial news,share market news india,stock market investing,indian economy,loans news,banking news,gold,bullion,commodities,art investment,sensex,nifty,nse,bse live,economic times,india business news,-indian market,india business,company news,indian industry,forex news,capital market,bombay stock exchange,indian stock market,indian business,equity research,world business,national stock exchange,international business,market news,stock market india,mutual funds in india,mutual funds,property,real estate news,ipo news” name=“keywords”><meta content=“PQ6sc1DJV+8wuapNsYGk 6DfMNUrdxsAzsgqfBsKt1gs=” name=“verify-v1”><meta content=“IE=EmulateIE7;IE=EmulateIE9” http-equiv=“X-UA-Compatible”><META content=“name= News;action-document.write(‘<s’+’cript language=“javascript” src=“http://netspiderads2.indiatimes.com/ads.dll/genptypead?slotid=36869&srands=‘+shosh Rnd+’&shtype=3”>‘+’</’+’s’+’cript>‘)

</script></body></html>

3.5.2 Plagiarism in Web Publishing

Copyright laws protect creative and economic interests of writers, musicians, and artists. In a democratic setup, creative works should be accessible but with proper monitoring and control. This implies that without taking proper permission, we cannot publish any material that belongs to others. Before uploading any file, it would be required to take proper care to see that all the rules and regulations are adhered to. A detailed discussion follows in the next section which will highlight different aspects of copyright issues in web publishing.

3.6 Legal and Ethical Issues in Web Publishing

There are several legal and ethical issues that need to be considered while publishing on the web page. This section deals with several practical aspects of web publishing so as to make the designers aware of these issues. Many times the designers subcontract the work of web design to several others; while accepting the subcontracted work, the main designers need to make other designers aware of these facts. This will save the publishers from many legal procedures and embarrassments later on. It might be a good idea to have a legal advisor so as to handle each and every publishing copyright issue. This will help to understand the consequences of publishing the work online. For example, if the intention is to publish a written work, then we need to have clear permissions from the previous publishers. This is so because many publishers will not like to publish in the web as this means distributing digitally to everyone without any commercial gains. These publishers might take legal actions against web publishers as web publications of their works would have reduced their earning potentials.

Even if there are files and web pages that have been designed by you and you own these files completely, still it might be a good idea to look at the legal restrictions that might be binding on these files. In this context, consideration of following points will be desirable:

- Are the files being published has already been published elsewhere?
- Are the files being published are modified versions of already existing and published files?
- Are the materials to be published are excerpts of existing materials (already published somewhere else)?
- Are there sufficient permissions to download the materials and then publish them as mine?
- Can the pictures and figures that have been published by someone else and available in the public domain be made available by another publisher (in partial or full display)?

There are several software tools (these tools available in different web sites to be used for checking the plagiarism; some of the domains where these tools are available are www.plagiarism-detector.com, www.writecheck.com, www.plagiarismchecker.com, www.dustball.com, www.plagiarisma.net) which can be used to detect plagiarism. This is advisable to be done before publishing the page to the web. The software gives details of the words and lines that have been copied verbatim and provides the source in the Internet, where these materials have been published earlier. At the time of going to the press, the available tools could only detect text and not the pictures and figures. We are sure with advancement of technology, the tools will be able to detect if pictures and figures have been copied from other sources.

As shown in Table 3.1, the summary of output of the plagiarism check is displayed.

The report starts with the name of the document which has been checked for plagiarism; here the name of the document which was checked for plagiarism is 'TQM and BPR' and the extension docx indicates that this is a Microsoft Office document (2007). It then indicates the percentage of plagiarism reported. In this case, 23% of the document has been found to be copied verbatim from different sources in the Internet (already published). It then lists the web sites from where the lines have been copied or similar lines are available in published formats. The

Table 3.1 Sample plagiarism report

TQM and BPR.docx (23%)
23% total score
17% http://www.answers.com/topic/tqm
17% http://www.scribd.com/doc/27472736/1-Total-Quality-Management-TQM-Refers-To
16% http://www.referenceforbusiness.com/encyclopedia/Thir-Val/Total-Quality-Management-TQM.html
17% http://www.scribd.com/doc/2919927/Total-Quality-Management
17% http://www.referenceforbusiness.com/small/Sm-Z/Total-Quality-Management-TQM.html
10% http://www.asqh.org/threads/108-TQM-Principles-and-Implementing
7% http://www.aibuma.org/journals/paper2_Quality_Management_Magutu.pdf
6% http://www.1000advices.com/guru/quality_tqm_14points_deming.html
6% http://www.witiger.com/internationalbusiness/TQM.htm

percentages written on the left side indicates the percentages of lines in the document found in a particular web site.

Before publishing any document to the web site, we need to check the contents for plagiarisms which can lead to copyright violation issues. These violations can lead to legal battles which not only can claim monetary penalties from the publishers but also can harm the image and reputations.

3.6.1 Copyright Basics

(Source: Indian Copyright Act, 1957, www.copyright.gov.in)
Ministry of Human resources, Government of India, Department of secondary education, and higher education has published a hand book of copyright law. This handbook does not intend to substitute copyright act and rules, but serves as information for enforcement agencies. The rational of copyright protection as explained in this handbook is produced here as under:

3.6.1.1 What is copyright?

Copyright is a right given by the law to creators of literary, dramatic, musical, and artistic works and producers of cinematograph films and sound recordings. In fact, it is a bundle of rights including, inter alia, rights of reproduction, communication to the public, adaptation, and translation of the work. There could be slight variations in the composition of the rights depending on the work.

3.6.1.2 Why should copyright be protected?

Copyright ensures certain minimum safeguards of the rights of authors over their creations, thereby protecting and rewarding creativity. Creativity being the keystone of progress, no civilized society can afford to ignore the basic requirement of encouraging the same. Economic and social development of a society is dependent on creativity. The protection provided by copyright to the efforts of writers, artists, designers, dramatists, musicians, architects, and producers of sound recordings, cinematograph films, and computer software, creates an atmosphere conducive to creativity, which induces them to create more and motivates others to create.

Is it not true that strict application of the principle of protection of copyright hampers economic and cultural development of the society?
Yes. If copyright protection is applied rigidly, it can hamper progress of the society. However, copyright laws are enacted with necessary exceptions and limitations to ensure that a balance is maintained between the interests of the creators and of the community.

To strike an appropriate and viable balance between the rights of the copyright owners and the interests of the society as a whole, there are exceptions in the law. Many types of exploitation of work which are for social purposes such as education, religious ceremonies, and so on are exempted from the operation of the rights granted in the Act. Copyright in a work is considered as infringed only if a substantial part is made use of unauthorized means. What is 'substantial' varies from case to case. More often than not, it is a matter of quality rather than quantity. For example, if a lyricist copy a very catching phrase from another lyricist's song, there is likely to be infringement even if that phrase is very short.

Does the law allow any use of a work without permission of the owner of the copyright, and, if so, which are they?
Subject to certain conditions, a fair deal for research, study, criticism, review, and news reporting, as well as use of works in library and schools and in the legislatures, is permitted without specific permission of the copyright owners. In order to protect the interests of users, some exemptions have been prescribed in respect of specific uses of works enjoying copyright. Some of the exemptions are the uses of the work,

i. for the purpose of research or private study,
ii. for criticism or review,
iii. for reporting current events,
iv. in connection with judicial proceeding,
v. performance by an amateur club or society if the performance is given to a non-paying audience, and
vi. the making of sound recordings of literary, dramatic, or musical works under certain conditions.

3.6.1.3 What is the Scope of Protection in the Copyright Act, 1957?

The Copyright Act, 1957 protects original literary, dramatic, musical, and artistic works, and cinematograph films and sound recordings from unauthorized uses. Unlike the case with patents, copyright protects the expressions and not the ideas. There is no copyright in an idea.

Does copyright apply to titles and names?

Copyright does not ordinarily protect titles by themselves or names, short word combinations, slogans, short phrases, methods, plots, or factual information. Copyright does not protect ideas or concepts. To get the protection of copyright a work must be original.

3.6.1.4 WORK: What is a Work?

A work means any of the following, namely, a literary, dramatic, musical, or artistic work, a cinematograph film, or a sound recording.

What is a work of joint authorship?
"Work of joint authorship" means a work produced by the collaboration of two or more authors in which the contribution of one author is not distinct from the contribution of the other author or authors.

What are the classes of works for which copyrights protection is available in India?
Copyright subsists throughout India in the following classes of works:

- Original literary, dramatic, musical, and artistic works;
- Cinematograph films; and
- Sound recordings.

What is an artistic work?
An artistic work means:

- a painting, a sculpture, a drawing (including a diagram, map, chart, or plan), an engraving, or a photograph, whether or not any such work possesses artistic quality;
- a work of architecture; and
- any other work of artistic craftsmanship.

What is a musical work?
"Musical work" means a work consisting of music and includes any graphical notation of such work but does not include any words or any action intended to be sung, spoken, or performed with the music. A musical work need not be written down to enjoy copyright protection.

What is a sound recording?
"Sound recording" means a recording of sounds from which sounds may be produced regardless of the medium on which such recording is made or the method by which the sounds are produced. A phonogram and a CD-ROM are sound recordings.

What is a cinematograph film?
"Cinematograph film" means any work of visual recording on any medium produced through a process from which a moving image may be produced by any means and includes a sound recording accompanying such visual recording and "cinematograph" shall be construed as including any work produced by any process analogous to cinematography including video films.

What is a government work?
"Government work" means a work which is made or published by or under the direction or control of,

- the government or any department of the government,
- any legislature in India, and
- any court, tribunal or other judicial authority in India.

What is an Indian work?
"Indian work" means a literary, dramatic, or musical work,

- the author of which is a citizen of India; or
- which is first published in India; or
- the author of which, in the case of an unpublished work is, at the time of the making of the work, a citizen of India.

3.6.1.5 Authorship and Ownership

Whose rights are protected by copyright?
Copyright protects the rights of authors, i.e., creators of intellectual property in the form of literary, musical, dramatic, and artistic works and cinematograph films and sound recordings.

Who is the first owner of copyright in a work?
Ordinarily the author is the first owner of copyright in a work.

Who is an author?

- In the case of a literary or dramatic work the author, i.e., the person who creates the work.
- In the case of a musical work, the composer.
- In the case of a cinematograph film, the producer.
- In the case of a sound recording, the producer.
- In the case of a photograph, the photographer.
- In the case of a computer generated work, the person who causes the work to be created.

Who all have rights in a musical sound recording?
There are many right holders in a musical sound recording. For example, the lyricist who wrote the lyrics, the composer who set the music, the singer who sang the song, the musician(s) who performed the background music, and the person or company who produced the sound recording.

Is it necessary to obtain any license or permission to use a musical sound recording for public performance?
A sound recording generally comprises various rights. It is necessary to obtain the licenses from each and every right owner in the sound recording. This would, inter alia, include the producer of the sound recording, the lyricist who wrote the lyrics, and the musician who composed the music.

Who is the owner of copyright in a government work?
In the case of a government work, government shall, in the absence of any agreement to the contrary, be the first owner of the copyright therein.

Who is the owner of copyright in the work of a public undertaking?
In the case of a work made or first published by or under the direction or control of any public undertaking, such public undertaking shall, in the absence of any agreement to the contrary, be the first owner of the copyright therein.

Who is the owner of copyright in works by journalists during the course of their employment?
In the case of a literary, dramatic, or artistic work made by the author in the course of his employment by the proprietor of a newspaper, magazine, or similar periodical under a contract of service or apprenticeship, for the purpose of publication in a newspaper, magazine, or similar periodical, the said proprietor shall, in the absence of any agreement to the contrary, be the first owner of the copyright in the work in so far as the copyright relates to the publication of the work in any newspaper, magazine, or similar periodical, or to the reproduction of the work for the purpose of its being so published, but in all other respects the author shall be the first owner of the copyright in the work.

Who is the owner of a work produced during the course of the author's employment?
In the case of a work made in the course of the author's employment under a contract of service or apprenticeship, the employer shall, in the absence of any agreement to the contrary, be the first owner of the copyright therein.

Who is the owner of the copyright in the case of a work produced for valuable consideration at the instance of another person?
In the case of a photograph taken, or a painting or portrait drawn, or an engraving or a cinematograph film made, for valuable consideration at the instance of any person, such person shall, in the absence of any agreement to the contrary, be the first owner of the copyright therein.

Is copyright assignable?
Yes. The owner of the copyright in an existing work or the prospective owner of the copyright in a future work may assign to any person the copyright either wholly or partially and either generally or subject to limitations and either for the whole term of the copyright or any part thereof.

What is the mode of assigning copyright?
It shall be in writing signed by the assignor or by his duly authorized agent. It shall identify the specific works and specify the rights assigned and the duration and territorial extent of such assignment. It shall also specify the amount of royalty payable, if any, to the author or his legal heirs during the currency of the assignment and the assignment shall be subject to revision, extension, or termination on terms mutually agreed upon by the parties.

Does an assignment lapse automatically?
Where the assignee does not exercise the rights assigned to him within a period of one year from the date of assignment, the assignment in respect of such rights shall be deemed to have lapsed after the expiry of the said period unless otherwise specified in the assignment.

What will be the period of assignment if not specifically stated in the assignments?
If the period of assignment is not stated, it shall be deemed to be five years from the date of assignment.

What will be the territorial extent of the assignment if not specified in the assignment?
If the territorial extent of assignment of the rights is not specified, it shall be presumed to extend within the whole of India.

Can an author relinquish copyright and, if so, how?
The author of a work may relinquish all or any of the rights comprising the copyright in the work by giving notice in the prescribed form to the Registrar of Copyrights.

3.6.1.6 Different Rights

Are copyrights same for all classes of works?
No. The rights vary according to the class of work.

What are the rights in the case of a literary work?
In the case of a literary work (except computer program), copyright means the exclusive right:

- To reproduce the work;
- To issue copies of the work to the public;
- To perform the work in public;

- To communicate the work to the public;
- To make cinematograph film or sound recording in respect of the work;
- To make any translation of the work;
- To make any adaptation of the work.

Is translation of an original work also protected by copyright?
Yes. All the rights of the original work apply to its translation also.

Are computer programs protected under Copyright Act?
Yes. Computer programs are protected under the Copyright Act. They are treated as literary works.

Are there any special rights in computer programs?
Yes. In addition to all the rights applicable to a literary work, owner of the copyright in a computer program enjoys the rights to sell or give on hire, or offer for sale or hire, regardless of whether such a copy has been sold or given on hire on earlier occasion.

What are the rights in a dramatic work?
In the case of a dramatic work, copyright means the exclusive right:

- To reproduce the work;
- To communicate the work to the public or perform the work in public;
- To issue copies of the work to the public;
- To include the work in any cinematograph film;
- To make any adaptation of the work;
- To make translation of the work.

What are the rights in an artistic work?
In the case of an artistic work, copyright means the exclusive right:

- To reproduce the work;
- To communicate the work to the public;
- To issue copies of the work to the public;
- To include the work in any cinematograph film;
- To make any adaptation of the work.

What are the rights in a musical work?
In the case of a musical work, copyright means the exclusive right:

- To reproduce the work;
- To issue copies of the work to the public;
- To perform the work in public;
- To communicate the work to the public;
- To make cinematograph film or sound recording in respect of the work;
- To make any translation of the work;
- To make any adaptation of the work.

What are the rights in a cinematograph film?
In the case of a cinematograph film, copyright means the exclusive right:

- To make a copy of the film including a photograph of any image forming part thereof;
- To sell or give on hire or offer for sale or hire a copy of the film;
- To communicate the cinematograph film to the public.

What are the rights in a sound recording?

- To make any other sound recording embodying it;
- To sell or give on hire, or offer for sale or hire, any copy of the sound recording;
- To communicate the sound recording to the public.

What is the right of reproduction?
The right of reproduction commonly means that no person shall make one or more copies of a work or of a substantial part of it in any material form including sound and film recording without the permission of the copyright owner. The most common kind of reproduction is printing an edition of a work. Reproduction occurs in storing of a work in the computer memory.

What is the right of communication to the public?
Communication to the public means making any work available for being seen or heard or otherwise enjoyed by the public directly or by any means of display or diffusion. It is not necessary that any member of the public actually sees, hears, or otherwise enjoys the work so made available. For example, a cable operator may transmit a cinematograph film, which no member of the public may see. Still it is a communication to the public. The fact that the work in question is accessible to the public is enough to say that the work is communicated to the public.

What is an adaptation?
Adaptation involves the preparation of a new work in the same or different form based upon an already existing work. The Copyright Act defines the following acts as adaptations:

a. Conversion of a dramatic work into a nondramatic work;
b. Conversion of a literary or artistic work into a dramatic work;
c. Rearrangement of a literary or dramatic work;
d. Depiction in a comic form or through pictures of a literary or dramatic work;
e. Transcription of a musical work or any act involving rearrangement or alteration of an existing work.

The making of a cinematograph film of a literary or dramatic or musical work is also an adaptation.

Can any person translate a work without the permission of the owner of the copyright in the work?
No. A person cannot translate a work enjoying copyright without the permission of the copyright owner.

Is there any copyright over news?
No. There is no copyright over news. However, there is copyright over the way in which a news item is reported.

3.6.1.7 Registration of Copyright

Is it necessary to register a work to claim copyright?
No. Acquisition of copyright is automatic and it does not require any formality. However, certificate of registration of copyright and the entries made therein serve as prima facie evidence in a court of law with reference to dispute relating to ownership of copyright.

What is the procedure for registration of a work under the Copyright Act, 1957?
Copyright comes into existence as soon as a work is created and no formality is required to be completed for acquiring copyright. However, facilities exist for having the work registered in the Register of Copyrights maintained in the Copyright Office of the Department of Education. The entries made in the Register of Copyrights serve as prima facie evidence in the court of law. The Copyright Office has been set up to provide registration facilities to all types of works and is headed by a Registrar of Copyrights and is located at B.2/W.3, C.R. Barracks, Kasturba Gandhi Marg, New Delhi- 110 003, Tel: 338 4387

What are the guidelines regarding registration of a work under the Copyright Act?
Chapter VI of the Copyright Rules, 1956, as amended, sets out the procedure for the registration of a work. Copies of the Act and Rules can be obtained from the Manager of Publications, Publication Branch, Civil Lines, Delhi or his authorized dealers on payment. The procedure for registration is as follows:

a. Application for registration is to be made on Form IV (Including Statement of Particulars and Statement of Further Particulars) as prescribed in the first schedule to the Rules;
b. Separate applications should be made for registration of each work;
c. Each application should be accompanied by the requisite fee prescribed in the second schedule to the Rules; and
d. The applications should be signed by the applicant or the advocate in whose favor a Vakalatnama or Power of Attorney has been executed. The Power of Attorney signed by the party and accepted by the advocate should also be enclosed.

Each and every column of the Statement of Particulars and Statement of Further Particulars should be replied specifically.

Both published and unpublished works can be registered. Copyright in works published before 21 January, 1958, i.e., before the Copyright Act, 1957 came in force, can also be registered, provided the works still enjoy copyright. Three copies of published work may be sent along with the application. If the work to be registered is unpublished, a copy of the manuscript has to be sent along with the application for affixing the stamp of the Copyright Office in proof of the work having been registered. In case two copies of the manuscript are sent, one copy of the same duly stamped will be returned, while the other will be retained, as far as possible, in the Copyright Office for record and will be kept confidential. It would also be open to the applicant to send only extracts from the unpublished work instead of the whole manuscript and ask for the return of the extracts after being stamped with the seal of the Copyright Office.

When a work has been registered as unpublished and subsequently it is published, the applicant may apply for changes in particulars entered in the Register of Copyright in Form V with prescribed fee.

3.6.1.8 Term of Copyright

Is copyright protected in perpetuity?
No. It is protected for a limited period of time.

What is the term of protection of copyright?
The general rule is that copyright lasts for 60 years. In the case of original literary, dramatic, musical, and artistic works the 60-year period is counted from the year following the death of the author. In the case of cinematograph films, sound recordings, photographs, posthumous publications, anonymous and pseudonymous publications, works of government, and works of international organizations, the 60-year period is counted from the date of publication.

3.6.1.9 Administration of copyright law

Is there any advisory body on copyright matters?
Yes. The government has set up a Copyright Enforcement Advisory Council (CEAC).

Are there special courts for copyright?
No. There are no special courts for copyright cases. The regular courts try these cases. There is a Copyright Board to adjudicate certain cases pertaining to copyright.

What are the powers of Copyright Board?
The Copyright Act provides for a quasi-judicial body called the Copyright Board consisting of a Chairman and two or more, but not exceeding fourteen, other members for adjudicating certain kinds of copyright cases. The Chairman of the Board is of the level of a judge of a High Court. The Board has the power to:

i. hear appeals against the orders of the Registrar of Copyright;
ii. hear applications for rectification of entries in the Register of Copyrights;

iii. adjudicate upon disputes on assignment of copyright;
iv. grant compulsory licenses to publish or republish works (in certain circumstances);
v. grant compulsory license to produce and publish a translation of a literary or dramatic work in any language after a period of 7 years from the first publication of the work;
vi. hear and decide disputes as to whether a work has been published or about the date of publication or about the term of copyright of a work in another country;
vii. fix rates of royalties in respect of sound recordings under the cover-version provision; and
viii. fix the resale share right in original copies of a painting, a sculpture, or a drawing and of original manuscripts of a literary or dramatic or musical work.

The present composition of the Board is at Appendix III.

Has the Registrar of Copyrights any judicial powers?
Yes. The Registrar of Copyrights has the powers of a civil court when trying a suit under the Code of Civil Procedure in respect of the following matters, namely:

a. summoning and enforcing the attendance of any person and examining him on oath;
b. requiring the discovery and production of any document;
c. receiving evidence on affidavit;
d. issuing commissions for the examination of witnesses or documents;
e. requisitioning any public record or copy thereof from any court or office;
f. any other matters which may be prescribed.

3.6.1.10 Performer's Rights

Who is a performer?
As per the Indian Copyright Act, a "Performer" includes an actor, singer, musician, dancer, acrobat, juggler, conjurer, snake charmer, a person delivering a lecture, or any other person who makes a performance.

What is a performance?
"Performance" in relation to performer's right, means any visual or acoustic presentation made live by one or more performers.

What are the rights of a performer?
A performer has the following rights in his/her performance:

- Right to make a sound recording or visual recording of the performance;
- Right to reproduce the sound recording or visual recording of the performance;
- Right to broadcast the performance;
- Right to communicate the performance to the public otherwise than by broadcast.

What is the term of protection of performer's rights?
Performer's rights subsist for 25 years.

What are the rights of a performer in a cinematograph film?
Once a performer has consented for incorporation of his performance in a cinematograph film, he shall have no more performer's rights to that performance.

3.6.1.11 Foreign Works

Is copyright of foreign works protected in India?
Yes. Copyrights of works of the countries mentioned in the International Copyright Order are protected in India, as if such works are Indian works.

Does copyright subsist in a foreign work?
Copyright of nationals of countries who are members of the Berne Convention for the Protection of Literary and Artistic Works, Universal Copyright Convention and the TRIPS Agreement are protected in India through the International Copyright Order. A list of such countries is at **Appendix IV**.

Which are the international copyright conventions of which India is a member?
Copyright as provided by the Indian Copyright Act is valid only within the borders of the country. To secure protection to Indian works in foreign countries, India has become a member of the following international conventions on copyright and neighboring (related) rights:

i. Berne Convention for the Protection of Literary and Artistic works.
ii. Universal Copyright Convention.
iii. Convention for the Protection of Producers of Phonograms against Unauthorized Duplication of their Phonograms.
iv. Multilateral Convention for the Avoidance of Double Taxation of Copyright Royalties.
v. Trade Related Aspects of Intellectual Property Rights (TRIPS) Agreement.

3.6.1.12 Collective Administration of Copyrights

What is collective administration of copyright?
Collective administration of copyright is a concept where management and protection of copyright in works are undertook by a society of owners of such works. Obviously no owner of copyright in any work can keep track of all the uses others make of his work. When he becomes a member of a national copyright society, that society, because of its organizational facilities and strength, is able to keep a better vigil over the uses made of that work throughout the country and collect due royalties from the users of those works. Because of the country's membership in

international conventions, the copyright societies are able to have reciprocal agreements with similar societies in other countries for collecting royalties for the uses of Indian works in those countries. From this, it can automatically be inferred that it will be in the interests of copyright owners to join a collective administration organization to insure better protection to the copyright in their works and for reaping optimum economic benefits from their creations. Users of different types of works also find it easy to obtain licenses for legal exploitation of the works in question, through the collective administrative society.

What is a copyright society?
A copyright society is a registered collective administration society. Such a society is formed by copyright owners. The minimum membership required for registration of a society is seven. Ordinarily, only one society is registered to do business in respect of the same class of work. A copyright society can issue or grant licenses in respect of any work in which copyright subsists or in respect of any other right given by the Copyright Act.

What are the functions of a copyright society?
A copyright society may:

i. Issue licenses in respect of the rights administered by the society;
ii. Collect fees in pursuance of such licenses;
iii. Distribute such fees among owners of copyright after making deductions for the administrative expenses;

Are there any registered copyright societies in India?
Yes. The following are the registered copyright societies in India:

i. Society for Copyright Regulation of Indian Producers for Film and Television (SCRIPT), 135, Continental Building, Dr. A.B. Road, Worli, Mumbai 400 018, (for cinematograph and television films).
ii. The Indian Performing Right Society Limited (IPRS), 208, Golden Chambers, 2nd Floor, New Andheri Link Road, Andheri (W), Mumbai- 400 058 (for musical works).
iii. Phonographic Performance Limited (PPL), Flame Proof Equipment Building, B.39, Off New Link Road, Andheri (West), Mumbai 400 053 (for sound recordings).

Is it necessary to obtain licenses from more than one society for exploitation of a work?
In many cases, it is necessary to obtain licenses from more than one society. For example, playing of the sound recording of music may involve obtaining a license from the IPRS for the public performance of the music as well as a license from the PPL for playing the records, if these societies have the particular work in their repertoire.

3.6.1.13 Moral Rights

What are the moral rights of an author?
The author of a work has the right to claim authorship of the work and to restrain or claim damages in respect of any distortion, mutilation, modification or other acts in relation to the said work which is done before the expiration of the term of copyright if such distortion, mutilation, modification or other act would be prejudicial to his honor or reputation. Moral rights are available to the authors even after the economic rights are assigned.

Do the author's moral rights remain after assignment of copyright?
Yes. The moral rights are independent of the author's copyright and remains with him even after assignment of the copyright.

Will failure to display a work infringe the moral rights of an author?
No. Failure to display a work or to display it to the satisfaction of the author shall not be deemed to be an infringement of the moral rights of the author.

3.6.1.14 Copyright Infringements

Which are the common copyright infringements?
The following are some of the commonly known acts involving infringement of copyright:

i. Making infringing copies for sale or hire or selling or letting them for hire;
ii. Permitting any place for the performance of works in public where such performance constitutes infringement of copyright;
iii. Distributing infringing copies for the purpose of trade or to such an extent so as to affect prejudicially the interest of the owner of copyright;
iv. Public exhibition of infringing copies by way of trade; and
v. Importation of infringing copies into India.

Has the owner of an auditorium or a hall any liability while renting out the place for communication to the public of a copyrighted work?
Yes. If a person permits for profit any place to be used for the communication of a work to the public, where such communication constitutes an infringement of the copyright in the work, unless he was not aware and had no reasonable ground for believing that such communication to the public would be an infringement of copyright, he will be deemed to have committed an offense under the Copyright Act.

What are the civil remedies for copyright infringement?
A copyright owner can take legal action against any person who infringes the copyright in the work. The copyright owner is entitled to remedies by way of injunctions, damages, and accounts.

Which is the court having jurisdiction over civil remedies in copyright cases?
The District Court concerned has the jurisdiction in civil suits regarding copyright infringement.

What is the proof of the authorship of a work?
Where, in the case of a literary, dramatic, musical, or artistic work, a name purporting to be that of the author or the publisher appears on copies of the work as published, or, in the case of an artistic work appeared on the work where it was made, the person whose name so appears or appeared shall, in any proceeding in respect of copyright in such work, be presumed, unless the contrary is proved, to be the author or the publisher of the work, as the case may be.

What are the rights of owner over infringing copies and equipments used for making infringing copies?
All infringing copies of any work in which copyright subsists and all plates used or intended to be used for the production of such infringing copies shall be deemed to be the property of the owner of the copyright.

What are the remedies in the case of groundless threat to legal proceedings?
Where any person claiming to be the owner of copyright in any work, by circulars, advertisements or otherwise; threatens any other person with any legal proceedings or liability in respect of an alleged infringement of copyright; any person aggrieved thereby may institute a declaratory suit that the alleged infringement to which the threats related was not in fact an infringement of any legal rights of the person making such threats; and may in any such suit:

a. obtain an injunction against the continuance of such threats; and
b. recover such damages, if any, as he has sustained by reason of such threats.

Is copyright infringement a criminal offense?
Yes. Any person who knowingly infringes or abets the infringement of the copyright in any work commits criminal offense under Section 63 of the Copyright Act.

What are the punishments for a criminal offense under the copyright law?
The minimum punishment for infringement of copyright is imprisonment for 6 months with the minimum fine of Rs. 50,000/-. In the case of a second and subsequent conviction the minimum punishment is imprisonment for one year and fine of Rs. 1,00,000/-.

Is copyright infringement a cognizable offense?
Any police officer, not below the rank of a sub inspector, may, if he is satisfied that an offense in respect of the infringement of copyright in any work has been, is being, or is likely to be committed, seize without warrant, all copies of the work and all plates used for the purpose of making infringing copies of the work, wherever found, and all copies and plates so seized shall, as soon as practicable be produced before a magistrate.

How are the seized infringing copies or plates disposed off?
The Court may order delivery to the owner of the copyright all such copies or plates.

Who is responsible for copyright offense committed by a company?
Every person who at the time the offense was committed was in charge of, and was responsible to the company for, the conduct of the business of the company, as well as the company shall be deemed to be guilty of such offense and shall be liable to be proceeded against.

Which court can try copyright offense cases?
No court inferior to that of a Metropolitan Magistrate or a Judicial Magistrate of the first class shall try any offense under the Copyright Act.

Can a police officer seize infringing goods without warrant?
Yes. A police officer not below the rank of sub inspector can seize without warrant all infringing copies of the work.

3.7 Summary

In this chapter, we learnt the steps for publishing web page in the public domain. For publishing the web pages, we can use many editors, but HTML editors are the best ones as it saves time and helps in increasing productivity with good quality web pages. After publishing the web pages, we can right click on the page and check the source information and if required correct the information there itself for final publishing. While publishing, copyright issues should be taken care of. Any material, if published in any other domain, should be published only after taking proper permission from the previous publishers.

3.8 Review Questions

1 What are the extensions of a web browser files?
2 What are copyright issues and why are they important?
3 What is meant by work or a previously published material?
4 How do we define foreign work?
5 What precautions should be taken before publishing web pages (hint:using plagiarism tool).

Chapter 4
Concepts in E-Commerce

4.1 Learning Objectives

At the end of the chapter, students would learn different concepts such as:

- What is e-commerce and different models in e-commerce
- Role of e-commerce in developing economy
- How e-commerce is different than e-business
- Internet security requirement for e-commerce
- Factors that would influence adoption of e-commerce
- What is m-commerce and how is it related to e-commerce
- Electronic payment system
- E-banking
- Legal and policy issues in e-commerce
- E-commerce and online publishing
- Factors that impact adoption of e-commerce among small and medium enterprises (SMEs)
- Regulatory monitoring required for e-commerce

4.2 Introduction

One of the many challenges facing the countries in the Asia–Pacific today is preparing their societies and governments for globalization and the information and communication revolution. Policy makers, business executives, NGO activists, academics, and ordinary citizens are increasingly concerned with the need to make their societies competitive in the emergent information economy.

The present chapter aims to provide readers with a clear understanding of the various terminologies, definitions, trends, and issues associated with the

S. Mohapatra, *E-Commerce Strategy*, Springer Texts in Business and Economics, DOI: 10.1007/978-1-4614-4142-7_4,

information age. The primers are written in simple, easy-to-understand language. They provide examples, case studies, lessons learned, and best practices that will help planners and decision makers in addressing pertinent issues and crafting policies and strategies appropriate for the information economy.

In the emerging global economy, e-commerce and e-business have increasingly become a necessary component of business strategy and a strong catalyst for economic development. The integration of information and communications technology (ICT) in business has revolutionized relationships within organizations and those between and among organizations and individuals. Specifically, the use of ICT in business has enhanced productivity, encouraged greater customer participation, and enabled mass customization, besides reducing costs.

With developments in the Internet and web-based technologies, distinctions between traditional markets and the global electronic marketplace-such as business capital size, among others-are gradually being narrowed down. The name of the game is strategic positioning, the ability of a company to determine emerging opportunities and utilize the necessary human capital skills (such as intellectual resources) to make the most of these opportunities through an e-business strategy that is simple, workable, and practicable within the context of a global information milieu and new economic environment. With its effect of leveling the playing field, e-commerce coupled with the appropriate strategy and policy approach enables small and medium scale enterprises to compete with large and capital-rich businesses.

On another plane, developing countries are given increased access to the global marketplace, where they compete with and complement the more developed economies. Most, if not all, developing countries are already participating in e-commerce, either as sellers or buyers. However, to facilitate e-commerce growth in these countries, the relatively underdeveloped information infrastructure must be improved. Among the areas for policy intervention is:

- High Internet access costs, including connection service fees, communication fees, and hosting charges for web sites with sufficient bandwidth;
- Limited availability of credit cards and a nationwide credit card system;
- Underdeveloped transportation infrastructure resulting in slow and uncertain delivery of goods and services;
- Network security problems and insufficient security safeguards;
- Lack of skilled human resources and key technologies (i.e., inadequate professional IT workforce);
- Content restriction on national security and other public policy grounds, which greatly affect business in the field of information services, such as the media and entertainment sectors;
- Cross-border issues, such as the recognition of transactions under laws of other ASEAN member-countries, certification services, improvement of delivery methods, and customs facilitation; and
- The relatively low cost of labor, which implies that a shift to a comparatively capital intensive solution (including investments on the improvement of the physical and network infrastructure) is not apparent.

It is recognized that in the Information Age, Internet commerce is a powerful tool in the economic growth of developing countries. While there are indications of e-commerce patronage among large firms in developing countries, there seems to be little and negligible use of the Internet for commerce among small and medium sized firms. E-commerce promises better business for SMEs and sustainable economic development for developing countries. However, this is premised on strong political will and good governance, as well as on a responsible and supportive private sector within an effective policy framework. This primer seeks to provide policy guidelines toward this end.

4.3 Concepts and Definitions

4.3.1 What is E-Commerce?

Electronic commerce or e-commerce refers to a wide range of online business activities for products and services. It also pertains to any form of business transaction in which the parties interact electronically rather than by physical exchanges or direct physical contact. E-commerce is usually associated with buying and selling over the Internet, or conducting any transaction involving the transfer of ownership or rights to use goods or services through a computer-mediated network. Although popular, this definition is not comprehensive enough to capture recent developments in this new and revolutionary business phenomenon. A more complete definition is: E-commerce is the use of electronic communications and digital information processing technology in business transactions to create, transform, and redefine relationships for value creation between or among organizations, and between organizations and individuals.

International data corp (IDC) estimates the value of global e-commerce in 2000 at US$350.38 billion. This is projected to climb to as high as US$3.14 trillion by 2004. IDC also predicts an increase in Asia's percentage share in worldwide e-commerce revenue from 5 % in 2000 to 10 % in 2004. Asia–Pacific e-commerce revenues are projected to increase from $76.8 billion at year-end of 2001 to $338.5 billion by the end of 2004.

4.3.2 Is E-Commerce the Same as E-Business?

While some use e-commerce and e-business interchangeably, they are distinct concepts. In e-commerce, ICT is used in inter-business or inter-organizational transactions (transactions between and among firms/organizations) and in business-to-consumer transactions (transactions between firms/organizations and individuals).

In e-business, on the other hand, ICT is used to enhance one's business. It includes any process that a business organization (either a for-profit, governmental, or non-profit entity) conducts over a computer-mediated network. A more comprehensive definition of e-business is: "The transformation of an organization's processes to deliver additional customer value through the application of technologies, philosophies and computing paradigm of the new economy".

Three primary processes are enhanced in e-business

1. Production processes, which include procurement, ordering, and replenishment of stocks; processing of payments; electronic links with suppliers; and production control processes, among others;
2. Customer-focused processes, which include promotional and marketing efforts, selling over the Internet, processing of customers' purchase orders and payments, and customer support, among others; and
3. Internal management processes, which include employee services, training, internal information-sharing, video-conferencing, and recruiting. Electronic applications enhance information flow between production and sales forces to improve sales force productivity. Workgroup communications and electronic publishing of internal business information are likewise made more efficient.

4.3.3 Is the Internet Economy Synonymous with E-Commerce and E-Business?

The Internet economy is a broader concept than e-commerce and e-business. It includes e-commerce and e-business. The Internet economy pertains to all economic activities using electronic networks as a medium for commerce or those activities involved in both building the networks linked to the Internet and the purchase of application services such as the provision of enabling hardware and software and network equipment for web-based/online retail and shopping malls (or "e-malls"). It is made up of three major segments: physical (ICT) infrastructure, business infrastructure, and commerce.

The center for research and electronic commerce (CREC) at the University of Texas has developed a conceptual framework for how the Internet economy works. The framework shows four layers of the Internet economy—the three mentioned above and a fourth called intermediaries (see Table 4.1).

4.4 Different Types of E-Commerce?

The major different types of e-commerce are: business-to-business (B2B); business-to-consumer (B2C); business-to-government (B2G); consumer-to-consumer (C2C); and mobile commerce (m-commerce).

Table 4.1 Internet economy conceptual frame

	Layer 1 - Internet	Layer 2 -	Layer 3 -	
	Layer 4 - Internet			
	Infrastructure:	Internet	Internet	
	Commerce:			
	Companies that	Applications	Intermediaries:	
	Companies that			
	provide the	Infrastructure:	Companies	sell
products or				
	enabling hardware,		Companies	
		that link e-	services directly	
	software, and	that make	commerce	to
consumers or				
	networking	software	buyers and	
		businesses.		
	equipment for	products that	sellers;	
	Internet and for the		facilitate Web	
		companies that		
	World Wide Web	transactions;	provide Web	
		companies	content;	
		that provide Web	companies that provide	
		development	marketplaces	
		design and	in which e-	
		consulting	commerce	
		services	transactions	
			can occur	

	Networking	Internet	Market Makers	E-
Tailers				
	Hardware/Software		Commerce	in
Vertical	Online			
	Companies	Applications	Industries	
		Entertainment		
	Line Acceleration	Web	Online Travel	and

(continued)

Table 4.1 (continued)

Professional				
	Hardware	Development	Agents	
		Services		
	Manufacturers	Software	Online	
		Manufacturers		
	PC and Server	Internet	Brokerages	
		Selling Online		
	Manufacturers	Consultants	Content	
		Airlines Selling		
	Internet Backbone	Online	Aggregators	
		Online Tickets		
	Providers	Training	Online	
		Fee/Subscription-		
	Internet Service	Search	Advertisers	
		Based		
	Providers (ISPs)	Engine	Internet Ad	
		Companies		
	Security Vendors	Software	Brokers	
	Fiber Optics	Web-Enabled	Portals/Content	
	Makers	Databases	Providers	
		Multimedia		
		Applications		
	Cisco	Adobe	e-STEEL	
	Amazon.com			
	AOL	*Microsoft	Travelocity e -	Dell
	AT&T	*IBM	Trade	
	Qwest	Oracle	Yahoo!	
			ZDNet	

Source Based on Center for Research in Electronic Commerce, University of Texas, "Measuring the Internet Economy", June 6, 2000; available from www.Internetindicators.com

4.4.1 B2B E-Commerce

B2B e-commerce is simply defined as e-commerce between companies. This is the type of e-commerce that deals with relationships between and among businesses. About 80 % of e-commerce is of this type, and most experts predict that B2B e-commerce will continue to grow faster than the B2C segment.

The B2B market has two primary components: e-frastructure and e-markets. E-frastructure is the architecture of B2B, primarily consisting of the following:

- Logistics—transportation, warehousing, and distribution (e.g., Procter and Gamble);
- application service providers—deployment, hosting, and management of packaged software from a central facility (e.g., Oracle and Linkshare);
- outsourcing of functions in the process of e-commerce, such as web-hosting, security, and customer care solutions (e.g., outsourcing providers such as eShare, NetSales, iXL Enterprises, and Universal Access);
- auction solutions software for the operation and maintenance of real-time auctions in the Internet (e.g., Moai Technologies and OpenSite Technologies);
- content management software for the facilitation of web site content management and delivery (e.g., Interwoven and ProcureNet); and
- Web-based commerce enablers (e.g., Commerce One, a browser-based, XML enabled purchasing automation software).

E-markets are simply defined as web sites where buyers and sellers interact with each other and conduct transactions.

The more common B2B examples and best practice models are IBM, Hewlett Packard (HP), Cisco, and Dell. Cisco, for instance, receives over 90 % of its product orders over the Internet.

Most B2B applications are in the areas of supplier management (especially purchase order processing), inventory management (i.e., managing order-ship-bill cycles), distribution management (especially in the transmission of shipping documents), channel management (i.e., information dissemination on changes in operational conditions), and payment management (e.g., electronic payment systems or EPS). The eMarketer projects an increase in the share of B2B e-commerce in total global e-commerce from 79.2 % in 2000 to 87 % in 2004 and a consequent decrease in the share of B2C e-commerce from 20.8 % in 2000 to only 13 % in 2004.

Likewise, B2B growth is way ahead of B2C growth in the Asia–Pacific region. According to a 2001 eMarketer estimate, B2B revenues in the region are expected to exceed $300 billion by 2004.

The impact of B2B markets on the economy of developing countries is evident in the following:

4.4.2 Transaction Costs

There are three cost areas that are significantly reduced through the conduct of B2B e-commerce. First is the reduction of search costs, as buyers need not go through multiple intermediaries to search for information about suppliers, products, and prices as in a traditional supply chain. In terms of effort, time, and money spent, the Internet is a more efficient information channel than its traditional counterpart. In B2B markets, buyers and sellers are gathered together into a single online trading community, reducing search costs even further. Second is the reduction in the costs of processing transactions, (e.g. invoices, purchase orders, and payment schemes), as B2B allows for the automation of transaction processes and therefore, the quick implementation of the same compared to other channels (such as the telephone and fax). Efficiency in trading processes and transactions is also enhanced through the B2B e-market's ability to process sales through online auctions. Third, online processing improves inventory management and logistics.

4.4.3 Disintermediation

Through B2B e-markets, suppliers are able to interact and transact directly with buyers, thereby eliminating intermediaries and distributors. However, new forms of intermediaries are emerging. For instance, e-markets themselves can be considered as intermediaries because they come between suppliers and customers in the supply chain.

4.4.4 Transparency in Pricing

Among the more evident benefits of e-markets is the increase in price transparency. The gathering of a large number of buyers and sellers in a single e-market reveals market price information and transaction processing to participants. The Internet allows for the publication of information on a single purchase or transaction, taking the information readily accessible and available to all members of the e-market. Increased price transparency has the effect of pulling down price differentials in the market. In this context, buyers are provided much more time to compare prices and make better buying decisions. Moreover, B2B e-markets expand borders for dynamic and negotiated pricing, wherein multiple buyers and sellers collectively participate in price-setting and two-way auctions. In such environments, prices can be set through automatic matching of bids and offers. In the e-marketplace, the requirements of both buyers and sellers are thus aggregated to reach competitive prices, which are lower than those resulting from individual actions.

4.4.5 Economies of Scale and Network Effects

The rapid growth of B2B e-markets creates traditional supply-side cost-based economies of scale. Furthermore, the bringing together of a significant number of buyers and sellers provides the demand-side economies of scale or network effects. Each additional incremental participant in the e-market creates value for all participants in the demand side. More participants form a critical mass, which is the key in attracting more users to an e-market.

4.4.6 B2C E-Commerce

Business-to-consumer e-commerce, or commerce between companies and consumers, involves customers gathering information; purchasing physical goods (i.e., tangibles such as books or consumer products) or information goods (or goods of electronic material or digitized content, such as software, or e-books); and, for information goods, receiving products over an electronic network.

It is the second largest and the earliest form of e-commerce. Its origins can be traced to online retailing (or e-tailing). Thus, the more common B2C business models are the online retailing companies such as Amazon.com, Drugstore.com, Beyond.com, Barnes and Noble, and ToysRus. Other B2C examples involving information goods are E-Trade and Travelocity.

The more common applications of this type of e-commerce are in the areas of purchasing products and information, and personal finance management, which pertain to the management of personal investments and finances with the use of online banking tools.

The eMarketer estimates that worldwide B2C e-commerce revenues will increase from US$59.7 billion in 2000 to US$428.1 billion by 2004. Online retailing transactions make up a significant share of this market. The eMarketer also estimates that in the Asia–Pacific region, B2C revenues, while registering a modest figure compared to B2B, nonetheless went up to $8.2 billion by the end of 2001, with that figure doubling at the end of 2002-at total worldwide B2C sales below 10 %.

B2C e-commerce reduces transactions costs (particularly search costs) by increasing consumer access to information and allowing consumers to find the most competitive price for a product or service. B2C e-commerce also reduces market entry barriers since the cost of putting up and maintaining a web site is much cheaper than installing a "brick-and-mortar" structure for a firm. In the case of information goods, B2C e-commerce is even more attractive because it saves firms from factoring in the additional cost of a physical distribution network. Moreover, for countries with a growing and robust Internet population, delivering information goods becomes increasingly feasible.

4.4.7 B2G E-Commerce

Business-to-government e-commerce or B2G is generally defined as commerce between companies and the public sector. It refers to the use of the Internet for public procurement, licensing procedures, and other government-related operations. This kind of e-commerce has two features: first, the public sector assumes a pilot/leading role in establishing e-commerce; and second, it is assumed that the public sector has the greatest need for making its procurement system more effective.

Web-based purchasing policies increase the transparency of the procurement process and reduce the risk of irregularities. To date, however, the size of the B2G e-commerce market as a component of total e-commerce is insignificant, as government e-procurement systems remain undeveloped.

4.4.8 C2C E-Commerce

Consumer-to-consumer e-commerce or C2C is simply commerce between private individuals or consumers. This type of e-commerce is characterized by the growth of electronic marketplaces and online auctions, particularly in vertical industries where firms/businesses can bid for what they want from among multiple suppliers. It perhaps has the greatest potential for developing new markets.

This type of e-commerce comes in following forms:

- auctions facilitated at a portal, such as eBay, which allows online real-time bidding on items being sold in the web;
- peer-to-peer systems, such as the Napster model (a protocol for sharing files between users used by chat forums similar to IRC) and other file exchange and later money exchange models; and
- classified ads at portal sites such as Excite Classifieds and eWanted (an interactive, online marketplace where buyers and sellers can negotiate and which features "Buyer Leads and Want Ads").
- Consumer-to-business (C2B) transactions involve reverse auctions, which empower the consumer to drive transactions. A concrete example of this: when competing airlines gives a traveler best travel and ticket offers in response to the traveler's post that she wants to fly from New York to San Francisco.
- There is little information on the relative size of global C2C e-commerce. However, C2C figures of popular C2C sites such as eBay and Napster indicate that this market is quite large. These sites produce millions of dollars in sales every day.

4.5 Understanding M-Commerce?

M-commerce (mobile commerce) is the buying and selling of goods and services through wireless technology—i.e., handheld devices such as cellular telephones and personal digital assistants (PDAs). Japan is seen as a global leader in m-commerce. As content delivery over wireless devices becomes faster, more secure, and scalable, some believe that m-commerce will surpass wireline e-commerce as the method of choice for digital commerce transactions. This may well be true for the Asia–Pacific where there are more mobile phone users than there are Internet users. Industries affected by m-commerce include: Financial services, including mobile banking (when customers use their handheld devices to access their accounts and pay their bills), as well as brokerage services (in which stock quotes can be displayed and trading conducted from the same handheld device).

Telecommunications, in which service changes, bill payment, and account reviews can all be conducted from the same handheld device. Service/retail, as consumers are given the ability to place and pay for orders on-the-fly; and Information services, which include the delivery of entertainment, financial news, sports, figures, and traffic updates to a single mobile.

Irctc.co.in has recently started its m-commerce operations. It asks customers (who are registered users in the site) to download an application to their mobiles. These mobile applications route the requests for buying rail tickets (irctc.co.in sells rail tickets online for Indian Railways) to a different server than that accessed by the regular online users. The mobile applications allow users to book and cancel rail tickets through their mobile devices. Thus, while this ensures mobility of the users, it also allows users to book their tickets on the go. It also allows users to enquire about ticket availability, train running information, etc. However, since payment related information will be passed through these applications, it requires Internet security so that confidential financial information can be protected. Hence, mobile commerce requires proper strategy to make it a sustainable one.

As mobile e-commerce is becoming popular, there is a need for a long term strategy for the organizations using them. One of the most critical considerations for this strategy is the software solution that the organization uses. From traditional solutions to iPhone applications, each software solution provides a unique set of advantages and disadvantages. These must be considered while designing long term strategy. With technologies changing fast, mobile solutions need to keep track of these changes as well. The mobile phone has evolved as 'all in one' device that threatens to replace many existing devices. With changing life style, mobility has become an integral part of the lives in all walks of population. As a result, banks are trying to create cost effective virtual distribution channel with rapid innovations so that they can extend their reach across segments. This will increase convenience without compromising security. While designing this strategy, banks need to contemplate how to go about exploiting the channel for increasing reach and what could be the best mobile solution that can be deployed so that both customers and banks can benefit. These benefits should be in terms of usage, reach, cost of installation, efforts and money for maintenance, upgradeability, and sustainability.

There is no right way of designing and implementing a mobile solution, but the solutions should be able to address the needs of all the players (including regulatory requirements). A bank is always required to remain competitive and improve customer reach. In such a scenario, a solution is adopted that can be deployed fast, and if required can be scalable. As the bank moves to further offerings in the m commerce, it has to take care of disparate systems, customized solutions, and maintenance cost. Thus, a long term strategy would help the bank to integrate these solutions and reduce IT investment cost.

M-commerce requires that the bank should choose a platform that easily integrates new services and allows banks to be flexible, while allowing the bank to reap benefits from the full potential of the mobile commerce. There are several platforms available for m commerce, each catering to a specific segment or purpose. These platforms could be catering to either of business requirements such as core banking solutions (Finacle mobile banking solution from Infosys), mobile banking solutions (Firethorn, Clairmail etc.), aggregating solutions capabilities for mobile commerce (Tyfone) and customized banking solutions (usually these solutions are developed in-house). Also, some solutions can integrate some of the above platforms to provide unique set of advantages for its customers.

Mobility solutions are still emerging and have far reaching consequences than others. This is not one time investment rather should have a clear vision and objectives for further growth and thus cannot adopt 'one size fits all' approach. With cloud computing services on the rise, choosing the right solution involves the right technology partner that can provide best services to its customers.

4.6 Factors Affecting E-Commerce

There are at least three major forces fuelling e-commerce: economic forces, marketing and customer interaction forces, and technology, particularly multimedia convergence. Economic forces, one of the most evident benefits of e-commerce is economic efficiency resulting from the reduction in communications costs, low-cost technological infrastructure, speedier and more economic electronic transactions with suppliers, lower global information sharing and advertising costs, and cheaper customer service alternatives.

Economic integration is either external or internal. External integration refers to the electronic networking of corporations, suppliers, customers/clients, and independent contractors into one community communicating in a virtual environment (with the Internet as medium). Internal integration, on the other hand, is the networking of the various departments within a corporation, and of business operations, and processes. This allows critical business information to be stored in a digital form that can be retrieved instantly and transmitted electronically. Internal integration is best exemplified by corporate intranets. Among the companies with efficient corporate intranets are Procter and Gamble, IBM, Nestle and Intel.

SESAMi.NET is Asia's largest B2B e-hub, a virtual exchange integrating and connecting businesses (small, medium or large) to trading partners, e-marketplaces, and internal enterprise systems for the purpose of sourcing out supplies, buying and selling goods, and services online in real time. The e-hub serves as the center for management of content and the processing of business transactions with support services such as financial clearance and information services. It is strategically and dynamically linked to the global trading web (GTW), the world's largest network of trading communities on the Internet. Because of this very important link, SESAMi reaches an extensive network of regional, vertical, and industry-specific interoperable B2B e-markets across the globe.

Market forces. Corporations are encouraged to use e-commerce in marketing and promotion to capture international markets, both big and small. The Internet is likewise used as a medium for enhanced customer service and support. It is a lot easier for companies to provide their target consumers with more detailed product and service information using the Internet.

Brazil's Submarino is a classic example of successful use of the Internet for improved customer service and support. From being a local Sao Paulo B2C e-commerce company selling books, CDs, video cassettes, DVDs, toys, electronic, and computer products in Brazil, it expanded to become the largest company of its kind in Argentina, Mexico, Spain, and Portugal. Close to a third of the 1.4 million Internet users in Brazil have made purchases through this site. To enhance customer service, Submarino has diversified into offering logistical and technological infrastructure to other retailers, which includes experience and expertise in credit analysis, tracking orders, and product comparison systems.

Technology forces. The development of ICT is a key factor in the growth of e-commerce. For instance, technological advances in digitizing content, compression, and the promotion of open systems technology have paved the way for the convergence of communication services into one single platform. This in turn has made communication more efficient, faster, easier, and more economical as the need to set up separate networks for telephone services, television broadcast, cable television, and Internet access is eliminated. From the standpoint of firms/businesses and consumers, having only one information provider means lower communications costs.

Moreover, the principle of universal access can be made more achievable with convergence. At present the high costs of installing landlines in sparsely populated rural areas is a disincentive to telecommunication companies to install telephones in these areas. Installing landlines in rural areas can become more attractive to the private sector if revenues from these landlines are not limited to local and long distance telephone charges, but also include cable TV and Internet charges. This development will ensure affordable access to information even by those in rural areas and will spare the government the trouble and cost of installing expensive landlines.

4.7 E-Commerce Components

E-commerce does not refer merely to a firm putting up a web site for the purpose of selling goods to buyers over the Internet. For e-commerce to be a competitive alternative to traditional commercial transactions and for a firm to maximize the benefits of e-commerce, a number of technical as well as enabling issues have to be considered. A typical e-commerce transaction loop involves the following major players and corresponding requisites:

- A corporate web site with e-commerce capabilities (e.g., a secure transaction server);
- A corporate intranet so that orders are processed in an efficient manner; and
- IT-literate employees to manage the information flows and maintain the e-commerce system.

The Seller should have the following components:
Transaction partners include:

- Banking institutions that offer transaction clearing services (e.g., processing credit card payments and electronic fund transfers);
- National and international freight companies to enable the movement of physical goods within, around, and out of the country.

For business-to-consumer transactions, the system must offer a means for cost-efficient transport of small packages (such that purchasing books over the Internet, for example, is not prohibitively more expensive than buying from a local store); and Authentication authority that serves as a trusted third party to ensure the integrity and security of transactions.

Consumers (in a business-to-consumer transaction) who:

- Form a critical mass of the population with access to the Internet and disposable income enabling widespread use of credit cards; and
- Possess a mindset for purchasing goods over the Internet rather than by physically inspecting items.
- Firms/Businesses (in a business-to-business transaction) that together form a critical mass of companies (especially within supply chains) with Internet access and the capability to place and take orders over the Internet.

Government, to establish:

- A legal framework governing e-commerce transactions (including electronic documents, signatures, and the like); and
- Legal institutions that would enforce the legal framework (i.e., laws and regulations) and protect consumers and businesses from fraud, among others.

And finally, the Internet, the successful use of which depends on the following:

- A robust and reliable Internet infrastructure; and

- A pricing structure that doesn't penalize consumers for spending time on and buying goods over the Internet (e.g., a flat monthly charge for both ISP access and local phone calls).

For e-commerce to grow, the above requisites and factors have to be in place. The least developed factor is an impediment to the increased uptake of e-commerce as a whole. For instance, a country with an excellent Internet infrastructure will not have high e-commerce figures if banks do not offer support and fulfillment services to e-commerce transactions. In countries that have significant e-commerce figures, a positive feedback loop reinforces each of these factors.

4.7.1 Internet and E-Commerce

The Internet allows people from all over the world to get connected inexpensively and reliably. As a technical infrastructure, it is a global collection of networks, connected to share information using a common set of protocols. Also, as a vast network of people and information, the Internet is an enabler for e-commerce as it allows businesses to showcase and sell their products and services online and gives potential customers, prospects, and business partners access to information about these businesses and their products and services that would lead to purchase.

Before the Internet was utilized for commercial purposes, companies used private networks—such as the EDI or Electronic Data Interchange-to transact business with each other. That was the early form of e-commerce. However, installing and maintaining private networks was very expensive. With the Internet, e-commerce spread rapidly because of the lower costs involved and because the Internet is based on open standards.

4.7.2 Intranet and E-Commerce

An intranet aids in the management of internal corporate information that may be interconnected with a company's e-commerce transactions (or transactions conducted outside the intranet). Inasmuch as the intranet allows for the instantaneous flow of internal information, vital information is simultaneously processed and matched with data flowing from external e-commerce transactions, allowing for the efficient and effective integration of the corporation's organizational processes. In this context, corporate functions, decisions, and processes involving e-commerce activities are more coherent and organized.

The proliferation of intranets has caused a shift from a hierarchical command and control organization to an information-based organization. This shift has implications for managerial responsibilities, communication and information flows, and workgroup structures. Aside from reducing the cost of doing business, what are the advantages of e-commerce for businesses? E-commerce serves as an "equalizer". It enables start-up and small- and medium-sized enterprises to reach the global market. Amazon.com is a virtual bookstore. It does not have a single square foot of bricks and mortar retail floor space. Nonetheless, Amazon.com is posting an annual sales rate of approximately $1.2 billion, equal to about 235 Barnes & Noble (B&N) superstores. Due to the efficiencies of selling over the web, Amazon has spent only $56 million on fixed assets, while B&N has spent about $118 million for 235 superstores. (To be fair, Amazon has yet to turn a profit, but this does not obviate the point that in many industries doing business through e-commerce is cheaper than conducting business in a traditional brick-and-mortar company).

However, this does not discount the point that without a good e-business strategy, e-commerce may in some cases discriminate against SMEs because it reveals proprietary pricing information. A sound e-business plan does not totally disregard old economy values. The dot-com bust is proof of this. According to Webmergers.com statistics, about 862 dot-com companies have failed since the height of the dot-com bust in January 2000. Majority of these were e-commerce and content companies. The shutdown of these companies was followed by the folding up of Internet-content providers, infrastructure companies, Internet service providers, and other providers of dial-up and broadband Internet access services.

From the perspective of the investment banks, the dot-com frenzy can be likened to a gamble, where the big money players were the venture capitalists and those laying their bets on the table were the small investors. The bust was primarily caused by the players' unfamiliarity with the sector, coupled with failure to cope with the speed of the Internet revolution and the amount of capital in circulation.

Internet entrepreneurs set the prices of their goods and services at very low levels to gain market share and attract venture capitalists to infuse funding. The crash began when investors started demanding hard earnings for sky-high valuations. The Internet companies also spent too much on overhead before even gaining a market share.

E-commerce makes "mass customization" possible. E-commerce applications in this area include easy-to-use ordering systems that allow customers to choose and order products according to their personal and unique specifications. For instance, a car manufacturing company with an e-commerce strategy allowing for online orders can have new cars built within a few days (instead of the several weeks it currently takes to build a new vehicle) based on customer's specifications. This can work more effectively if a company's manufacturing process is advanced and integrated into the ordering system.

E-commerce allows "network production". This refers to the parceling out of the production process to contractors who are geographically dispersed but who are connected to each other via computer networks. The benefits of network production include: reduction in costs, more strategic target marketing, and the facilitation of selling add-on products, services, and new systems when they are needed. With network production, a company can assign tasks within its noncore competencies to factories all over the world that specialize in such tasks (e.g., the assembly of specific components).

4.8 E-Commerce and Consumers

In C2B transactions, customers/consumers are given more influence over what and how products are made and how services are delivered, thereby broadening consumer choices. E-commerce allows for a faster and more open process, with customers having greater control.

E-commerce makes information on products and the market as a whole readily available and accessible, and increases price transparency, which enable customers to make more appropriate purchasing decisions.

4.9 Business Transformation Through E-Commerce

E-commerce transforms old economy relationships (vertical/linear relationships) to new economy relationships characterized by end-to-end relationship management solutions (integrated or extended relationships).

4.9.1 Linking Stakeholders Through E-Commerce

E-commerce facilitates organization networks, wherein small firms depend on "partner" firms for supplies and product distribution to address customer demands more effectively.

To manage the chain of networks linking customers, workers, suppliers, distributors, and even competitors, an integrated or extended supply chain management solution is needed. Supply chain management (SCM) is defined as the supervision of materials, information, and finances as they move from supplier to manufacturer to wholesaler to retailer to consumer. It involves the coordination and integration of these flows both within and among companies. The goal of any effective supply chain management system is timely provision of goods or services to the next link in the chain (and ultimately, the reduction of inventory within each link).

There are three main flows in SCM, namely:

- The product flow, which includes the movement of goods from a supplier to a customer, as well as any customer returns or service needs;
- The information flow, which involves the transmission of orders and the update of the status of delivery; and
- The financial flow, which consists of credit terms, payment schedules, and consignment and title ownership arrangements.

Some SCM applications are based on open data models that support the sharing of data both inside and outside the enterprise, called the extended enterprise, and include key suppliers, manufacturers, and end customers of a specific company. Shared data resides in diverse database systems, or data warehouses, at several different sites and companies. Sharing this data "upstream" (with a company's suppliers) and "downstream" (with a company's clients) allows SCM applications to improve the time-to-market of products and reduce costs. It also allows all parties in the supply chain to better manage current resources and plan for future needs.

4.10 Components of E-Business

An e-business model should have

- A shared digital business infrastructure, including digital production and distribution technologies (broadband/wireless networks, content creation technologies and information management systems), which will allow business participants to create and utilize network economies of scale and scope;
- A sophisticated model for operations, including integrated value chains—both supply chains and buy chains
- An e-business management model, consisting of business teams and/or partnerships; and
- Policy, regulatory, and social systems-i.e., business policies consistent with e-commerce laws, teleworking/virtual work, distance learning, incentive schemes, among others.

4.11 E-Commerce Applications: Issues and Prospects

Various applications of e-commerce are continually affecting trends and prospects for business over the Internet, including e-banking, e-tailing, and online publishing/online retailing.

A more developed and mature e-banking environment plays an important role in e-commerce by encouraging a shift from traditional modes of payment (i.e., cash, cheques or any form of paper-based legal tender) to electronic alternatives (such as e-payment systems), thereby closing the e-commerce loop.

4.12 E-Commerce in Developing Countries

In most developing countries, the payment schemes available for online transactions are the following:

4.12.1 A. Traditional Payment Methods

- Cash on delivery. Many online transactions only involve submitting purchase orders online. Payment is by cash upon the delivery of the physical goods.
- Bank payments. After ordering goods online, payment is made by depositing cash into the bank account of the company from which the goods were ordered. Delivery is likewise done the conventional way.

4.12.2 B. Electronic Payment Methods

- Innovations affecting consumers include credit and debit cards, automated teller machines (ATMs), stored value cards, and e-banking.
- Innovations enabling online commerce are e-cash, e-cheques, smart cards, and encrypted credit cards. These payment methods are not too popular in developing countries. They are employed by a few large companies in specific secured channels on a transaction basis.
- Innovations affecting companies pertain to payment mechanisms that banks provide their clients, including inter-bank transfers through automated clearing houses allowing payment by direct deposit.

4.13 Electronic Payment System

An electronic payment system (EPS) is a system of financial exchange between buyers and sellers in the online environment that is facilitated by a digital financial instrument (such as encrypted credit card numbers, electronic cheques, or digital cash) backed by a bank, an intermediary, or by legal tender. EPS plays an important role in e-commerce because it closes the e-commerce loop. In developing countries, the underdeveloped electronic payments system is a serious impediment to the growth of e-commerce. In these countries, entrepreneurs are not able to accept credit card payments over the Internet due to legal and business concerns. The primary issue is transaction security.

The absence or inadequacy of legal infrastructures governing the operation of e-payments is also a concern. Hence, banks with e-banking operations employ service agreements between themselves and their clients. The relatively undeveloped credit card industry in many developing countries is also a barrier to e-commerce. Only a small segment of the population can buy goods and services over the Internet due to the small credit card market base. There is also the problem of the requirement of "explicit consent" (i.e., a signature) by a card owner before a transaction is considered valid-a requirement that does not exist in the US and in other developed countries.

4.13.1 Security Issues in E-Payment System

Many developing countries are still cash-based economies. Cash is the preferred mode of payment not only on account of security but also because of anonymity, which is useful for tax evasion purposes or keeping secret what one's money is being spent on. For other countries, security concerns have a lot to do with a lack of a legal framework for adjudicating fraud and the uncertainty of the legal limit on the liability associated with a lost or stolen credit card. In short, among the relevant issues that need to be resolved with respect to EPS are: consumer protection from fraud through efficiency in record-keeping; transaction privacy and safety, competitive payment services to ensure equal access to all consumers, and the right to choice of institutions and payment methods. Legal frameworks in developing countries should also begin to recognize electronic transactions and payment schemes.

4.14 Understanding E-Banking

E-banking includes familiar and relatively mature electronically based products in developing markets, such as telephone banking, credit cards, ATMs, and direct deposit. It also includes electronic bill payments and products mostly in the developing stage, including stored-value cards (e.g., smart cards/smart money) and Internet based stored value products.

4.14.1 E-Banking in Third World Countries

E-banking in developing countries is in the early stages of development. Most banking in developing countries is still done the conventional way. However, there is an increasing growth of online banking, indicating a promising future for online banking in these countries. Below is a broad picture of e-banking in three ASEAN countries.

4.14.2 The Philippine Experience

In the Philippines, Citibank, Bank of the Philippine Islands (BPI), Philippine National Bank, and other large banks pioneered e-banking in the early 1980s. Interbank networks in the country like Megalink, Bancnet, and BPI Expressnet were among the earliest and biggest starters of ATM (Automated Teller Machines) technology. BPI launched its BPI Express Online in January 2000. The most common online financial services include deposits, fund transfers, applications for new accounts, Stop Payment on issued cheques, housing and auto loans, credit cards, and remittances.

4.14.3 The Singapore Experience

In Singapore, more than 28 % of Internet users visited e-banking sites in May 2001. Research by NetValue (an Internet measurement company) shows that while the number of people engaging in online banking in Singapore has increased, the average time spent at sites decreased by approximately 4 min from March 2001 to May 2001. This decline can be attributed to the fact that more visitors spend time completing transactions, which take less time than browsing different sites. According to the survey, two out of three visitors make a transaction.

All major banks in Singapore have an Internet presence. They offer a wide range of products directly to consumers through proprietary Internet sites. These banks have shifted from an initial focus on retail-banking to SME and corporate banking products and services.

Among the products offered are:

- Fund transfer and payment systems;
- Integrated B2B e-commerce product, involving product selection, purchase order, invoice generation, and payment;
- Securities placement and underwriting and capital market activities; Securities trading; and Retail banking.

4.14.4 The Malaysian Experience

E-banking in Malaysia emerged in 1981 with the introduction of ATMs. This was followed by telebanking in the early 1990s where telecommunications devices were connected to an automated system through the use of Automated Voice Response (AVR) technology. Then came PC banking or desktop banking using proprietary software, which was more popular among corporate customers than retail customers.

On June 1, 2000, the Malaysian Bank formally allowed local commercial banks to offer Internet banking services. On June 15, 2000, Maybank (www.maybank2U.com), one of the largest banks in Malaysia, launched the country's first Internet banking services. The bank employs 128-bit encryption technology to secure its transactions. Other local banks in Malaysia offering e-banking services are Southern Bank, Hong Leong Bank, HSBC Bank, Multi-Purpose Bank, Phileo Allied Bank and RHB Bank. Banks that offer WAP or Mobile banking are OCBC Bank, Phileo Allied Bank and United Overseas Bank.

The most common e-banking services include banking inquiry functions, bill payments, credit card payments, fund transfers, share investing, insurance, travel, electronic shopping, and other basic banking services.

4.15 Factors of the Growth of E-Banking in Developing Countries

Human tellers and automated teller machines continue to be the banking channels of choice in developing countries. Only a small number of banks employ Internet banking. Among the middle and high-income people in Asia questioned in a McKinsey survey, only 2.6 % reported banking over the Internet in 2000. In India, Indonesia, and Thailand, the figure was as low as 1 %; in Singapore and South Korea, it ranged from 5 % to 6 %. In general, Internet banking accounted for less than 0.1 % of these customers' banking transactions, as it did in 1999. The Internet is more commonly used for opening new accounts but the numbers are negligible as less than 0.3 % of respondents used it for that purpose, except in China and the Philippines where the figures climbed to 0.7–1.0 %, respectively.

This slow uptake cannot be attributed to limited access to the Internet, since 42 % of respondents said they had access to computers and 7 % said they had access to the Internet. The chief obstacle in Asia and throughout emerging markets is security. This is the main reason for not opening online banking or investment accounts. Apparently, there is also a preference for personal contact with banks.

Access to high-quality products is also a concern. Most Asian banks are in the early stages of Internet banking services, and many of the services are very basic.

4.16 Future Trend in E-Banking in Third World Countries

There is a potential for increased uptake of e-banking in Asia. Respondents of the McKinsey survey gave the following indications:

- Lead users: 38 % of respondents indicated their intention to open an online account in the near future. These lead users undertake one-third more transactions a month than do other users, and they tend to employ all banking channels more often.
- Followers: An additional 20 % showed an inclination to eventually open an online account, if their primary institution were to offer it and if there would be no additional bank charges.
- Rejecters: 42 % (compared to the aggregate figure of 58 % for lead users and followers) indicated no interest in or an aversion to Internet banking. It is important to note that these respondents also preferred consolidation and simplicity, i.e., owning fewer banking products and dealing with fewer financial institutions.

- Less than 13 % of the lead users and followers indicated some interest in conducting complex activities over the Internet, such as trading securities or applying for insurance, credit cards, and loans. About a third of lead users and followers showed an inclination to undertake only the basic banking functions, like ascertaining account balances and transferring money between accounts, over the Internet.

4.17 Understanding E-Tailing

E-tailing (or electronic retailing) is the selling of retail goods on the Internet. It is the most common form of business-to-consumer (B2C) transaction. The year 1997 is considered the first big year for e-tailing. This was when Dell Computer recorded multimillion dollar orders taken at its web site. Also, the success of Amazon.com (which opened its virtual doors in 1996) encouraged Barnes & Noble to open an e-tail site. Security concerns over taking purchase orders over the Internet gradually receded. In the same year, Auto-by-Tel sold its millionth car over the web, and CommerceNet/Nielsen Media recorded that 10 million people had made purchases on the web.

4.17.1 Trends and Prospects for E-Tailing

Jupiter projects that e-tailing will grow to $37 billion by 2002. Another estimate is that the online market will grow 45 % in 2001, reaching $65 billion. Profitability will vary sharply among web-based, catalog-based, and store-based retailers. There was also a marked reduction in customer acquisition costs for all online retailers from an average of $38 in 1999 to $29 in 2000.

4.18 Online Publishing and E-Commerce

Online publishing is the process of using computer and specific types of software to combine text and graphics to produce web-based documents such as newsletters, online magazines and databases, brochures and other promotional materials, books, and the like, with the Internet as a medium for publication.

4.18.1 Advantages of Online Publishing to Business

Among the benefits of using online media are low-cost universal access, the independence of time and place, and ease of distribution. These are the reasons why the Internet is regarded as an effective marketing outreach medium and is often used to enhance information service.

4.18.2 Issues in Online Publishing

The problems in online publishing can be grouped into two categories: management challenges and public policy issues. There are two major management issues:

- The profit question, which seeks to address how an online presence can be turned into a profitable one and what kind of business model would result in the most revenue; and
- The measurement issue, which pertains to the effectiveness of a web site and the fairness of charges to advertisers.

The most common public policy issues have to do with copyright protection and censorship. Many publishers are prevented from publishing online because of inadequate copyright protection. An important question to be addressed is: How can the existing copyright protections in the print environment are mapped onto the online environment? Most of the solutions are technological rather than legal. The more common technological solutions include encryption for paid subscribers, and information usage meters on add-in circuit boards, and sophisticated document headers that monitor the frequency and manner by which text is viewed and used.

In online marketing, there is the problem of unsolicited commercial e-mail or "spam mail". Junk e-mail is not just annoying; it is also costly. Aside from displacing normal and useful e-mail, the major reason why spam mail is a big issue in online marketing is that significant costs are shifted from the sender of such mail to the recipient. Sending bulk junk e-mail is a lot cheaper compared to receiving the same. Junk e-mail consumes bandwidth (which an ISP purchases), making Internet access clients slower and thereby increasing the cost of Internet use.

4.19 E-Commerce in Developing Countries

For SMEs in developing countries e-commerce poses the advantages of reduced information search costs and transactions costs (i.e., improving efficiency of operations-reducing time for payment, credit processing, and the like). Surveys show that information on the following is most valuable to SMEs: customers and markets, product design, process technology, and financing source and terms. The Internet and other ICTs facilitate access to this information. In addition, the Internet allows automatic packaging and distribution of information (including customized information) to specific target groups.

However, there is doubt regarding whether there is enough information on the web that is relevant and valuable for the average SME in a developing country that would make investment in Internet access feasible. Underlying this is the fact that most SMEs in developing countries cater to local markets and therefore rely heavily on local content and information. For this reason, there is a need to substantially increase the amount and quality of local content (including local language content) on the Internet to make it useful especially to low-income entrepreneurs.

The eMarketer estimates that SME e-business revenues will increase: from \$6.53 billion to \$28.53 billion in Eastern Europe, Africa, and the Middle East combined; \$127.25 billion in 2003 to \$502.69 billion by 2005 in the Asia–Pacific region; \$23.51 billion in 2003 to \$89.81 billion by 2005 in Latin America; from \$340.41 billion in 2003 to \$971.47 billion by 2005 in Western Europe; and from \$384.36 billion in 2003 to \$1.18 trillion by 2005 in Northern America.

4.19.1 How is E-Commerce Useful to Developing Country Entrepreneurs?

There are at least five ways by which the Internet and e-commerce are useful for developing country entrepreneurs:

1. It facilitates the access of artisans and SMEs to world markets.
2. It facilitates the promotion and development of tourism of developing countries in a global scale.
3. It facilitates the marketing of agricultural and tropical products in the global market.
4. It provides avenues for firms in poorer countries to enter into B2B and B2G supply chains.
5. It assists service-providing enterprises in developing countries by allowing them to operate more efficiently and directly provide specific services to customers globally.

Developing country SMEs in the services sector have expanded their market with the increased ability to transact directly with overseas or international customers and to advertise their services. This is especially true for small operators of tourism related services. Tourism boards lend assistance in compiling lists of service providers by category in their web sites.

In addition, for SMEs in developing countries the Internet is a quick, easy, reliable, and inexpensive means for acquiring online technical support and software tools and applications, lodging technical inquiries, requesting repairs, and ordering replacement parts or new tooling.

The Internet is also instrumental in enabling SMEs in developing countries to join discussion groups with their peers across the globe who are engaged in the same business, and thereby share information, experiences, and even solutions to specific technical problems. This is valuable especially to entrepreneurs who are geographically isolated from peers in the same business.

4.19.2 Adoption of E-Commerce Among SMEs

Currently, the Internet is most commonly used by SME firms in developing countries for communication and research; the Internet is least used for e-commerce. E-mail is considered an important means of communication. However, the extent of use is limited by the SMEs' recognition of the importance of face-to-face interaction with their buyers and suppliers. The level of confidence of using e-mail for communication with both suppliers and buyers increases only after an initial face-to-face interaction. E-mail, therefore, becomes a means for maintaining a business relationship. It is typically the first step in e-commerce, as it allows a firm to access information and maintains communications with its suppliers and buyers. This can then lead to more advanced e-commerce activities.

ICT usage patterns among SMEs in developing countries show a progression from the use of the Internet for communication (primarily e-mail) to use of the Internet for research and information search, to the development of web sites with static information about a firm's goods or services, and finally to use of the Internet for e-commerce. Many firms use the Internet to communicate with suppliers and customers only as a channel for maintaining business relationships. Once firms develop a certain level of confidence on the benefits of e-mail in the conduct of business transactions and the potential of creating sales from its use, they usually consider the option of developing their own web site.

Studies commissioned by The Asia Foundation on the extent of ICT use among SMEs in the Philippines, Thailand and Indonesia, show common use patterns, such as:

1. wide use of the Internet for e-mail because of the recognized cost and efficiency benefits;
2. use of web sites more for promotion than for online sales or e-commerce, indicating that SMEs in these countries are still in the early stages of e-commerce;
3. common use of the Internet for basic research; and
4. inclination to engage more in offline transactions than in e-commerce because of security concerns.

SMEs go through different stages in adopting e-commerce. They start with creating a web site primarily to advertise and promote the company and its products and services. When these firms begin generating traffic, inquiries and, eventually, sales through their web sites, they are likely to engage in e-commerce.

In addition, many web sites providing market and technical information, agronomic advice and risk management tools for SMEs (to coffee and tea farmers in developing countries, for example) have emerged.

4.19.3 Issues in Adopting E-Commerce by SMEs

According to recent surveys conducted in select Southeast Asian countries, the perceived external barriers to e-commerce include the unfavorable economic environment, the high cost of ICT, and security concerns. The internal barriers are poor internal communications infrastructure within SME firms, lack of ICT awareness and knowledge as well as inadequacy of ICT-capable and literate managers and workers, insufficient financial resources, and the perceived lack of relevance or value-added of ICTs to their business. In general, the main issues of concern that acts as barriers to the increased uptake of information technology and e-commerce are the following:

4.19.4 Lack of Awareness and Understanding of the Value of E-Commerce

Most SMEs in developing countries have not taken up e-commerce or use the Internet because they fail to see the value of e-commerce to their businesses. Many think e-commerce is suited only to big companies and that it is an additional cost that will not bring any major returns on investment.

4.19.5 Lack of ICT Knowledge and Skills

People play a vital role in the development of e-commerce. However, technology literacy is still very limited in most developing countries. There is a shortage of skilled workers among SMEs, the key issue in moving forward with using information technology in business. There are also doubts about whether SMEs can indeed take advantage of the benefits of accessing the global market through the Internet, given their limited capabilities in design, distribution, marketing, and post-sale support. While the Internet can be useful in accessing international design expertise, SMEs are not confident that they can command a premium on the prices for their goods unless they offer product innovations. They can, however, capitalize on returns on the basis that they are the low cost providers.

Furthermore, more often than not, the premium in design has already been captured-for example, in the textile products industry-by the branded fashion houses. SMEs doubt whether web presence will facilitate their own brand recognition on a global scale.

- Financial costs. Cost is a crucial issue. The initial investment for the adoption of a new technology is proportionately heavier for small than for large firms. The high cost of computers and Internet access is a barrier to the uptake of e-commerce. Faced with budgetary constraints, SMEs consider the additional costs of ICT spending as too big an investment without immediate returns.

Many SMEs find marketing on the Internet expensive. Having a web site is not equivalent to having a well-visited web site. One reason is that there may be no critical mass of users. Another reason is the challenge of anonymity for SMEs. Because of the presence of numerous entrepreneurs in the Internet, it seems that brand recognition matters in order to be competitive. Moreover, it is not enough that a web site is informative and user-friendly; it should also be updated frequently. Search engines must direct queries to the web site, and news about the site must be broadly disseminated. Significantly, the experience of many OECD countries attests to the fact that the best e-marketing strategies are not better substitutes for the conventional form of media. One solution may be to encourage several SMEs to aggregate their information on a common web site, which in turn would have the responsibility of building recognition/branding by hyperlinking or updating, for example.

- Infrastructure. The national network/physical infrastructure of many developing countries is characterized by relatively low teledensity, a major barrier to e-commerce. There are also relatively few main phone lines for business use among SMEs.
- Security. Ensuring security of payments and privacy of online transactions is the key to the widespread acceptance and adoption of e-commerce. While the appropriate policies are in place to facilitate e-commerce, lack of trust is still a barrier to using the Internet to make online transactions. Moreover, credit card usage in many developing countries is still relatively low.

  Also, consumers are reluctant to use the Internet for conducting transactions with SMEs due to the uncertainty of the SMEs' return policy and use of data.

- Other privacy- and security-related issues. While security is commonly used as the catch-all word for many different reasons why individuals and firms do not engage in extensive e-commerce and use of Internet-based technologies, there are other related reasons and unresolved issues, such as tax evasion, privacy and anonymity, fraud adjudication, and legal liability on credit cards. In many countries, cash is preferred not only for security reasons but also because of a desire for anonymity on the part of those engaged in tax evasion or those who simply do not want others to know where they are spending their money. Others worry that there is lack of legal protection against fraud (i.e., there is no provision for adjudicating fraud and there may be no legal limit on liability, say, for a lost or stolen credit card). It is necessary to distinguish these concerns from the general security concerns (i.e., transaction privacy, protection, and security) since they may not be addressed by the employment of an effective encryption method (or other security measure).

4.20 Women Entrepreneurs and E-Commerce

In general, the Internet and e-commerce have empowered sectors previously discriminated against. Women have gained a foothold in many e-commerce areas. In B2C e-commerce, most success stories of women-empowered enterprises have to do with marketing unique products to consumers with disposable income. The consumers are found largely in developed countries, implying that there is a need for sufficient infrastructure for the delivery of products for the business to prosper and establish credibility. For example, if an enterprise can venture into producing digital goods such as music or software that can be transmitted electronically or if such goods can be distributed and/or delivered locally, then this is the option that is more feasible and practicable.

There are many more successful cases of e-commerce ventures that the women sector can emulate. Some concrete examples are: Tortasperu.com http://www.tortasperu.com.pe), a business involving the marketing of cakes in Peru run by women in several Peruvian cities; Ethiogift (http://ethiogift.com), involving Ethiopians buying sheep and other gifts over the Internet to deliver to their families in other parts of the country, thereby dispensing with the physical delivery of goods abroad; and the Rural Women's Association of the Northern Province of South Africa, which uses the web to advertise its chickens to rich clients in Pietersburg.

While most of the examples involve B2C e-commerce, it must be noted that women are already engaged in wholesale distribution businesses in developing countries. Thus, they can begin to penetrate B2B or B2G markets.

4.21 Role of Government in the Development of E-Commerce in Developing Countries

While it is generally agreed that the private sector should take the lead role in the development and use of e-commerce, the government plays an instrumental role in encouraging e-commerce growth through concrete practicable measures such as:

1. Creating a favorable policy environment for e-commerce; and
2. Becoming a leading-edge user of e-commerce and its applications in its operations, and a provider to citizens of e-government services, to encourage its mass use.

Among the public policy issues in electronic commerce that governments should take heed of are:

- "bridging the digital divide" or promoting access to inexpensive and easy access to information networks;
- legal recognition of e-commerce transactions;
- consumer protection from fraud;
- protection of consumers' right to privacy;

- legal protection against cracking (or unauthorized access to computer systems); and
- protection of intellectual property.

Measures to address these issues must be included in any country's policy and legal framework for e-commerce. It is important that government adopt policies, laws, and incentives that focus on promoting trust and confidence among e-commerce participants and developing a national framework that is compatible with international norms on e-commerce (covering for instance, contract enforcement, consumer protection, liability assignment, privacy protection, intellectual property rights, cross-border trade, and improvement of delivery infrastructure, among others).

4.22 How Can Government Use E-Commerce

Government can use e-commerce in the following ways:

- E-procurement. Government agencies should be able to trade electronically with all suppliers using open standards-through 'agency enablement' programs, 'supplier enablement' programs, and e-procurement information systems.
- Customs clearance. With the computerization of customs processes and operations (i.e., electronic submission, processing, and electronic payment; and automated systems for data entry to integrate customs tables, codes, and pre-assessment), one can expect more predictable and more precise information on clearing time, and delivery shipments, and increased legitimate revenues.
- Tax administration. This includes a system for electronic processing and transmission of tax return information, online issuances of tax clearances, permits, and licenses, and an electronic process registration of businesses and new taxpayers, among others.

More often than not, the e-commerce initiatives of government are a barometer indicating whether or not the infrastructure supports e-commerce use by private firms. This means that if government is unable to engage in e-procurement, secure records online, or have customs fees remitted electronically, then the private sector will also have difficulties in e-commerce uptake. Virtually, the benefits from e-commerce accrue to the government, as the experiences of some countries reflect.

4.23 Regulatory Monitoring for E-Commerce

Unfortunately, the existing legal systems in most developing countries are not sufficient to protect those engaged in e-commerce. For instance, with respect to contracts, existing laws were conceived at a time when the word "writing", "document" and "signature" referred to things in paper form. On the other hand, in today's electronic business transactions paper is not used for record-keeping or entering into contracts.

Another important and common legal issue faced by many developing countries is uncertainty regarding whether the courts will accept electronic contracts or documents and/or electronic signatures as evidence. One view is that the issue of admissibility of electronically generated evidence will not be resolved unless a law specifically referring to it is passed. This gap in existing legal systems has caused the emergence of at least two divergent views: one bordering on the conservative interpretation of the word "document" as to exclude non-paper-based ones; and the other involving a liberal construction, which allows electronic counterparts of documents.

In the ASEAN region, only three countries-Singapore (Singapore Electronic Transactions Act), Malaysia (Cyberlaws), and the Philippines (Philippine E-commerce Act)-have a legal framework for e-commerce. These frameworks provide for the legal recognition of electronic documents and signatures and penalize common crimes and offenses committed in cyberspace.

Other policy issues concern basic prerequisites of infrastructure for successful e-commerce, as follows:

1. Telecoms pricing and performance

   One of the aims of telecommunications policy and legislation should be to ensure that the public has access to basic telecommunications services at a reasonable cost. The goal should ultimately be universal access or widespread access to reliable information and communication services at a reasonable cost and its availability at a reasonable distance.

   To enhance the quality of telecommunications services, policies should encourage:

   - open access, which refers to the absence of non-competitive practices by network providers;
   - open architecture, which pertains to the design of a system that facilitates interconnection among different systems and services currently and as they develop over time; and
   - flexible access, which pertains to interconnected and interoperable networks of telecommunications, broadcasting, and electronic publishing, where the format will be digital and the bandwidth will be adjusted according to the demands of the user and the character of communications.

2. Quality and speed of distribution logistics (i.e., roads and bridges)

   Roads and bridges, especially in developing countries, still form part of the e-commerce infrastructure. Very few goods are delivered over the information infrastructure or the Internet (the exceptions are music and software). Most of the goods purchased over the Internet are still delivered the conventional way (i.e., physical delivery). Hence, poor roads and bridges, inefficient transport systems, coupled with the high cost of international parcel services and bureaucratic customs clearance processes, are major obstacles in the uptake of e-commerce in developing countries. Government should therefore create a policy environment that will:

- encourage investments in the national physical and transport infrastructure;
- and provide for electronic customs clearance processing to streamline the bureaucracy and allow for more transparent, predictable and efficient customs operations.

Both of these will contribute to the reduction of distribution and logistics costs.

4.24 Policies for SMEs for E-Commerce Adoption

The following are the more relevant areas for government intervention with respect to SME uptake of e-commerce. The following are the more relevant areas for government intervention with respect to SME uptake of e-commerce.

- E-SME Development. The market ultimately drives e-commerce development, but it is the private sector that fuels it. Government can provide incentives to encourage widespread e-commerce use by SMEs. An "e-SME development program" in which various sectors can provide technical assistance to SMEs to promote e-commerce uptake, can also be developed. Banks, financial lending and training institutions, and corporations should be encouraged to develop "SME desks" that will address the specific needs of SMEs. In particular, steps should be taken to:
- provide incentives to individuals to become entrepreneurs by lowering borrowing rates;
- provide incentives to SMEs that intend to use e-commerce in their business operations;
- broaden credit extension facilities to SMEs in order for them to use ICT and e-commerce; and
- offer discounts on business solution software packages and software licenses.

Moreover, big businesses and corporations should be encouraged to transfer technology to SMEs by offering them free training in ICT and e-commerce. Awareness Campaign. Evidence suggests that SMEs have insufficient knowledge of information technology and e-commerce. Many SMEs have identified their lack of knowledge of technology as one of the main barriers to using e-commerce. Government and private sector partnerships can engage in a campaign to disseminate information to SMEs about e-commerce policies, best practices, success stories, and opportunities, and obstacles relating to the use of ICTs and e-commerce. These awareness campaigns could include free training courses and workshops on e-commerce, security, and privacy, awards programs, and information centers to assist SMEs. Ultimately, this information campaign should come in the form of an overall e-commerce development strategy for the economy, focusing on its various innovative applications for SMEs.

E-Government. Government should be the lead user of e-commerce if various business and private sector related activities are to be prompted to move online.

In effect, government becomes a positive influence. E-government can take the form of various online transactions such as company registration, taxation, applications for a variety of employee- and business-related requirements, and the like.

Network Infrastructure and Localization of Content. A developed national information infrastructure is a necessary, though not a sufficient, condition for e-commerce uptake of SMEs. Without reliable and inexpensive telecommunications and other information services, SMEs will not be able to go online. An important strategy in this regard is the construction of "telecenters" or electronic community centers that would serve as a community-shared access and connectivity platform especially in the rural areas (e.g., an electronic agriculture information center which provides market information to farmers in rural areas). These telecenters can also be a venue for capacity building, skills enhancement, training, communications, and content development. Government can also adopt agglomerative approaches to Internet use to reduce costs (e.g., export aggregators, such as B2B or B2C portals/exchanges for SMEs, which will facilitate trading with fellow SMEs and with other companies in the international market). Strengthening Consumer Protection. Among the more common trust-related issues that SMEs take note of in considering whether to engage in e-commerce are: where and how payment takes place (whether real or virtual); when settlement takes place (before, during or after the transaction); who settles; whether the transaction is B2B or B2C; and whether settlement can be traced. Generally, however, among e-commerce users in developing countries, including SMEs, there is very low willingness to provide sensitive financial information over the Internet. On the other hand, consumers have reservations about transacting with SMEs through the Internet due to the lack of a clear policy on returns and use of data. To address this concern, government can encourage companies/SMEs to make their privacy policy explicit in their web sites.

A more comprehensive measure that government can undertake to ensure security in e-commerce transactions is the establishment of a Certification Authority, which verifies seller and buyer identities, examines transactions and security procedures, and issues digital certificates to those who are able to meet the set security standards. A good example of this government effort is Singapore's Certification Authority, Netrust. This suggestion does not to discount the importance of private-driven security solutions such as web sites like Hypermart, which host and build storefronts for SMEs while providing them a common system for secure payments. Government can also provide guidelines for SMEs in the development of a system of collaborative ratings, which these entrepreneurs can display on their web sites not only to inform but also to assure their consumers of security. For instance, in electronic exchanges, customers should be able to rate suppliers in terms of quality of product or service and speed of delivery, among others. To minimize fraud, certain safeguards should be built into the rating system like imposing the requirement of presenting evidence of purchase before one's rating can count, with ratings of regular customers having more weight. Trends in ratings and comments should be made readily available to all users. SMEs should also be encouraged through appropriate government incentive schemes to participate in internationally accredited web-based online rating schemes.

Government can also design and establish a legal and judiciary framework that provides for minimum standards of and requirements for transparency, impartiality, and timeliness. While in many developing countries this may be a very ambitious goal, in the medium term SMEs may use self-regulated codes of conduct covering, for example, return policy, data protection, and acceptable forms of content, that are applicable within associations, cooperatives or their respective groups of peers, and e-entrepreneurs. It is important to have not only a rating system but also an enforcement regime that people trust.

Human Resources Development. The government can initiate pilot projects and programs for capability-building, training, and e-commerce support services, such as web design. In Kenya, for instance, the youth from Nairobi's slums are being trained in web design skills.

In general, government initiatives should be in line with current efforts in the foregoing areas of concern. Coordination with development cooperation agencies is important to avoid any duplication of initiatives and efforts.

4.25 Case: IPL—A New Saga in E-Commerce

Cricket is known as a Gentlemen game. The game was initially played in England only; with colonization the game came to different countries and slowly became popular in India. The game, initially, had one format. This format was known as "Test" matches where two teams (mostly representing their countries played against each other. The game was played for 5 days; at the end of 5 days there was no certainty that there will be a result meaning there was no certainty that there will be a winner. To make the game more interesting another format was introduced where the game was played for certain 'overs' (one over means six deliveries by the bowling team) by each team. The winner was decided based on the runs scored within these overs. Of late, a new variant has been framed where the teams have to play only 20 overs and the winner will be declared based on the results of these matches. One such popular tournament where teams play only 20 overs against each other is known as IPL (short form of Indian Premier League). This is organized by Board of Cricket Control of India (BCCI).

IPL is a fast paced game where fitness of the players will be crucial to the success of their teams. This is because, a number of cricket matches needs to be played by each team to go the next round. This calls for energy, focus, and skills with a bit of luck. These aspects make audience go crazy about supporting their favorites. The audience enthusiasm and involvement has made this tournament into big business. The players are paid on average INR 5 million; the fees can vary depending on the profile of the players. Some of the players get paid to the tune of INR 30 million for the season. Every win will result in more cash awards for the players and the team. These numbers and the formats have excited the audience to quite an extent; with the use of e-commerce, the team management as well as BCCI have been able to open up new business models.

The popularity of the IPL is primarily because of the usage of e-commerce channels along with the usage of technology to increase awareness among the audience. For example, by using technology, statistical data are collected and organized. Videos are recorded for each and every match from different cameras which have been positioned at different angles to capture the actions. The web site gives information related to each ball being bowled; for example, the web site reveals information related to the bowler who bowled, the batsman facing the ball, the detailed profile of the bowler and batsman, who is the non-striking batsman, how many runs were scored, etc. All these were tagged by the web site designer so that they can be indexed and future searches were made easier. A host of information through the site attracted many to visit the sites. At the site, several commodities were sold using e-commerce channels. The jersey (i.e. the clothes worn by the players), the bat used in the match, the balls that have been discarded but was used for taking wickets, the stumps used in the match, the gears (protective gears) used by the players, etc. were made available for sale. Sometimes, these sales were done through online auctioning in the web site.

Kolkata Knightriders (KKR), a team in IPL T20 tournaments, used e-commerce to sell its merchandise; using a promotional video, where the song was performed by senior team members of KKR and the promoter of KKR, Shah Rukh Khan (SRK), and the web site attracted many buyers (http://www.kkr.in/). They could download the song as ring-tone (mobile ring tone), buy bat, ball, dress, gears etc. which have the KKR logo on all these merchandise. The fans were enthusiastic and KKR earned in more than 10 million in sale of these commodities through its e-commerce site. The web site also used a slogan which when translated to English meant 'we will fight and win'.

The official theme of the team is (in Bengali) Korbo, Lorbo, Jeetbo Re (English translation means We will do it, Fight for it, Win it) and the official colors are purple and gold. As per a study done by a UK based brand valuation company (Brand Finance, UK), Kolkata Knight Riders are ranked as the second most valuable franchise brand at US$46 million. "The IPL brand alone has risen significantly from the previous year's valuation providing tremendous economic value to its owner BCCI", Brand Finance, the brand valuation consultancy, said in a media release.

"In comparison to international benchmarks for sporting business such as EPL (English Premier League) which is valued at $12 billion, the IPL juggernaut, in a short span of 3 years, is valued at $4 billion and has the potential to grow further", said Unni Krishnan, Managing Director of Brand Finance India. "A huge amount of intellectual property is being created by the complete IPL ecosystem which was sustained despite last year's difficult economic conditions. This demonstrates the exponential value of IPL and the brand potential in a cricket loving country like India and other global cricketing countries", Brand Finance said in a release.

Similarlly, other franchises have been a part of this growth through the e-commerce phenomenon. Chennai Super Kings (CSK), has emerged the most valued franchise in 2010. The CSK franchise has moved up the ladder to number one with a valuation of USD 48.4 million. The Rajasthan Royals, co-owned by Bollywood actress Shilpa Shetty comes in third with USD 45.2 million. The Royal Challengers Bangalore, owned by Vijay Mallya, is ranked fourth with a valuation of USD 41.9 million and is followed by the Mumbai Indians (USD 40.8 million), Delhi Daredevils (USD 40.5 million) and Kings XI Punjab (USD 36.1 million). The Deccan Chargers are at the base with a valuation of USD 34.4 million. All these achievements in IPL have been possible through e-commerce and using technology to open new business avenues and electronic channels for selling the merchandise. Observing the love and franticness for this mega event, eBay India came up with an initiative to offer a unique opportunity for die-hard cricket fans. They partnered with several branded apparel companies, so that cricket fans all across the world can access IPL merchandise of all eight teams (Kings XI Punjab, Kolkata Knight Riders, Royal Challengers Bangalore, Chennai Super Kings, Delhi Daredevils, Mumbai Indians, Deccan Chargers and Rajasthan Royals) at a click of a button. IPL merchandise on offer were T-shirts, jerseys, caps, backpacks, footwear, key chains, collectibles, cheering sticks, wrist bands, and many more. E-commerce company like iStreet (http://www.istreetnetwork.com), realized catering to the wide interests of online shoppers, who are die-hard cricket fans. The e-commerce site assisted eBay India in its operations of selling the goods through electronic channel. Successfully, together, they managed to assist eBay in selling most IPL merchandises. This was done through product image management, catalog pricing, listing management, and fulfillment. More importantly, key performance metrics were used in the entire process right from market assessment to implementation to achieve the desired result.

Like other businesses, the T20 cricket faced problems such as high cost of players' salaries, high degree of required skills. However, by using e-commerce, it has become a survival model for the BCCI and has shown the way for others to follow (other tournaments such as English Premier League have started using e-commerce sites) for increasing the revenue.

Review Questions

1. Was there a need to change traditional format of cricket? How did a new business model evolved out of it?
2. How could BCCI have sustained this business model? Was there a need for e-commerce- Discuss.
3. How all the stakeholders were benefited by technology based cricket format?

4.26 Case Jet Airways: Always with E-Commerce

Jet Airways is known for its 'on schedule' operations. In recent past while discussing with a British national, I was surprised that he preferred Jet airways for travel to India to other airlines. He liked the pricing, 'on schedule' operations, and ease of booking. In domestic market, Jet is also a preferred flight as it operates around 400 flights to more than 40 destinations. In international circuit, it operates to multiple countries (UK, USA, Canada, and Singapore to name a few). The airline has introduced wide bodied planes so that it can increase its number of destinations and flights. It is being considered as the most successful airline. Many of the success are attributed to the ability of the airline to monitor and control its operations using information system. The information system uses its e-commerce site (all the passengers interact with the airline through this site only).

The airline has always been keen in maintaining a good relationship with its customers. In keeping with the commitment to customer service excellence, Jet Airways has introduced a set of key e-commerce initiatives. With a clear focus on customer satisfaction, the airline has been keen on adopting the most advanced, cutting-edge technology. The software used helped it to integrate many services and be able to act on customer feedback immediately. By using e-commerce technology initiative, the airline has become the first Indian carrier ever to implement Bar-coded boarding passes (BCBP), an IATA standard solution. The BCBP can be automatically scanned at the boarding process, avoiding manual boarding and thus enabling multiple flights to be handled at a single gate. This reduced error, seat allocation without any manual error, and customers have to spend less time at check-in counters. After successfully implementing the BCBP system in Singapore, where a scanned boarding pass data is immediately uploaded to the main database, the airline introduced the same system at all other check-in counters. As per CEO Sudheer Raghavan, this has helped them meeting security standards as well increase productivity with less error. Moreover, the information was available to the relatives of the passengers as well.

In an effort to improve customer satisfaction, the airline has improved the features in its web site, http://www.jetairways.com. It has a new look, enhanced usability, and performance with easy to use interface with the customers. The new web site provides information in different languages such as Chinese and also provides information on live weather updates with forecast for next five days.

The information has been integrated with http://www.weather.com to provide live weather information. The airline's attractive online promotional scheme currently offers passengers who make online bookings on jetairways.com a chance to win different prizes apart from offering several discount coupons. For customers who register in the web site and also those who are frequent travelers, the site offers several freebies such as discounted holiday packages, chance to redeem their mileage points. Also, from time to time, they take opinion poll from these registered customers through the web sites and use the feedback to improve their services. Many times they declare winners from the opinion polls through lucky draw and invite them to participate in different celebrations.

Using the e-commerce web site, the airline has introduced an international web check-in facility for the convenience of its international travelers at London, Hong Kong, Singapore, Kuala Lumpur, Bangkok, and Brussels, wherein passengers holding e-tickets can check-in on the web and print their boarding passes. The facility is also now available for frequent flyers in domestic circuit as well. The airline plans to extend this facility to its North American destinations with the receipt of the requisite security clearances.

The airline's JetPrivilege members may now redeem their JPMiles online at jetairways.com in real time, pay via credit card, and print their award tickets online. Although the service is available on the airline's India web site only, it will be opened to other country sites shortly. Using the same web site, Jet also plans to offer e-ticketing facilities on all its flights, spanning 60 destinations in India, and around the world. The airline also launched its much-awaited Infant e-ticketing facility recently.

In order to increase its passenger base, it has tied up with several international airlines to offer partner benefits to the travelers. It also has expanded its partnership programs to hotels and retail categories. The loyalty program known as JetPrivilege, announced three exciting new opportunities for its members to earn JPMiles, with the addition of three new partners in the ever expanding publishing, hotel, and retail categories. In the Publishing category, Jet Airways has partnered with an Indian publishing house. JetPrivilege members can earn 150 JPMiles for a 1-year subscription for magazines from that publishing house at a special price of INR 499. In the Hotel category, Jet Airways has partnered with Citrus Hotels Limited. Citrus Hotels comprises seven hotels in seven singular locations spanning the length and breadth of the country. The hotel offers distinctive style and connects at best value in any location they are situated in. Each resort is different in location, look, mood, and guest experience. Jet Airways' JetPrivilege members can earn 300 JPMiles per stay, as well as enjoy 15 % discount on room rate, applicable on different room tariffs and 10 % discount on food & beverage, including in-room dining. In the e-Retail category, Jet Airways has partnered with myZingo eCommerce Service Pvt. Ltd. Jet Airways JetPrivilege members can earn 5 JPMiles for every INR 100 spent at myZingo web site, Guest delight is at the core of Jet Airways' strategy to offer better value creation for its JetPrivilege members. This partnership further cements Jet position as arguably the leading airline frequent flyer program in the country with the high value it offers members and the wide range of product choices. Through this association esteemed JetPrivilege members can enjoy a fine brand experience as well as earn JPMiles.

The airline also uses the same site to do cargo booking, to provide internal information to its employees on crew rosters and flight schedule. Using the web site, the maintenance crew can locate possible problems at different locations and troubleshoot them from remote servers. With its ambitious plan to grow its operations, the e-commerce applications will hold the key to their business consolidation and sustained business model.

Review Questions

1. What are the issues Jet Airline face for consolidating its operations?
2. What is the necessity of e-commerce web sites?
3. What are the benefits of using e-commerce web sites? How does it help passengers?

4.27 Summary

4.27.1 Review Questions

1. What do you understand by e-commerce?
2. What are the differences between e-commerce and e-business?
3. What are different types of e-commerce being practiced?
4. What is m-commerce and how is related to e-commerce?
5. What are the factors that affect adoption of e-commerce?
6. What is the role of Internet in e-commerce?
7. How companies can use intranet for e-commerce?
8. What is the role of e-commerce in developing countries? What benefits does it provide to economy
9. What is electronic payment system and how does it vary from traditional payment system?
10. What are the benefits of e-banking? How does e-commerce help in e-banking?
11. What is e-tailing and what are its prospects?
12. What is online publishing?

Part II
Strategy

Chapter 5
Understanding E-Commerce Product Design Strategy

5.1 Learning Objectives

At the end of the chapter, the students would learn:

- Benefits of Internet-based marketing;
- When a product can be marketed over Internet;
- Design criteria for selecting Web-enabled supply channels

5.2 Introduction

There is a saying which means it is not advisable to force fit a solution—"YOU CANNOT PUSH A SQUARE PEG THROUGH A ROUND HOLE". As we know, for sales and marketing teams, channels used for marketing is quite important (they are referred here as holes). Channels as we know are the different conduits that are used to reach end users. Examples are salespersons, distributors, retailers, the Internet. When a particular product or service is designed, which is referred to as 'peg' here, channel selection becomes quite important. A correct fitment of products and channels will ensure lower selling costs, availability of products at the right time, and fewer customer problems. Today, technology is changing the shape of the channel by enhancing the capability of existing channels and creating new ones. Marketers need to design and make their products ready to be easily sold, marketed, and serviced through these "technology enabled" channels. In the new economy, this fitment is becoming critical.

Product marketers need to define strategy which would be enabled by technology. For marketers, the Internet forces them to rethink in terms of the nature and mix of channels which they use for selling after completing packaging and designing of their offerings. If the strategy is well tuned toward enabling Internet,

S. Mohapatra, *E-Commerce Strategy*, Springer Texts in Business and Economics, DOI: 10.1007/978-1-4614-4142-7_5,

then with correct design, all products can take advantage of the Web enabled. The unique benefits offered by "web-enabled" channels like the Internet helps simple products that easily fit such as digital music, news, financial services, and computer software, but also creates easy brand awareness among consumers. Marketers from different organizations (from cars to detergents to raw goods for industry) can take advantage of Web-enabled selling channels, if they take different perspectives of the traditional four Ps of marketing (packaging, promotion, placement, and pricing). In order to take advantage of the potential of new or Web-enhanced channels, organizations in the new economy have started to look at the channels with new perspectives. This chapter discusses design criteria that will be useful to marketing strategists entrusted to redesign their products and services for technology-enabled supply channels. A classic case has been Dell Computer, one of the early birds to redesign its selling approach using technology and one of the pioneers who showed others how this strategy can work.

5.3 Benefits of Web-Enabled Channels

Every related literature talks about Dell as the pioneer for reaping benefits from Web-enabled channels. This is because it pioneered the concept of redesigning products as per the requirements of the new channel. This success mantra can be adopted by others who redesign their products to fit better in the new channel. Technology is enhancing existing selling channels and creating new ones in every industry. These changes will ultimately change the way offerings are packaged and designed. In other words, the "peg" (product) remains the same, but the shape of the hole (the channel) is changing. For example, most large companies are automating their sales forces and call centers with Customer Relationship Management (CRM) solutions. This is forcing product marketers to "digitize" product catalogs and making them available to all. These catalogs can be digitally displayed through sales peoples' laptops as well as in different web sites (using banner advertisements). This also has forced many to rearchitect product specifications so that they can be well understood by end users and can be seen as "customer configured" on their computer screen.

To start with the concept of Web-enabled channels, we should understand that to be successful in e-marketing, the organization needs to have a strategy in place. This strategy creates different types of demands on products and its features. New Internet storefronts and online marketplaces that sell products directly online are forcing product marketers to digitize their features. This means that the ways the products are represented or delivered are changed so that these products can be displayed on electronic shelves. Some other features are changing price as customers customize and try out different combinations of features. This also can help to keep up with the rapid-fire bidding during online auctions. As seen above, designing strategy to make products ready for technology-enabled channels, represents an opportunity to marketers because most organizations are so focused on building technology-enabled selling channels that they have little time or money to focus on developing specialized offerings that fit those channels. To come out of the selling products from its present format to develop strategies for improving features of the product for digitization is a paradigm shift. The concept of making products ready for channels is not yet on the radar screen of most organizations.

Ultimately, things will have to change. The previous assumption that only certain products (e.g., CDs, books, travel) are Web ready will be proven wrong. For instance, Maruti–Suzuki puts a lot of energy into designing products and developing strategy so that they can use online channels to support the sale of their products. Car manufacturers like Chrysler and General Motors have aggressively looked deeper into dealer inventories and ultimately assemble custom cars. Professional services are another industry that can take advantage of the Internet. Executive search marketplaces, such as Monster.com, are among the most successful online marketplaces because of the Internet's ability to aggregate job hunters in one place and transport resumes and job postings with no proper or manpower. In the late 1990s an accounting firm, Ernst and Young, even started delivering tax consulting online through a website tool called "Ernie", inspiring a raft of imitators in all parts of consulting.

In the short term, marketers can begin simply by sorting out which products "fit" better in online channels, and which ones do not. For example, when Herman Miller, the office furniture producer, started building their electronic channels, they offered only a few simple home office products that were easy to buy online. Once they had gained some familiarity with online selling, Heman Miller added more products for home office users and offered an Internet configuring too. It was not fancy: just a downloadable "Room Planner" that helped buyers to figure out whether the desks and chairs they wanted to by would actually fit in their cramped home offices. But it was important because the tool made it easier for remote customers to visualize and confidently select furniture for their home-based businesses. As a result, online sales at Herman Miller started growing at 38 % each month.

Over the long haul to gain a competitive edge, product marketing professionals will have to embrace two priorities:

1. Enabling product configuration and assembly that is fast and transparent to the customer;
2. Designing products and services that can be sold through any channel or mix of channels.

5.4 E-Commerce Considerations

To begin to make their products ready for technology-enhanced selling channels, product marketers must first understand the capability of the channel that they are trying to use. This means looking outside their organizations to find the new information that can be used by product design teams. During this assessment, distribution requirements have to be considered into product design. For example, if an automobile manufacturer wants to use a Web-enabled channel, then they have to first put the features in an interactive mode so that all customers can get a virtual experience and then supply the orders through the nearest dealer. Here, the size, shape, and weight of cars are dictated by how these products will fit into railroad carriers and containers. The standardized containers and pack sizes offered by courier services did not meet the customization required by its customers. As a result, if a courier organization has to design a channel, then first it has to strategize to design features of the boxes that can fit the requirements. They also have to relate to how they will be stacked in airplane cargo holds. Designing in response to external factors creates a competitive advantage when it can result in efficiencies in product delivery.

5.4.1 Understanding Consumer Behavior

Once customers get used to the benefits of buying through the Internet, they become a new kind of customer. This new customer expects, if not demands, highly personalized products, personalized services, and immediate delivery. Adapting existing products to meet such high expectations will involve changes in how organizations package, distribute, and configure products. For example, customers will shop at online marketplaces that allow them to compare prices and products of many different suppliers, and then select a vendor at a single mouse click. As a result, manufacturers of commodity products such as steel, paper, chemicals, and plastics, and purveyors of indirect materials, such as packaging equipment and maintenance supplies, must tailor their products for online transactions. In simplistic terms, this involves providing digital product specifications and even visual screen demonstrations on web sites to encourage virtual experience and provides "extra information" that may influence a buyer. Eventually, competitive bidding in these online markets will force marketers to become better at adjusting product pricing on the fly while still managing profit margins.

Online customers expect an increasingly wider selection of products and services through self-service electronic channels. But customers differ when it comes to the level of the self-service they desire. Some customers will require a great deal of assistance when they buy anything from a fishing hat to a mainframe. Other customers prefer minimal assistance and find no joy interacting with human telephone representatives. Slowly, organizations will have to become experts in managing a bigger collection of offerings for self-services.

5.4.2 Benchmarking Your Competitors

The example of Dell shows that marketers who look closely at how a product is sold have a good chance of gaining a sustainable competitive advantage.

Competitors are trying to create unique selling propositions by using technology in the sales and marketing process. For example, in consumer financial services, new players like Sharekhan and Moneycontrol were able to enter the market by breaking apart the traditional financial services product to take advantage of the unique benefits of the Internet channel. These innovators divided and conquered by separating stock transactions from financial advice and research. They offered lower transaction costs, more self-service, and more options online to customers who wanted cheap trades and did not require advice. They passed on the commission that was usually paid to middle agents on to customers and attracted them. New business models will create value in different ways by building services into structured pricing. Competitors typically accessorize mature products with desirable services—anything from automatic replenishment ordering, free returns, and free delivery, to 24 h technical support. Experiments in this zone also include leasing arrangements for products traditionally purchased, automatic free product upgrades, trade-ins, or creative financing for the buyer.

5.4.3 Understanding Technical Capabilities of the Channel

To design products that fit well in new technology enabled channels, organizations will need to better understand the technical capabilities of these channels. The four Ps of marketing (packaging, price, placement, and promotion) still apply to product development. Technology, however, influences these Ps. New product design teams should keep abreast of new methods to digitally represent and distribute products that were previously available only in a more physical form. For example, online channels are transforming the packaging of all written, audio, graphic, and video products. New media such as HTML, writable CDs, multimedia, flash video files, and wireless are merely alternate formats to paper books, plastic records, drawn decorative artwork, and video cassettes. Both the publishing and the music industry are in the process of modifying their offerings for digital distribution in a variety of electronic formats such as digital MP3 audio, .flv files, and video files. Publishers are also exploring new ways of pricing by considering time, medium, and context, which may have relevance to many other products and services. For example, the India Today group allows its online customers to buy either their online edition or printable edition or both. This takes advantage of the Web's unique ability to sell content in very small quantities. Accomplishing this same strategy at the newsstand would not be physically possible.

A case of selling groceries through Web: Companies that can successfully modify their products to take advantage of new channels can open up new markets. One of the earliest success stories is that of the Future Bazaar group which tried to sell groceries through the Web. Selling groceries through the Internet required some attention to technical requirements of the new distribution channel. For example, they could only ship groceries that could be safely stored at room temperatures and had a shelf life which was more than the time required to deliver.

This meant that Future bazaar could sell a limited number of groceries (less than that sold in the food bazaar) but at a substantially discounted price. To attract customers to this model, the organization used FM channels to advertise as the local residents were the primary target customers.

Once an organization has measured or assessed the capabilities of the available technology and its fitment capability to products being offered, it would be desirable to redesign products and enhance available products with features that will allow its complete potential to be exploited through Web technology. To do this, product managers will need to rethink the criteria they use to redesign products. This also implies that organizations need to sort and modify their offerings based on the type of channel being used. For example, even though books were among the first products to move online in large numbers, several material changes to the product were necessary. In the retail channel, the binder art on the side of the book is important because it sits on a bookstore shelf. This is often the only part the customer sees while browsing. In online channels some new things are important. The theme and content of the book must be made available to the potential customers. Also, it is better to program good search engine "keywords" and other interactive links that make sure readers with interest find the book easily. Good graphics and charts bring the content to life and make it look better online. And a large number of impartial, open-source reviews and referrals from actual customers are keys to making the sales. In the short term, this means resegmenting and repackaging products based on where they sell best. In the long run, this means redesigning products based on a new set of "channel readiness" criteria. Amazon.com is an example, where a person can browse through the front cover and inside cover to understand the theme of the book. To enable this, publishers now insist that their authors provide details related to the book and the biography of the author as 'inside front cover' and 'back cover' respectively. This is clearly a case where the products (here books) have been redesigned so that readers can access related information for buying the books and take decisions accordingly.

5.4.4 Making Products Easier to Sell and Buy Online

Before a product is sold over the Internet through E-commerce, the products need to be redesigned so that they can become E-commerce savvy. This involves improving the ease with which customers are able to select, configure, and buy products over the Internet. As is evident, all products can be sold over the Internet. As of now, very simple, digital products or services standard products can be delivered entirely through Internet channels. With the introduction of 3G technologies, the capability of E-commerce will increase as customers can feel the products over the Internet and take decisions without going to retail stores. Marketers who take the extra step of making it easier for customers to select, configure, and buy their more complicated products, (not just simple ones) can gain competitive advantage. Standardization and availability of catalogs over the

Internet can improve the capability to improve product sales. Simplifying the way products are listed and categorized can also make it easier for customers to find, understand, select, and buy the products through E-commerce.

5.4.5 Technological Features

Using different features such as natural language search and artificial intelligence can improve E-commerce features. These technology features allow customers to formulate questions about what they want in plain English as well as in their local language. Using artificial intelligence, the company can suggest, guide, and assist customers as well as anticipate customer questions. The intelligence is developed based on customers' past buying history as well as buying patterns. The process of purchasing a video cassette recorder, for example, may trigger a screen prompt for a sale on blank videocassettes. Amazon.com uses this feature very well, where for every buy, the customer is prompted with suggestions for related products as well.

5.4.6 Mass Customization

The mass customization concept involves designing/redesigning products to be readily configured and assembled as per customer specifications. All the products offered through E-commerce route have to be assembled. A good strategy for E-commerce will design products that can be more easily "configured" to meet the needs of customers. Salesforce.com has allowed its customers to configure required software services and pay accordingly. This led to the Software as Service (SaS) model. Another example, General Mills permitted customers to customize their own breakfast cereal through the web site myCereal.com. This gave cereal eaters the choice of millions of possible varieties. Thus, General Mills could offer swift delivery of an individualized product, thanks to the use of product configuration tools.

Using this strategy, firms can provide buyers with facilities to request the ingredients, textures, packaging, and choose delivery schedule. A family takes a family photograph and puts the photograph on a mug. The color of the mug can be chosen by the family and delivered to their house. Thus, the firm is able to factor in large amounts of customer information into the design of the product, including health, diet, portion size, allergies, and demographics. For all these customizations, the customers will not mind paying extra the usual price.

Other experiments in the packaged goods area include personalized cosmetics from Procter & Gamble (Reflect.com) and customized sneakers online: Customatix and Nike. Dell also provides customization in the assembly of components and delivers a product as per customer requirements. Chrysler's web site tracks 220 specific car options, features, and other attributes across its customer and prospect base. While it does not make personalized cars yet, it currently uses this information to model and forecast demand and reduce the cost of "mass customizing" its most popular cars in the factory. As a result, Chrysler takes a leadership position in mass customization. Mattel enables Barbie fans to custom configure their doll with hundreds of possible permutations (e.g., hair and eye color, outfits, accessories) on its Barbie.com site.

5.4.7 Dynamic Pricing

This strategy means using dynamic pricing models to deliver fast and accurate market pricing and to calculate product profitability as per the configuration demanded by the customer. As flexible pricing rapidly becomes a competitive necessity, marketers will have to take advantage of technologies. They need to collaborate with partners such as Micro payments/digital rights management, which allows customers to pay for increasingly smaller increments of usage. Other technology partners could include providers of auctioning software, which help organizations to participate in dynamic trading communities by enabling hundreds of different, market-based pricing structures. Other partners such as data mining/segmentation software providers will provide data analysis tools that would allow marketers to better understand customer price sensitivity and value perceptions. This will help frame marketing policy to enable individualized or customized pricing tiers. This approach has also led to what is known as value packaging.

Value packaging means defining how value is created for customers. Instead of selling a product, the value package shows the true worth of money from the customers' viewpoint. This means, the firms will have to rethink the "boundaries" they draw around their product to take advantage of the ways technology will be able to enhance the sales channels and exploit new forms of distribution. Taking this concept further, we find Hyundai not only offers its products (cars), but also arranges vehicle financing for the customers. Chevrolet has offered 3 years' 'no money charged' servicing for its vehicles. Maruti and also other vehicle manufacturers have offered vehicle insurance along with their products. These value packages, when offered through the E-commerce route need to attract customers through its distribution channels.

Online sellers often gain an advantage when they bundle products with other features and provide a package. Organizations must redefine the boundaries of their products so that they can optimally align the value to the customer ("value creation") with the basis for payment to the seller ("value capture"), with respect to specific channels. However, this is not an easy task. For example, auto manufacturers like Ford are being forced to unbundle, or separate, their used and new car sales from Ford's in-house financing, and will forego the option of giving customers a "branded" service. This has been done so that they can participate in independent car-shopping portal web sites and online trading communities such as Auto-bytel and Cars. com.

Customers have become more knowledgeable and demanding forcing firms to innovate new 'values' for customers. The firms will find ways to redefine value boundaries in many ways, including repackaging traditional product bundles into smaller units for more customer flexibility, assembling new and innovative bundles of services and products into solutions, and experimenting with new compensation and payment models.

5.4.8 Channel Distribution

For E-commerce to be successful, the distribution channel needs to be redesigned. A hybrid channel needs to be defined which will take care of traditional and Internet-based distribution channels. This is required as traditional products such as refrigerators, shirts, and kitchen appliances need to be marketed through E-commerce. With the introduction of E-commerce, there is a need to package products for more than one distribution channel. This means adapting and designing products for easy distribution through a variety of channels, including electronic and online business partners as well as traditional supply channels.

For example, many products viz., booking tickets for travel, online stock brokerage, buying personal computers, and note books are currently sold through a variety of channels at the same time. Firms which are marketing these products need to coordinate all the elements of product design across more than one channel. The channel design becomes complicated with differential pricing for different channels. Even packaging for these products will be different for different channels.

Designing hybrid channels is important because of preferences for both traditional and online channels. While many customers still prefer the traditional channel, tech savvy and jet set executives prefer to buy products online. Sending flowers through online portals has become a practice for many customers, while still many customers would prefer to pick up the bouquets from shops (traditional channel). Similarly, a customer might buy on the Web, complain on the phone, return to the store, and ultimately write a "snail mail" letter to the president looking for a rebate. The risk of not making products ready and consistent for all channels means losing potential customers. Also, customers will complain when the change of address they input on a firm's web site is not reflected in snail mails. Firms must design products for easy distribution through an increasing variety of electronic channels as well as for third-party business partners. This may require product simplification, better product information, or new delivery, and payment mechanisms.

5.4.9 Online Billing

For E-commerce strategy to be successful, the firms need to plan for preparing computerized billing online, accepting electronic checks, credit card payments, tie-ups with banks, and credit card payment gateways as well as warehousing and logistics to manage rapid delivery and returns.

5.4.10 Technology

Firms need to plan and use technologies that can fit through many different channels and media. These technologies use a variety of software programs designed to package products for meeting the technical parameters of online delivery. Some of the examples are Adobe PDF, MP3, and RealNet works, which allow documents to be ported, presented in good digital formats. Foxit, Adobe MP4, MPEGs have helped in digitizing artwork and music that were quickly accepted as the standards. India Post, the Government postal services in India has planned that it would create a standardized method to certify the delivery of electronic documents. We are sure this will have implications for private companies, such as Blue Dart, Federal Express, and DHL, as India Post will force them to reduce the money that they were charging for similar courier services.

In addition, firms that plan to migrate products from physical channels of distribution to electronic channels must also consider warehousing and logistics to manage rapid delivery and returns. Also, firms need to implement collaborative CRM using technology. These technologies facilitate online collaboration between customers and live agents during the product sale. Fabmall, Makemytrip, etc., use specific technologies such as voice-over IP, co-browsing, automated call back, page push, and customer service chat.

Best-in-class E-commerce marketers will work to embed service into products such that proper guidelines for installation, troubleshooting are provided in detail. Panasonic cordless telephones, Apple ipods, provide the requisite service knowledge using the network, memory, and database technology to build instructions, help-desk support, and service into products themselves. While strategizing for E-commerce, firms should make self-service products with embedded service capability through substantial investments in self-serve technical support, customer service, and frequently asked questions (FAQ) database accessed over the Internet or embedded within the product.

Firms also should use technology for mail response management. This class of technology uses artificial intelligence and business rules to read, sort, and respond to electronic inquiries, so that marketers can respond more quickly to online customers and online prospects. ICICI bank, iMINTpoints (reward point redemption) use these types of technologies.

5.4.11 Service and Support

Firms must plan for building customer service into products. This involves matching the level of product service and support to the requirements of the customer and to the technical needs of a selling channel. For example, IT product manufacturers Microsoft, Symantec, etc., have overcome the lack of retail sales support by embedding self-help knowledge bases and easy online customer support into their products. Popular products such as Windows operating system, Microsoft Office, Symantec Anti virus products have provided online support for faster customer service. Firms must invest in technologies to provide some level of automated buying support.

5.5 Case of Dell Computer: Early Bird in Web Enablement

Market dynamics have changed substantially over the decades. Most of these changes have happened because of adoption of technology. In the early 1980s, a few innovators changed the personal computer industry. Visionaries such as Stephen Jobs of Apple Computer and Michael Dell of Dell, Inc. tried to address complexities involved in owning personal computers (PCs). They wanted to try out making PCs simpler. Also, Bill Gates wanted to try out bringing PCs that would be affordable, user friendly, and for which customers need not be experts to be able to use them. All of them wanted to execute these visions in different ways and set about the tasks using different approaches. Bill and Jobs simplified the computer itself by inventing the Microsoft and Apple MacIntosh, respectively, with its easy point and click instructions. Dell did something equally interesting and had a different approach altogether. He wanted to pass on the benefits to the customer in terms of price. He also simplified how PCs were sold. While Jobs and Bill revolutionized the design of products and influenced how PCs would be manufactured in the future, Dell revolutionized the distribution channel and influenced how PCs would be sold in the future.

Jobs and Bill built computers from scratch. Dell, on the other hand, using his imagination, did not build computers rather he assembled them from parts. He did this while he was a college student and did the assembly in his college dormitory. This perspective allowed him to reach his customers through a different channel. He decided to customize PCs and sell them to individuals with different product configurations. Product configuration would be decided by the customer and then Dell would assemble in his room and sell them. He concluded that since all the parts were basically the same, there would be value in buying a bunch of parts and then building a product configured to suit the needs of an individual consumer.

Over time, this focus on "configuring" products rather than building them let Dell as a company get very good at helping customers navigate thousands of possible PC system combinations available for sale. By applying this concept to the selling process, Dell learned how to translate the needs of customers, who were not technical, but end users such as common business persons (without computer background) and household users. He translated what the customer wanted in plain nontechnical language into a product recommendations or a customized computer built just for them. Dell made it easier for the average person without a technical degree to select and buy personal computers. All these business transactions were completed without displaying products in retail outlets, but rather through sales representatives who were rather expensive. This meant that in practice, Dell could take orders through telephone and then assemble and through sales representatives, ship these assembled ones to the customers' place. In contrast, other computers were still being sold through retail stores. To make this happen, they laid out options in a print catalog so that customers could see the choices they had; they used software to help call center agents calculate the costs of options and add-ons on the fly while talking to prospects. And Dell used technology to immediately send proposals back to the prospects at the push of a button. As a result, Dell's selling costs were a third less than the competition, a significant gap in a business where margins were shrinking, as the price of personal computers continued to drop in the wake of the low-cost Apple product line.

In the mid-1990s, when the Internet came along, Dell found that the discipline of making the personal computer "ready" for the phone channel also helped them make it ready for online channels. To adapt the PC for sale in online channels, they used new third-party software called "product configuration software" that automated this process of selection. This new "third party" of softwares (these were marketed by companies like Trilogy and Calico) did the permutation and combination for assembling these parts and came up with the final PC. The softwares helped to consider all possible alternatives and came up with the best set of options for a client. At Dell, this tool helped online customers navigate and understand very large and complicated product lines. They also helped to understand the universe of PC products and embedded features, which increased the level of involvement of the customers. This was the first of its kind and customers liked their experience as they felt like experts assembling their own PCs. They were proud to display their creations to their colleagues and this created a euphoria. This also reduced the burden on the call center representatives. Assistants were available who helped these customers through the buying process over the phone. In addition, Dell's focus on configuration allowed them to become leaders in product customization and personalization because of the amount of information that could be processed quickly, and then translated as customer orders were sent directly to the factory.

Armed with these tools, Dell began to sell computers over the Internet in 1996 and was soon averaging over a million dollars in online sales a day. By the turn of the century they were doing over $13 billion in online sales a year, half of their total sales. This focus on making products ready for Web-enabled channels helped Dell to grow faster for less money. By simplifying their products, which could be understood by common persons, they alienated so-called techie persons, but succeeded in getting huge numbers. As a result, they could be sold through low-cost telephone and Web channels. Dell was able to get more margin out of every sale compared with their competitors such as Compaq, IBM, HP, and even Apple. By the end of the decade, they were growing at twice the rate as the rest of the industry and became the number one seller of PCs in the United States. Their competitors are still scrambling to restructure and change their selling approach to close the cost-to-sell gap.

5.6 Summary

This chapter explains the different parameters that need to be considered before getting ready for E-commerce. Simply making a web site portal available for product information and buying and selling will not be sufficient. It has to be complemented by designing product features, hybrid channels for distributions, differential pricing for products meant for different channels, and mass customization. Mastering the discipline of product channel readiness will become critical to success when new selling routes are used. The firms also need to factor in how using the Internet technology will change the nature and mix of channels; the firms also need to redesign packaging as well as their service offerings.

5.7 Review Questions

1. What are the different parameters that need to be considered while designing E-commerce strategy?
2. Give examples of products that have been designed for hybrid channels?
3. Discuss a product that has differential pricing for E-commerce and for traditional channel.
4. Dell—is it a case of mass customization or using hybrid channel? Discuss in detail.
5. What is importance of dynamic pricing for E-commerce?
6. Why do firms need to understand consumer behavior?

Chapter 6
E-Commerce and Online Auctions

6.1 Learning Objectives

At the end of the chapter, students would understand

- What is online auction
- Importance of online auction in the industry
- Role of e-commerce in online auction

6.2 Introduction

Online auctions, buying and selling articles through social network sites, business-to-business exchanges, and other forms of electronic trading are slowly becoming the marketing options for new age firms. As the penetration of Internet is making inroads to every household as well as business house, online marketing becomes inevitable for millions of businesses worldwide. As the trend continues, more and more buyers have started using them. Coal India, for example, will buy about $55 billion worth of goods and services in 2008. The company plans to make almost one-third of these purchases through online marketplaces. The trend is catching up as firms from different domains have started online marketing and in future a significant percentage of their day-to-day customer interactions will occur through online marketplaces over the next 2–3 years.

This has pros and cons for firms. It is bad news because these online market-places will shift the balance of power from the seller to the buyer. This is so as there will be transparency with respect to price, transaction volume, etc. If Coal India wants to buy in online markets, a seller must react. The seller has to register first, even if it means paying a fee for posting his price list in a digital catalogue. This can expose seller to more competition than ever before. The good news is that online marketplaces offer sellers the opportunity to access global markets and

S. Mohapatra, *E-Commerce Strategy*, Springer Texts in Business and Economics,
DOI: 10.1007/978-1-4614-4142-7_6,

define new markets. Firms need to understand how to blend online marketplaces with traditional selling channels (e.g., field sales, telechannels, distributors, and virtual Internet storefronts) to reach more markets and match the way customers want to buy. Online marketing creates knowledge repository about sale volume and unit pricing. As a result, ultimately, the real winners will find ways to use the information generated in these marketplaces to their own advantage, or add to their business by offering new, profitable services to buyers in these markets.

The next sections in this chapter deal with different parameters for defining strategy for e-commerce and online marketing.

6.3 Asian Paints: E-Commerce for Online Marketplaces

In the INR 5,000 crore plus paints industry, traditional method of selling is now tried with online marketing practices. About 12 % of corporate buyers currently purchase paints online. A growing number of online marketplaces, including early players such as eBay.com, amazon.com, and ChemMatch, were set up to make it easier to buy and sell products online at a global scale. Because the paints market is very fragmented a very few producers must sell to a large number of international buyers, ranging from household customers, industrial houses, producers of plastic soda bottles to producers of automobiles. These online marketplaces offered paint manufacturers the opportunity to reach this diverse group of buyers economically.

Asian Paints, manufacturer of paints for different customers, saw online marketplaces as a new sales channel to complement its field sales force, its network of global distributors, and its new electronic commerce channel. Already noted for its strong field sales force, Asian Paints had recently added e-commerce as a new direct sales channel. As a result, within months of its launch, the new online store-front had registered more than 500 customers and produced INR 10 crore in sales. Asian Paints understands that online market is in its infancy stage and is an "immature" channel. As a part of its strategy, it airs a number of awareness programmes through customer meets, advertisements and seminars. It continues to re-evaluate all of the online marketplaces it sells, for their usefulness and longevity.

Asian Paints currently projects that online marketplaces will account for 20 % of its international sales by 2011. In the long run, as these marketplaces add value-added services such as 'mix your own paint', professional painting services, the firm should be poised to maximize margins and gain revenue through participation as well as through its equity stake.

6.4 Why Customers Will Use Online Marketing

The paints industry is not an isolated example. After the dot-com bust, in the year 2003, billions of dollars of online sales transactions, involving thousands of companies, were conducted through over 750 online marketplaces. Industries such as recruitment agencies, agricultural products to secondhand factory equipment are being marketed or sold through these online marketplaces every day. The eBay uses its portal to let customers buy and sell virtually everything. Online marketplaces may be slow out of the gate and still have some growing up to do, but it is likely that many of customers are starting to buy through them. On business-to-business (B2B) sales front, the impact of online marketing will be great. *Purchasing Magazine's* annual reader survey showed that 16 % of buyers participated in third-party online marketplaces in the year 2000. A recent IMT Strategies survey of 260 businesses showed that 80 % intended to either participate in an online marketplace or build one themselves.

As it can be seen, there is shift in consumer preferences. The Internet makes shopping and buying things much simpler and more cost-effective. As an example, at online marketing place, it is easy to match expectations of online buyers and sellers, compare different features of available products, and exchange information. Early consumer marketplaces, such as Priceline.com or eBay, illustrate clearly how online marketplaces do a good job getting many buyers and sellers into one place. The online auction site eBay conducted over $40 billion in transactions in 2005. It has more than one million registered participants who are mostly individual customers who are interested in purchasing and do bargains in secondhand merchandise.

At online market place, technology supports more flexible and efficient pricing. Traditional commodity auction places used to be a physical gathering with lot of shouting to be heard correctly. With introduction of sites such as icicidirect.com, sharekhan.com, etc. a virtual trading place has been created. From earlier times, when it used to be physical display of items for auctions, online market place can be carried out at the comfort of your home. Earlier "real-time" pricing were restricted to "elbow-to-elbow" bidding at stock exchange trading floors and elite auction houses. Today, networks like the Internet allow most businesses to take advantage of these efficient "market-based" pricing tools. Here, you are allowed to set the limits for your products and name your price for buy and sell activities. For example, Pricellne.com popularized the "reverse auction" pricing mechanism (cleverly marketed as "naming your own price") and as a result sold over 3 % of all airline tickets. Twenty-five percent of corporate buyers already use or plan to use auctions and real-time bidding when they negotiate prices with their suppliers, according to the 2000 *Purchasing Magazine* reader survey.

For these buyers, the efficiency of Internet markets can translate into fairer prices, reduced transaction costs, shortened cycle times, and unproved information flow. Industrial buyers are already seeing significant benefits from buying through marketplaces as 15–25 % savings have been reported for different business transactions.

6.5 Types of Online Marketing and E-Commerce

Online marketing has become a marketing strategy for many firms to increase customer base. E-commerce has helped online marketing to become what it is now—a strategic management tool. Success of online marketing, to a large extent, depends on e-commerce success. There are different variants of online marketing practices which have been used in a variety of industries, most notably in commodities (e.g., specialty chemicals, steel, paper) secondary markets (e.g., parts, capital equipment, telephone bandwidth) and functional specialties (e.g., indirect procurement, energy management). These portals have registrations which range from small to large customer base as well as private and public. As the strategy catches on, there can be more variants as well. In countries like India, where purchase power of consumers have become higher and they are more tech savvy now, this strategy should give more returns to the firms. To take care of this ever increasing customer base, e-commerce should support thousands of specialized marketplaces.

However, this poses problems because the firm has to take care of both technology related issues (such as e-commerce) and marketing issues (online marketing). In a way, it distracts sales management from the real issue finding the best ways of using online markets to sell more. These online marketing places are known by different terms such as exchanges, or "integrated captive supply chain". Online marketing can be grouped into five primary flavors of online marketplaces, serving both the business-to-business and business-to-consumer markets. Based on practices adopted in these marketing, there are five different types of services available for online marketing.

1. Buying Services: These online services offer support during the awareness and demand generation phases of the selling process. These services are available in any of these forms such as 'ask me', 'contact us', 'live chat', etc. Here the potential customer can get more information about buying process including availability of products, cost, discount, etc.
2. Auctions: Auctions are online markets that are good at aggregating demand and matching buyers and sellers for a wide range of B2B and B2C products. This service helps in showing details of quantity available, price range, etc. This helps both seller and buyer to take their positions dynamically.
3. B2B Exchanges: Business-to-business (B2B) exchanges are independent trusted intermediaries that support most aspects of business-to-business commerce with vertical market and product-specific expertise. The expert service includes logistics, pricing, up and horizontal sale features.
4. Industry-sponsored Exchanges: In this service, major buyers such as Coal India use online marketing portal to buy their raw materials from all of their suppliers. This helps in tracking delivery status and helps the purchase department to place order as per the economic order quantity (EOQ), lead time for purchasing and approved vendor list. This service helps all the approved vendors to be members of the portal and then they can work with the purchase department of the buyer.

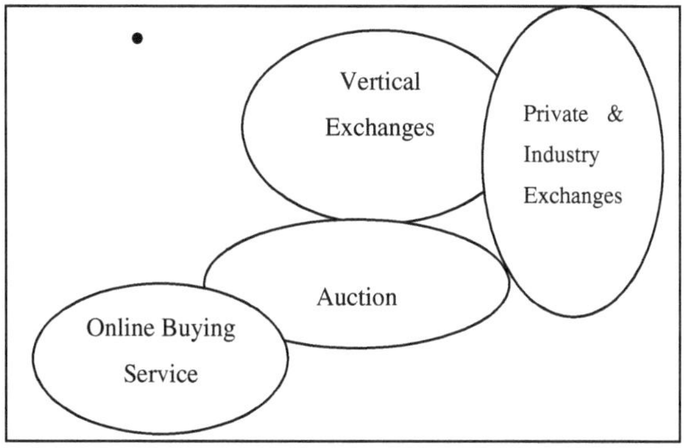

Fig. 6.1 Types of e-commerce versus consumer category

5. Private Exchanges: This is where individual companies like Wal-Mart and Hewlett–Packard, who deal with a large number of suppliers and command a lot of buying power, create their own "private" or "captive" online marketplaces to reduce costs and improve information flow in their supply chains.

6.6 E-Commerce Services

Online marketing through e-commerce has made it easier for marketers and consumers to sell and but things. For e-commerce to be effective, a process can be defined which should be followed by different stakeholders (consumers, marketers, etc.) (Please refer to Fig. 6.1). The process generally starts with a prospective buyer thinking about buying something (product consideration). They then move toward contacting a seller to investigate the specifics of the offering (demand generation). If the product or service meets a particular need, a sales transaction occurs (sales and fulfillment) and a relationship begins (service and support). However, this can be successful only if the needs of different consumers are kept in mind.

The process for effective e-commerce design can be as follows:

- Make Price and features of products to be sold completely transparent. This helps in increasing the ability to easily locate and compare products and prices.
- Tie up with suppliers who can supply depending on the varying needs of the consumers. The suppliers should be able to match the customization requirements of the customers. These customizations would have been ordered through Internet by the customers while ordering their products. This can be possible by convenient and reliable transactions, by matching buyer and seller orders, and accommodating a wide range of pricing alternatives such as different types of auction formats or real-time bidding. These are often called "market-making mechanisms".

- Apart from base products, marketers should provide a wide range of value-added services. These value-added services should include all details which are associated with the selling process such as logistics, inventorying, financing, forecasting, advertising, catalog management, and more.

However, different e-commerce sites differ from each other in designing their selling strategy. They provide different levels of information to the buyer and seller such as price, availability, or range of substitutes. Some will provide more services than others such as quality assurance, financing credit risk, and customer support. They also differ in offering different varieties of pricing formats such as Dutch auctions, reverse auctions, real-time transactions, 'and collaborative negotiations. Individual e-commerce vendors will also differ by products sold and markets served, as well as by size and scope. Moreover, e-commerce firms differ in vertical markets and also differ in offering different levels of control to the buyer, seller, and market facilitator, as well as defining the role of each player in a slightly different manner.

There are different services that a strategist for e-commerce should keep in mind. These services will be able to differentiate between two companies offering products through e-commerce. These are:

6.6.1 Comparative Online Information for E-Commerce Transactions

These services offer comparative price and product information to prospective buyers in their web sites. Through this information, e-commerce strategists can create product awareness and product demand. For example, cardekho.com (http://www.cardelho.com) offers analyst reviews of new and used cars in India. Also the e-commerce site solicits customer opinions through member reviews. Their web sites help introduce buyers to new products and usually include product reviews by experts and analysts, product recommendations, or other selection aids.

Online buying services primarily target to consumers, as well as to small business/home office (i.e., (Business-to-Business and Business-to-Customers (B2B and B2C) markets. Most do not have transaction capabilities but will provide (usually for a fee) a link to a seller's commerce sites or a different site where transactions can be done. They can be a useful way to introduce a product to a geographically dispersed audience.

6.6.2 Internet Auctions

In online auctions, transactions materialize where needs of both buyers and sellers are matched. These needs matching could be between business-to-business and business-to-consumer buyers and sellers. They are popular and employ a variety of needs-matching mechanisms. Examples of these mechanisms are reverse auctioning (where buyer buys from the seller who offers best price), open auctioning (where buyers bid their prices and the highest bidder gets the product), direct selling (where the product features, quantity available and their prices are mentioned) and open buying (where the buyer puts forward his requirements and the prices that he is willing to pay for).

Online auctions are viable for sellers in retail, cosmetic products, apparels, spot purchases of commodities and raw materials; and used capital equipment. The eBay started as a one-on-one, individual auction offering an array of used, one-of-a-kind, collectible products. Today, it is also used by wholesalers offering small lots of different products.

6.6.3 Business-to-Business (B2B) Services

B2B ("business-to-business") e-commerce transactions are independent, trusted intermediaries that support business commerce with product-specific expertise. These e-commerce transactions deal with specific market and product categories. They offer real-time, dynamic pricing, and considerable product information in their realm of specialty. For instance, an e-commerce portal in India helps 1,700 members buy and sell steel products such as hot-rolled, cold-rolled, coated, and plated steel. This e-commerce portal is a neutral organization and is not affiliated with any industry player. It has created a niche as a trusted intermediary, serving all members of the steel supply chain including producers, distributors, fabricators, converters, trading companies, and large end-users. Other early examples of vertical exchanges in United States of America (USA) are Paper-Exchange.com (pulp and paper), e-Chemicals, CheMatch (industrial chemicals), DoveBid.com (capital assets), InterXion (bandwidth), and FreeMarkets (industrial materials). These online marketplaces are used for raw material procurement, spot purchases of commodities and raw materials, capital equipment, secondary markets, distressed inventory, perishables, and some direct materials such as semifinished and engineered products.

There are also e-commerce sites which are engaged in marketing services. These are called Functional e-commerce sites and the e-commerce transactions do not market products, but market services or solutions that automate or support specific business functions or processes (such as human resources benefits management or energy management). EmployEase is one example of a functional exchange that helps companies that manage employee benefits and administrative services to sell their services to human resource executives who are looking for efficient ways to outsource these tasks. A web site that aggregates jobseekers and corporate search firms, such as HotJobs.com or Monster.com would also be an example of a functional exchange that pulls in individuals as well as businesses. Other examples in a variety of service industries include e-Choupal, tradehub (import/export), Imark.com (capital equipment and raw materials purchasing),

Celarix (global logistics), YOUtilities (energy management), MRO.com (MRO purchasing), and Citadon.com (building/real estate project management).

6.6.4 Industry Specific E-Commerce Sites

These online marketplaces are usually launched by industry forums. In industries where buying power is concentrated with a small group of buyers, use these e-commerce sites to view different vendors who can sell the required raw materials. For example, in early 2000, the big three automotive manufacturers-GM, Ford, and Daimler Charysler (and subsequently joined by Renault and Nissan) announced shared sponsorship of Covisint to create a parts buyers paradise for the participating automakers. Cargill and Dupont teamed up to develop Rooster.com to serve agricultural markets.

Small industrial suppliers can join industry exchanges to create a forum and use e-commerce strategy to find a level playing field so that they will not be dictated by big-time buyers. Some of the examples are GlobalnetXchange (uniting retailers such as Sears and Carrefour) and Exostar (aerospace). It should be expected that corporations that set up industry exchanges will keep the exchange close to its forum in order to increase confidence among its members and use combined selling power to directly control industry supply chains.

Private Exchanges

An e-commerce portal designed by one buyer that deals with many suppliers, that already have established strong, established business relationships. Many large companies like Maruti-Suzuki, ICI Paints, Hewlett–Packard, and Wal-Mart cannot wait for "public" online marketplaces to grow up. They have set about building private e-commerce exchanges that seek to achieve the benefits of online marketplaces within their own supplier base. According to an annual Purchasing Magazine reader survey in 2000, most purchasing managers showed a preference for automating existing supplier relationships through private e-commerce sites than participating in third-party managed e-commerce transactions. For example, ICI paints buys so much chemicals for its paints that it has set up an e-commerce site that buys chemicals cheaply in bulk quantities and supplies them sub-assembly suppliers. These e-commerce exchanges help to benefit all stakeholders through better logistics management. Companies like Pantaloon, Tesco are so large they can gain large benefits just from getting thousands of their own suppliers to use the private e-commerce web site which will reduce purchasing costs and inventories.

6.7 E-Commerce and Customer Satisfaction

Customers get more information through e-commerce sites and shifts information power away from the seller to the buyer. The information will provide greater control over their suppliers and reduce operational costs. For example, in industries where buying power is concentrated but suppliers are numerous (as in the automotive industry, where there are handful of major producers who are served by thousands of parts suppliers), buyer-managed e-commerce sites (an example of this in the USA was Covisint, which was formed as a partnership of Ford, GM, Renault, and Daimler-Chrysler) will become a battleground where all sellers, big and small, compete for market share. In 2010, India witnessed a similar e-commerce site known as futurebazar.com, where electronic sellers such as Nokia, LG, Motorola, and Spice mobile fought for customer attention). In the year 2000, several e-commerce sites were announced in different domains viz. automotive, aerospace, travel, consumer packaged goods, retail, agriculture, energy. The total business transactions in the year 2000–2001 were more than $700 billion. There were several repeat businesses from returning customers, which indicated that they were satisfied with transparency provided in sharing information through these web sites.

Alternately, where both buyers and sellers are fragmented (such as in the small business market or a variety of aftermarkets), independent intermediaries ("middlemen") may step into create and manage exchanges that are theoretically neutral trading ground. These exchanges are often called "butterfly," or "vortex" markets. Since, independent trading sites make their income from transaction fees, their focus is also to encourage repeat purchase from returning customers, these e-commerce strategists provide enough information power to customers.

In industries, where a few sellers have a high degree of control over market supply (such as specialty chemicals, personal computers, insurance and airline travel), sellers can take the advantage by banding together to build "seller-biased" or "supplier-managed" exchanges. Makemytrip.com and Yatra.com are examples where e-commerce transactions are controlled by supply of limited air tickets. These sites provide different promotional offers which induce customers to buy air tickets as well as rent hotel rooms rather than purchasing these services from company owned web sites. As these e-commerce sites have total control on the pricing of these services, they cleverly offer packaged services to their loyal customers at a great discount than that offered by individual companies. Similarly, Orbitz, a consortium of five airlines (Delta, United, Northwest, Continental, and American Airlines) account for an estimated 85 % of all US air travel. The Orbitz e-commerce web site sells airline ticket reservations online, and competes successfully against the individual airline web site.

In general, online marketplaces increase the number of competitors, expose price differences, and often allow buyers to pool their buying power against sellers. In both business and consumer arenas, price information on online exchanges is routinely available and can be updated in minutes. Competing prices become transparent.

6.8 Risk Associated with E-Commerce Introduction

E-commerce strategists need to decide whether to have their private e-commerce portal or participate in the existing e-commerce portals which buy services for a group of participating companies. Small businesses and growth-oriented companies should not miss a potential opportunity to redefine their industry or expand into new regional and global markets. Hence, a faster decision on this will help executing the growth plans faster.

It has been found that very small selling organizations were eager to design their e-commerce web sites. These organizations anticipated getting new customers, increased visibility, and access to buyers through e-commerce. These small players felt they had nothing to lose in competing with rivals in a new arena. On the other hand, larger companies were more reluctant to participate through e-commerce route. The larger firms feared price exposure, erosion of margin, and cutthroat competition from faster-moving, upstart rivals. These bog firms had legacy systems and traditional distribution systems. As a result, these large organizations were worried about conflicts between new e-commerce and existing channels, changing existing selling processes. Some of the old employees were also worried about loss of power because of new e-commerce channel being introduced and losing control over product margins.

Other risks associated with e-commerce introduction were exclusion from existing markets, loss of margins due to product and price transparency, greater potential for customer dissatisfaction (as they started demanding more information on price, quality and become more knowledgeable). There are also risks associated with channel conflicts as online marketplaces overlap with and edge out traditional channels and distributors. This will upset already settled business partners and will bring in unpredictability in business model. There may be drop in market capitalization of the firm as the weary investors may not risk investment till business model becomes stable.

6.9 Considerations for Private E-Commerce

There are several advantages of private e-commerce such as control, increase in brand equity of the firm; the firm can also decide the degree to which it can share information related to price, products, product features without losing its competitiveness. However, participating in a public e-commerce portal will reduce maintenance cost; make the firm to increase operation effectiveness by adhering to standards that have already been set by the public e-commerce portal. But before taking a decision on whether to have private or participate in public e-commerce portal, it would be prudent to go through the following considerations.

6.9.1 Understand E-Commerce Readiness for Its Target Customers

E-commerce strategists and sellers understand that online marketplaces are being driven chiefly by buyers. Therefore, if an e-commerce can provide more (information) power to buyers by forcing its suppliers to provide more online information related to features and price of products, then it would attract more and more buyers (read customers). The more buying power a company can exert by forcing its suppliers to compete online, the more transparent it can be. For example, one of the leading automobile manufacturers bought more than 5 crores of raw materials from 12 different auctions. Thus, before deciding how to participate, selling organizations must first understand the changing customer-buying behavior. The trick for e-commerce strategists is to accurately anticipate and monitor how and how quickly their buyers are adopting online marketplaces. This is the only way to avoid being left out, and the best way to gain first mover advantage in certain online marketplaces.

6.9.2 Identify E-Commerce Readiness of Potential Market

There are many domains where traditional route of selling is required. For example, automobiles, consumer goods such as refrigerators, washing machines, etc. need to be touched, felt and if possible tried before making a purchase. In such domains, it is necessary to judge the degree of readiness of the domain. Similarly, real estate agents need to make their products have a concrete shape so that prospective customers can visualize and then buy the product. It is also necessary to make the sales force ready with the goals of expanding market coverage and unearthing new opportunities. Every organization wants to increase its customer base and make more sales more efficiently. Leaders will be recognized by their ability to pick the right e-commerce strategies for their organizations.

6.9.3 Margins Versus Volume

E-commerce strategists will have to decide if they are willing to trade lower profit margins for the greater customer access offered through online marketplaces. Many suppliers, who sell in reverse auction, prefer increasing customer base to lower product margins. By reducing retail price through e-commerce, they can easily attract more customers to their web site. For example, products sold through futurebazar.com are priced lesser than that of retail outlets. This strategy results in reduced customer acquisition cost and increased loyalty resulting in repeat business.

6.9.4 Ease of Doing Business Versus Efficiency

As we see an increase in Internet penetration in India, we find that all products do not require retail sale. For example, stationery items such as paper clips and most of the fast moving goods are too inexpensive and commoditized to justify the effort. The time and effort required for buyers to find the savings on the price tags by visiting stores was high, and hence it is more sensible to buy these products through e-commerce sites. However, some items in a product line may not be eligible for e-commerce transactions because they are part of "preconfigured" purchases engineered subassemblies for aircraft and automotive products. These types of products will not attract large buyer groups. In these cases, ease of doing business the old way will tend to outweigh pure price competitiveness. Similar arguments can be put forward for industrial product marketing such as marketing of cooling towers, sale of furnaces, etc. which require one to one marketing and cannot be carried out through e-commerce web site.

6.9.5 Market Share Versus Market Control

An e-commerce web site provides the opportunity to cover more untapped market, but it may also result in less corporate control over the sales process. In auctions where prices are "dynamic," the seller will have less control over price changes. Sellers also have little control over product information (for example, in product reviews that are published online). The typical control by marketers involve selling basket of goods with price mix and this approach allow the marketers (in fast moving consumer goods) to have complete control over day-to-day business decisions. However, in e-commerce, business logic will be applicable to all and sundry and hence the traditional control over the market is diluted.

6.9.6 Risk of Arbitrage

There are chances that there could be possibilities of e-commerce web sites will create information asymmetry that will allow middlemen to take advantage of price differences across global markets. For example, a global marketplace may expose the fact that certain electronic products such as laptops, movie cameras sells for 50 % less than in India. This will create middlemen, who would bring these products and sell them in India. *Verma* market in Chennai is an example where such cost arbitrage has been used by middlemen for their advantage.

Marketplaces involve more than just conducting transactions on the Internet. Relationships, information, and power come into play. In order for e-commerce to happen, buyers and sellers need to know things like "Who is selling?" "Which products are the best?" "How limited is supply?" and "How much are buyers willing to spend?" The good marketplace host should be recognized broadly for its expertise and ability to provide this "value-added information." Organizations that already publish reports or provide inspection, licensing, or quality certification services may be ahead of the game here.

6.9.7 Liquidity

The volume of sales transactions that happen in the market is vital for survival. Organizations that already gather and attract large numbers of buyers or sellers will find it easier to build the high volume of transactions required for a successful liquidity condition. Organizations that already do a lot of buying from smaller companies may find sufficient players to justify building their own "private" online marketplace for goods and services. Similarly, organizations that dominate their markets or hold unique market positions also have an edge. Organizations that currently provide financing or help their buyers or suppliers manage credit may have the "power" to move these functions to e-commerce marketing as well.

6.9.8 Redefine Value Boundaries

Profit margins erode and pricing becomes "transparent" when online markets allow customers to easily make apples-to-apples comparisons between products by supplying ratings, reviews, or other kinds of product comparison information. Marketers can transcend competition on price by cleverly bundling solutions, increasing minimum order sizes, or establishing pricing tiers to make things "apples to oranges" again. Marketers can develop proprietary or complex pricing schemes that discourage comparison shopping. Building customer-specific products, redrawing market segments, or negotiating exclusive volume purchase agreements (VPAs) can all be used to justify different prices. For instance, the airline industry has created pricing schedules that "discriminate" against business travelers by scaling prices against specific rates, short cycle times, and length of stay. Pricing practices can usually be justified by geography (delivery issues), unit volume (frequent-buyer or volume-buyer discounts), or acknowledged supply-and-demand peaks (seasonal or weekday/weekend, etc.).

E-commerce marketers should add on value-added service to every product they offer through an online marketplace. Online customers routinely pay higher prices for "free" delivery, liberal returns, product guarantees, service warranties, online user support, and other perceived value-adds. Retail and distributors can justify service premiums on commodity products since most online marketplaces today offer few services beyond matching buyers with sellers and providing some product and price information. For example, because few online marketplaces today offer customer support or on-site service, there is a potential advantage for distributors in bundling service into pricing and creating a local service company that customers can drive to.

6.9.9 Speed of Delivery

E-commerce can help in differentiating the products by offering speedier delivery. A component delivered in 8 h is worth more to some buyers than the same component delivered 8 days from now. In both consumer and business markets, faster fulfillment has proven to be a plus factor in pricing. Faster pricing can provide an edge. Marketers who become good at developing costs in "real time" can react more quickly to changes in demand and high-speed bidding. For instance, superior pricing models and capabilities will allow sellers to quickly decide where to participate (or rationally decide not to) and better understand and optimize margins in fast-paced bidding.

6.9.10 Induce Purchase

E-commerce can induce first time purchasers by choosing a product that is likely to appeal to first-time customers. The e-commerce strategists can use a loss leader (e.g., extremely low-priced) product as a way of acquiring customers. Depending on customer lifetime value, a lower cost of customer acquisition may offset low or even negative product margins.

6.9.11 Positioning

E-commerce web site strategists should gain favorable positioning in an online marketplace. This is always a viable strategy when dealing with online buying services such as product review sites. Paying for prime position or public relations exposure is one option, but do not rule out gaming—the software. For instance, American Airlines garnered 35 % of transactions on its captive Saber exchange, where, coincidentally, all airlines were listed alphabetically. To become an effective part of the selling equation, online marketplaces need to be viewed as a potentially powerful new selling channel that augments existing sales resources such as direct field sales, third-party distributors, and Internet e-commerce. To be complementary, not a source of conflict, online marketplaces must be managed in concert with these other methods of selling.

6.10 Case: eBay in Action

The eBay is a completely new phenomenon, where the customer can buy and sell products through bidding. The customers are spread all over the world. Due to its popularity, it has established web sites in different countries and has been successful. In September 1995, the eBay was founded in San Jose, California. Millions of collectibles, appliances, computers, household items, furniture, equipment and even vehicles are sold and bought through the eBay. Anything can be sold as long as it is not illegal or does not violate the eBay Prohibited and Restricted Items policy. Services and intangibles can be sold, too. Many organizations such as IBM use the eBay to sell their products on auction which is used for setting the price.

The eBay used to receive calls from its customers from all over the places. The volume of incoming calls was understandably high and eBay had to employ a large staff to handle these calls. Still there were complaints from customers that the service quality was not up to their expectations. In fact, eBay struggled to keep up with its own success and match its online customer growth with online customer service excellence. The number of registered customers was around 3.8 million in its first 2.5 years of operations. The eBay had to change its strategic orientation for handling such a large number of calls.

As the popularity and business grew, eBay started receiving e-mails to the tune of 2,000 per week, which slowly crosses 75,000 e-mails per week. These e-mails and other forms of messages had requests for submission for bids, reply from buyers and sellers. To handle these calls, eBay introduced automatic e-mail response system. In this system, the queries were categorized and at the first level, depending on the queries, automated responses were sent which helped the customers to troubleshoot. If there was a need for going to the next level of interaction, then the customer care executives stepped in. This ensured there was a prompt response to the queries, which assured the customers that his queries are being attended to. Internally, eBay defined a work flow system, by which, these queries were assigned to different executives. Service Level Agreements (SLA) were defined for different category of query; these SLAs ensured that within the define time period, the executives have to find solutions to the queries. Till the customer was satisfied, the allocations were kept open. So not only there was automation in the mail response system, query allocation was also automated through work flow mechanism. Automation of allocation of queries through work flow ensured that all the queries were dealt with. This resulted in customer satisfaction and increase in registered customer and subsequently number of business transactions also increased.

The eBay also created an automated knowledge management system for query handling. Kana Communication (now acquired by Broad base) helped eBay build a "knowledge base" of seals and support content that describes the rules and requirements for using the auction site services. The combination of knowledge management system, automated work flow mechanism and mail response system increased productivity by more than 50 %. This was achieved by routing queries to appropriate specialists and routine queries were dealt by using ready made contents in the knowledge management system.

The next level automation eBay was done in collaboration with customers. The eBay provided what was known as self service by providing online frequently asked questions (FAQs). This FAQ was constantly modified with inputs from customers. It also introduced rating system for the business transactions. The customers rated buyers, sellers, and the quality of the products based on their personal experience. This provided an automated credit rating system for the sellers and buyers. Since there was no direct contact for transactions in eBay, this helped to provide confidence to its users. This also reduced chances of unsatisfied customers. Other automated systems include online help, account management, item engine search, forums and chats in different topics.

The case gives an example as to how to use automation in customer care and convert traditional business model of auctioning over electronic channel.

Review Questions

1. The eBay cannot survive without e-commerce, discuss.
2. How can customer care department benefit from e-commerce?
3. What are the benefits to different stakeholders through e-commerce web sites?

6.11 E-Seva, Hyderabad, Andhra Pradesh

Background

The project was started as a pilot in the twin cities of Hyderabad and Secunderabad, and was thus called TWINS (Twin Cities Integrated Network Systems). It was started at a cost of Rs 10 million, fully funded by the Government of Andhra Pradesh. The project provided services such as registration of birth and death certificates, registration of vehicles and learners' driving licenses. After a successful pilot, 10 centers were started on 25 August 2001 and then the project was renamed as e-Seva (Electronic Service in Hindi). On 10 October 2001, a portal—http://www.esevaonline.com—was launched. Currently, there are 33 centers operating in the twin cities.

Objectives and Goals

- To provide real-time online transactions.
- To improve government-customer interface at all levels.

- To improve service quality and innovation.
- To improve operational efficiency.
- To provide cost-effective services.

Planning

It was planned on the lines of Singapore Online (http://www.singaporeonline.com), a well-known web portal that provides information about so many items such as job vacancies and business opportunities.

Services Provided

Presently, the e-Seva centers provide around 46 services such as payment of water and sewerage bills, property taxes, commercial taxes, income taxes, phone bills, registration of vehicles, issue of learner driving licenses, transfer of ownership of vehicles, registration of new trade licenses, renewal of trade licenses, registration of birth and death, birth and death certificates, filing of passport applications, collection of examination fees, registration of documents and stamps (non-judicial), sale of bus tickets, sale of non-judicial stamps, collection of small savings, etc. The services are provided within 60–120 s. The centers operate on working days from 8 am to 8 pm and on public holidays from 9 am to 3 pm. Citizens are not charged for any utility payments. Services like the payment of electricity/water/telephone bills and transport/property taxes are available on a 24 $\times$ 7 basis on the Web portal.

Target Group and Intended Beneficiaries

Citizens of the twin cities of Hyderabad and Secunderabad are the target group and intended beneficiaries.

Institutional Arrangements

The Directorate of e-Seva is headed by a director and has two deputy directors, one assistant director (technical), one assistant director (promotion), three senior assistants, one grievance officer and two helpers. Almost all the hardware and software services have been outsourced. A PPP was envisaged at the outset, in 2001. Global tenders were called for entrepreneurs to take up e-Seva centers. CMS

Computers Ltd got the tender for managing the centers. Software was designed at a cost of Rs 2.5 million by another company called RAM Informatics. The Government provided the premises and the managerial staff. The managing company provided the hardware, networking solutions, operators (with salary paid by the Government), engineering staff, help-desk staff and security staff at all the centers. The Government provided updated databases concerning the services while the company paid all telecom/leased line bills and electricity dues. A Memorandum of Understanding (MoU) was signed between the Government and the company for 5 years. On each transaction, Rs 5 as a user charge is collected from the concerned department out of which 75–80 % is paid back to the private partners. Earlier, four new-generation banks—Global Trust Bank, ICICI, HDFC and UTI—were selected to facilitate net-transactions of the payments. Later, two more banks, IDBI and Centurian Bank, also joined. A 4 % surcharged was charged on every credit card transaction, which has been reduced to 1.5 %.

Technologies

The network architecture is designed as an Intranet on a Wide Area Network (WAN). The network is designed in three tiers. The first tier for the client-end is located at the e-Seva centers. The front end is Java-based. All the centers are on 64 kbps dedicated leased lines, with ISDN backup. The second tier has two Sun E250 model and two Compaq ML530 model data servers. The second tier also consists of Application Servers (using Oracle GiAS and running on Sun Solaris 8 Operating System), Database Servers (using Oracle 8i R3 and running on MS Windows 2000 Operating System), Network Monitoring Servers (using Cisco Works and WhatsupGold on MS Windows 2000 Operating Systems), Management Servers (using MS putin), Firewall (using Cheuqn) and Web Servers (using Apache). All the machines used in this tier are Intel machines, along with Cisco switches and routers. The third tier is made of Departmental servers with an Oracle database as the backend in the concerned departments (Electricity, Municipality, Passport Office, Transport Department, Registration, Commercial Tax, etc.). These servers keep consolidated databases. They are linked with 64 Kbps DB link (except the Electricity Department server which has a 2 Mbps pipeline). The network architecture provides dedicated leased lines, with ISDN backup.

Primary Access Points

Primary access points for e-Seva services are the e-Seva centers, which are established on spacious premises. Each center has a waiting foyer, help desk, token counter and 8–15 operator counters. Six of the e-Seva centers have ATMs (two each of State Bank of Hyderabad, State Bank of India and Andhra Bank). Citizens can excess the portal from their households as well to avail of the services online.

Capacity Building

All the operators are given four-day operational training on the operator terminal. Some efforts have been made in providing IT training in the concerned departments. The Government and its numerous departments have paid little attention toward creating an e-workforce. There is an over-dependence on private technological partners, CMS Computers Ltd and RAM Informatics Ltd, for all technological solutions. The dependence on RAM Informatics Ltd and Jyothy Computers to provide all e-worker needs to be rectified by building the capacity and skills of redundant government employees. This becomes important in the context of a proposed expansion of 237 new e-Seva centers and the fact that the Government has to pay monthly salaries to all the operators engaged in these 237 centers.

Constraints and Implementation Challenges

The initial resistance came from vested interest groups, especially government officials and middlemen. The central success factors are political will, bureaucratic support, e-support of departments and infrastructure, and public demand. The revenue database of numerous government departments has been exposed (without impregnable safety measures) by multiple agencies (e-Seva operators, banks, citizens from the Web, technological partners). The project has not yet shown its technological and financial sustenance in poor and rural settings.

Project Outcomes

In the year up to the time of the study, the number of transactions for the year doubled and the payments increased six times. Between 18 July 2002 and 17 July 2003 (in one year), 8.27 million transactions took place in the e-Seva centers and Rs 32.796 billion were collected as payment from these transactions.

Key Lessons Learned

The e-Seva is India's pioneering e-governance project. It has paved the way for others to follow. It has also embarked on a sustainable PPP. This project has a very sound business model. The project has provided integrated multi-departmental government services at one stop. The software, hardware, and networking technology has been functioning satisfactorily well since the inception of the project with almost no instance of breakdown (uptime percentage is 99.6 %). It has shown the importance of laying down a reliable telecommunication infrastructure for the success of e-governance efforts.

Sustainability

This project is financially sustainable. The government, private entrepreneur and users, are all winners in this project. The huge acceptance by the public of e-Seva counters also confirms its future sustainability. The organizational reengineering and management practices adopted are also favorable for its sustainable existence.

Replication and Scaling Up

It is very unfortunate that the country's most successful e-governance project has not been seriously replicated in any other parts of India. The Government has decided to add 13 new e-Seva centers in the twin cities. This project is also going to be scaled-up with the installation of 237 new e-Seva centers (including all 117 municipalities) in the rest of the 23 districts in the state of Andhra Pradesh. These new centers fall in six zones (four zones are taken up by CMS Technologies, one zone by United Telecom Limited, and one by CCS Technologies). Each district will be a separate Intranet to start with, which will eventually be integrated into the Internet. Six new e-Seva centers have already been started in Rajmundri (Western Godavari district) on 30 July 2003. New services like railway reservations, sale of movie tickets, payment for traffic related offenses, payment of degree examination fees of the Open University, collection of bill payments of private landline and cellular companies, issue of encumbrance certificate, market value assistance, general insurance, reservation of tourism tickets for accommodation, call centers, Indian Airlines ticket reservation, life insurance premium payment, issue of caste certificates, sale of Indira Vikas Patra, renewal of drug licenses, issue of bus passes, etc., are also planned to be added. All the ATMs of the State Bank of Hyderabad, State Bank of India and Andhra Bank will be converted to e-Seva centers.

Recommendations

The project is highly recommended for replication and upscaling into the urban and semi-urban areas of India. Presently, the project is using the Java platform, which requires creation of an interface to integrate databases that are in diverse formats. It is recommended that the data structure be kept uniform for all government departments. The Government should coordinate billing procedures for all the relevant departments, so that citizens receive bills of different utilities at the same time, and the citizen has to travel only once a month to e-Seva centers for clearing them. This would increase citizen satisfaction and would take care of the customer load on the network. The bandwidth of the communication lines between ICSCs and the Data Centre at Khairatbad, as well as between the Data Centre and Departmental Servers of utility providers may be increased (to say, 128 Kbps), based on a network audit, which should also show the density of traffic flowing in each segment.

All departmental servers should be shifted to the Khairatabad center, which should be developed as a full-fledged data center with a 'server-farm' maintained on 24×7 basis, with due disaster-recovery and business continuity provisions. e-Seva centers started in ATMs need to be revitalized and the procedures simplified, as only 12 transactions have taken place in the 2 years prior to the study, though there are six ATMs providing the services. The usage of e-Seva centers in poor areas is very low (e.g., the Bahadur Pura center has less than 300 transactions per month against an average of 25,000 in any other center). Special efforts should be made to popularize the services among the poor and also to include services more relevant to the lower income groups. To reduce the huge expenses incurred in expanding the project, it is recommended that a change to Linux open-ended software be made. Basic amenities like toilets should be set up in all the centers, as half of them still lack toilets.

The expansion of 229 new e-Seva centers in 21 districts is planned to start on a WAN. Instead, it would be more cost-effective for the Government and more convenient for the citizens if the expansion is carried on the Internet. It is also important to take steps toward discouraging cash transactions and encourage the plastic-money culture, especially with a view to attracting increasingly more number of customers. A co-branded e-Seva Debit Card (on lines of Petro Card) could be developed, in association with major tech-savvy banks. With such a Card, it would also be possible to introduce innovative schemes for inducing citizens to pay their bills promptly, like the accumulation of 'usage points', 'loyalty points', 'timely-payment points' which could perhaps be redeemed as a certain percentage discount on the bills. There has been no effort toward the introduction of Smart Cards in the project, which could safeguard the transactions against frauds. The expansion of the services in the project is more focussed on services involving payments and revenue collections. Social-centric services are taking a backseat, but should be further considered.

Human Interest Stories

Catch-22

S. Raghawan, 28 years of age, is an operator at Vanasthalipuram e-Seva center and is facing a. After completing a Masters in Geology, he started working as a Medical Representative and earning Rs 9,000 per month. He had an interest in computers and had earlier done a six-month course in Java and Oracle. When the e-center was started in his locality in August 2002, he took a four-day training course and joined as an operator. But now he is only earning Rs 2,500 per month. He wants to quit the job due to the reduction in his earning. But his love for computers and the smile his work brings to his people is keeping him in the job.

A Short Walk from the Hospital

Sudhakar Reddy, 55 years old, was blessed with a son recently. He was in the nursing home with his wife and his first child. He was very happy and was planning a celebration for his relatives when he got back home. His wife insisted that he should take a walk to the e-Seva center in the locality (LB Nagar) and make his electricity bill payment. He showed some hesitation, as he was not willing to leave his wife in that condition. He walked down to the center and deposited Rs 228, in 45 s flat and was able to rush back to the hospital.

All Cash, No Files

S. Yadagiri, a 51-year-old accountant from the Vanasthalipuram e-Seva center, takes his responsibility of handing over the cash collected daily to the agent of CMS Securities, Phani Kumar, very seriously. He makes bundles of currency notes and cheques separately. On this particular day, Rs 1.88 million was collected in cash and Rs 0.24 million in cheques. He had only one small printout in front of him, from which he cross-checked collections from each of the seven counters. After cross-checking, he handed over all the cash and cheques to the agent, took the receipt of the printout and filed it in his monthly folder. That is it. His work was done. There was absolutely no file on his table or in his cabinet. He is happy that he has got rid of innumerable files, which used to be dumped on to him when he was working as a junior accountant in the Irrigation Department earlier. He is handling cash, and no files in the e-Seva center.

Review Questions

1. The e-Seva is a case of using e-commerce technology in Government services. Do you agree? Please support your answer with examples.
2. The e-Seva has increased productivity, transparency in different Government services. Please support the statement with examples.
3. What are the quantitative and qualitative benefits of e-Seva?
4. Can e-Seva be emulated in other states in the country?

6.12 E-Choupal, Ujjain, Madhya Pradesh

Background

ITC Limited is one of India's leading diversified conglomerates. Traditionally a tobacco and cigarette producer, it has grown into a conglomerate dealing in hotels, packaging, agribusiness, information technology, and fast moving consumer goods (FMCGs). ITC initiated its e-Choupal project in 2000 to streamline its dealings with Indian farmers. This is a project on a massive scale that ultimately aims to cover every sixth Indian village. Each choupal covers around six villages and 36,000 villages have been covered to date in Madhya Pradesh, Uttar Pradesh, Maharashtra, Rajasthan, Karnataka, and Andhra Pradesh.

Objectives and Goals

e-Choupal aims to provide Indian farmers ready access to crop-specific real-time information and customized knowledge in their native language. By doing so, ITC wants to improves the farmers' decision-making ability, thereby helping them to better align their farm output to the projected demand in Indian and international markets.

Planning

E-Choupal, the Web-based initiative of ITC's International Business Division, offers the farmers of India all the information, products, and services they need to enhance farm productivity, improve farm-gate price realization, and cut transaction costs. Farmers can access the latest local and global information on weather, scientific farming practices and market prices at the village itself through the Web portal—all in Hindi. The e-Choupal also facilitates the supply of high quality farm inputs as well as the purchase of soybeans at the farmers' doorstep. ITC plans to operate such kiosks so that they can create an electronic stock exchange for the marketing of agricultural commodities through the use of ICTs.

Services Provided

E-Choupals help farmers realize larger harvests by providing them with the latest weather reports and best farming practices. The information is retrieved from the Internet or caches on hard disks, and is made available in the relevant local languages. Static content is installed on hard disk while setting up the Choupals or is made available on CDs. The e-Choupals also offer other critical services such as soil- and water-testing, which can further help the farmers to enhance their yields. Apart from providing information on soya, the kiosks also have information about FMCGs and help the villagers buy various products such as motorbikes, bicycles, tractors, etc. Importantly, insurance is one of the common products that are being sold across the network. e-Choupals have a facility for providing life insurance policies, goods insurance and other policies to the villagers. This service has added an extra benefit to the villagers in terms of minimizing their cost on travel. The e-Choupal portals are based on Indian languages: Hindi, Marathi, Kannada, and Telugu. Through the e-Choupal portals, farmers can access the latest local and global information on weather, scientific farming practices, and market prices at the village level. The e-Choupals also facilitate the supply of high quality farm inputs as well as purchases of produce at the farmers' doorstep.

Target Group and Intended Beneficiaries

The e-Choupal initiative strives to transform the Indian farmer into a knowledge-seeking producer. The farmer will have access to information, which will help them make the right choice about farm inputs and agricultural commodities. The major focus of e-Choupal is on small and marginalized farmers.

Institutional Arrangements

The management of the e-Choupal network is looked after by the International Business Division of ITC Limited. Sanchalaks, the trusted local farmers who run the individual Choupals, are not official employees of ITC but serve as extended parts of the ITC organization, and simultaneously as commodity brokers and consumer goods salesmen.

ITC leverages the knowledge of the Sanyojaks who are grain merchants or wholesale dealers co-opted into the project. They are familiar with the land and have long-standing relationships with the villagers. They help manage the logistics of the e-Choupal network. Sanyojaks assist ITC teams in setting up new e-Choupals by conducting village surveys and helping identify the best Sanchalaks. They also help facilitate transactions by maintaining records, collecting price data from local mandis, and managing the physical flow of goods. In this manner, they still serve to compensate for infrastructure gaps along the supply chain, but no longer obstruct the flow of information and market signals. The Sanyojaks are paid commissions based on the services they render, and typically make more money as part of the e-Choupal network than they did independently.

Technologies

Typically, the Choupals use Pentium computers along with a dot matrix printer and a UPS (500VA). ITC had initially upgraded telephone exchanges by using RNS (RAX Network Synchronization) kits, but eventually in most of the e-Choupals, wireless VSAT links have been installed by bypassing the exchanges. Even with these improvements, the bandwidth often remains limited. Hence, e-Choupals have started compensating by caching static content locally. ITC also uses a specially designed template for managing data combined with new imaging techniques in order to speed up downloads and to optimize bandwidth use. To overcome the problem of sporadic electricity, several kiosk computers use backup batteries recharged with solar panels.

Primary Access Points

Primary access points for the farmers are the e-Choupals each located between six villages (42 such kiosks in Ujjain district). The kiosk has a web site http://www.echoupal.com which contains all the information regarding agricultural products.

Capacity Building

ITC has been successful in building the capacity of the farmers by increasing their knowledge in cultivating various agricultural crops and related information. Kiosks also provide information on land and soil, weather forecast, news, e-mails, etc. The Sanyojaks are given basic training on using the computer, the Internet and the printer by the engineer deputed for each district.

S/H 1: Constraints and Implementation Challenges

The biggest challenge for the project has been to familiarize the first-time users in remote areas of rural India with computers and the Internet. When the e-Choupal concept was first proposed, there was some initial hesitation on the part of the farmers. Imparting training to the Sanchalaks on the use of the computer has also posed some problems and hence it takes a minimum of 2 months for them to learn how to use the computers. The other major challenge for this project is to recruit a suitable person from each village who has leadership qualities and minimum education.

The project also has to surmount regulatory barriers. The Agricultural Produce Marketing Committee (APMC) Act prohibits the purchase of specified commodities (including several that ITC deals in) from any source other than at government-designated mandis. ITC has overcome this challenge by convincing the political and bureaucratic leadership of various state governments that the ‘spirit’ of the Act (to benefit the farmers) is better served through e-Choupals. As a result, some states have amended the Act, while others have allowed specific exemptions for such new business models.

Project Outcomes

- Enhanced relationship with the farming community across 36,000 villages so far.
- Reduced transaction cost for its agri-commodity purchases.
- Information on inventory retained by the farmers that can improve the quality of trading decisions.
- Provided means to expand the reach to the rural markets through the cross-selling of the company’s products and services.
- Capacity building of the farmers.
- Increase of knowledge due to the use of computers, the Internet.

Key Lessons Learned

E-Choupals deliver relevant technology in the hands of the farmers, which can improve the economic condition of the entire village. The e-Choupal is one of the very few ICT projects in India that has effectively utilized e-commerce transactions for poverty alleviation. One of the key lessons is that ICT can reduce the number of middlemen involved between agriculture commodity producers and final consumers. Another key factor is that very simple technology solutions are available to create networks in rural areas, which can function as virtual agricultural commodity marketplaces.

Sustainability

The project is financially sound and sustainable as the cost incurred on the establishment of the kiosk was recovered by the company in less than 2 years from profit generated by avoiding numerous tiers in agricultural commodity transitions. The recurring costs are born by the kiosk operators who receive commission on each transaction. The project is vibrant and sustainable, and has a bright future.

Replication and Scaling Up

There is ample scope to scale up this project due to the wide range of services provided at the doorsteps of the villagers. This project has been successfully replicated in states like Uttar Pradesh, Rajasthan, Karnataka, Maharashtra and Andhra Pradesh.

Recommendations

It is recommended that e-Choupals be converted into one-stop shops wherein the villagers can also get other relevant and essential services from the kiosk. It is recommended new e-governance, e-education, and e-health services be added on along with entertainment and computer education at these kiosks. It is also recommended that the commission agent recognized by ITC for each region be eliminated and replaced by a cooperative society or a cooperative bank. Other recommendations include linking up to various agricultural prices prevalent in major marketplaces in India so that the farmers have access to all the markets; and that GoI should facilitate similar kiosks wherein farmers can make transactions and these kiosks become small electronic exchanges with each other. Information regarding the kiosks among the villagers is not widespread. There is a need to conduct proper Gram Sabhas before installing e-Choupals in the villages. Importantly, more emphasis should be placed on the involvement of women due to their active participation in the fields. Better planned course curricula for learning computers should be implemented for the Sanyojaks to further training to the villagers.

Human Interest Stories

International Market Intelligence can Lead to Profits

Bhavarlal, a soybean grower in the Devgadh village of Ujjain district, earned a good profit due to the e-Choupal. He learned from the Internet that Indonesia had produced a lot of palm oil that year and hence would be selling it in the Indian markets. Knowing this, he assumed that the rates in the local mandis would fall and therefore he sold his soybeans in good time to make his profit. This shows that timely information can help farmers, not only in improving their yields but also in getting better prices.

Review Questions

1. Is e-Choupal initiative a sustainable one? What are the issues and challenges faced by e-Choupal?
2. What are the objectives of e-Choupal? Have these objectives been achieved?
3. Who are major stakeholders in e-Choupal?
4. What are the benefits accrued by the farmers?

6.13 Summary

Sales and marketing executives will have to change their approaches to pricing, channel management, and marketing in order to sell through online marketplaces like Internet auctions and business-to-business exchanges. To make e-commerce strategy a successful one, the strategists should consider readiness of the product as well as the market. The strategists also design value-added services as well provide information power to buyers so that the buyers will come back to the e-commerce site again and again. Finally, e-commerce strategy will not be the ideal for all domains such as industrial products and thus, cannot be force fitted for every category of products.

6.14 Review Questions

1. Why should customers use e-commerce? What are the benefits?
2. What are different e-commerce services?
3. What are different types of e-commerce?
4. What are considerations for designing e-commerce sites?

Chapter 7
E-Commerce Strategy

7.1 Learning Objectives

At the end of the chapter, the students would learn.

- Strategic positioning of e-commerce
- Competitive advantage from e-commercc

7.2 Introduction

The Internet has changed our lives and it has changed the way we used to interact with friends and carry out our business operations. The Internet has also changed marketing, advertisement, and promotional activities. Similarly, the impact of the Internet on brand equity is quite high. As more and more customers are surfing the net, strategists have used the Internet for creating competitive advantage. It has changed the competitive playing field by helping to establish brands in online channels. New companies that have launched e-commerce sites competed to achieve brand awareness forcing established companies to build brand awareness in online markets through the e-commerce route. The strategies have helped them in dragging their existing brand assets online and repositioning these assets to build a new brand through competitive e-commerce initiatives.

E-commerce strategies have become an attraction for Internet savvy customers. To become relevant to online buyers and take full advantage of new media, e-commerce strategists must rethink their brand investments. They must intelligently balance their brand strategies between the physical and online worlds. They must cleverly blend traditional media with online approaches to provide customers with a rich, interactive experience.

S. Mohapatra, *E-Commerce Strategy*, Springer Texts in Business and Economics,
DOI: 10.1007/978-1-4614-4142-7_7,

7.3 Case: Strategic Initiatives by Indian Railways—Indian Railways Catering and Tourism Corporation Limited

Beginning with an Anecdote

What is gone are the days when one had to wait in a long queue for hours, with a token number allocated, to buy railway tickets.

When you are on the Internet, just log onto the IRCTC site.

REGISTER once, give your personal details (Name, Address, Age, Sex, etc.), and get your username and password entered. Now, you have a Web-enabled ticketing counter right at your doorstep. The ticket reaches you by courier quickly within 24 h. You have three options available:

- Collect the ticket personally;
- Have it delivered through courier or;
- Collect it just before boarding the train

It is a thrilling experience, very advanced, the state-of-the-art technology, and of course, Indian Railways has been always experimenting with new technologies.

7.3.1 Introduction

The Indian Railways is one of the largest and highly networked railway systems in the world. Indian Railways carries about 6 billion people every year and 7 billion tons of freight is also transported. The Indian Railways Catering and Tourism Corporation Limited (IRCTC) is a public sector company, set up and fully owned by the Ministry of Railways, Government of India. This company has been formed to function as a subsidiary unit of the Indian Railways to enhance, professionalize, increase accountability, and manage the catering and hospitality services at railway stations and within trains running across the country. IRCTC's objectives also include promoting domestic and international tourism through development of budget hotels, special tour packages, and online reservation systems. Indian Railways' hospitality and catering services serves 13 million passengers in trains everyday and generates a total business of over Rs 6,000 crores per year.

The Indian Railways Catering and Tourism Corporation is a subsidiary of the Indian Railways that provides a best-in-class catering service for its express trains and food stores. IRCTC is more known for changing the process of Rail Ticket Reservation in India. It pioneered the online rail ticket booking in India through its web site 'www.irctc.co.in', and providing the convenience of booking railway tickets through various unconventional modes like mobile phones, SMS, etc. IRCTC recently launched a loyalty program through its web site for the regular users of its services, called 'Shubhyatra' and has also started online services for booking Mumbai Suburban Season Tickets.

Within a short span of its going online, this web site, www.irctc.co.in has become the largest and fastest growing e-commerce web site in the Asia Pacific region and the web site with the maximum number of transactions in this part of the world. Indian Railways' rules for reservation and ticket booking apply to all such transactions along with special conditions imposed for Internet-based booking. On Dec 6 2008, IRCTC started its online hotel bookings in partnership with Cleartrip. Under the new partnership, Cleartrip became the exclusive service provider of hotel information, availability, and pricing to the Indian Railways.

With the purpose of developing and managing rail catering and hospitality, IRCTC Ltd. went operational for sufficiently harnessing the tourism and catering potential in the country, worth Rs 500 crores. For the same purpose, a memorandum of understanding (MoU) was signed between IRCTC Ltd. and Indian Railways that came into effect on 12 April 2002. IRCTC has many objectives, from being customer focused and sensitive to the required changes to maintaining quality assurance. IRCTC is required to be aware of the scenario and heritage of the travel and improve the same through innovative marketing. It is expected to maximize the efficiency of its services provided through public–private partnerships.

7.3.2 Vision

IRCTC's vision for the tourism business states "To be the leading provider of a complete spectrum of consistently high quality tourism products".

7.3.3 Background

The past 2 years have witnessed considerable improvements in various areas in tourism and catering services including passenger amenities, increase in the number of new trains, new services offered, and extension of services and the proficient use of technology. Faced with complaints of downgraded food supplied in trains, the railways decided to set things right by setting up the IRCTC to become more efficient and accountable. It is subsidized by the Indian Railways, and has come into existence to provide for the catering needs of rail travelers. IRCTC has been a successful effort on the part of the Ministry of Railways to professionalize the services available.

Currently, IRCTC is running 53 food outlets, along with private parties on public–private-partnership basis. Catering facilities are provided through 10,752 catering units in 260 pairs of trains through the pantry cars available and in 80 trains through vendors. The total catering units under zonal railways are 56 and those under IRCTC are about 1,426. Private catering units under zonal railways stand at 3,473 and under IRCTC at 5,797.

IRCTC packages its own brand of drinking water called Rail Neer. Indian Railways Catering facilities are provided in all passenger trains in India. All meals on the trains are served according to the orders received from the passengers. The chief person-in-charge makes a round of the train beforehand, and takes orders, and the meals are delivered accordingly. IRCTC has time and again introduced variations in its meals and services.

- '*Kullads*', as they call it colloquially or earthen cups were introduced to serve tea at stalls. This initiative provided employment opportunities to even potters.
- *The A La Carte menu*: IRCTC introduced a special menu that covers food items not appearing in the main menu. The products have a reasonable and accessible price setting keeping in mind the huge volume of economy-class travelers.

Besides, on the luxury and also on the economy tourist trains, the quality of food and service is average, with the focus being on serving reasonably tasty and cost-effective meals. The high-class travelers on the other hand demand better quality, which is supplied through more customized menus and personalized service.

7.3.4 IRCTC's Range of Products and Services

- Luxury tourist trains
- Chartering of special trains and coaches over the network
- Special tour packages
- Bharat Darshan—Special tourist trains for the budget travelers
- Budget Hotels—near important railway stations all over India
- Car on rent
- E-ticketing for travel over Indian Railways
- Call Centers—for rail- and tourism-related information
- On-board catering on trains across the country
- Multicuisine food plazas at important railway stations
- Rail Neer—packaged drinking water

Availability of this wide range of services under its own web site puts IRCTC in the most competitively advantageous position of being able to offer standardized as well as customized packages to meet the requirements of all segments of the travel and tourism industry.

Luxury Tourist Trains—IRCTC works with other public and private organizations, in the tourism sector, for running luxury trains over the Indian Railway network. Besides the trains already running, a number of new trains are planned to be launched in the coming year.

Online Train Reservation—IRCTC provides an online booking facility through its web site. Customers can book tickets online either with a credit card or a debit card or an Internet banking account by creating their own account in the IRCTC site. The web site also contains information about ticket delivery, cancelation procedures, security mechanisms, agents, general rules, and policies, and terms and conditions. More than 2 million railway tickets are booked through the IRCTC web site, www.irctc.co.in every month. IRCTC's current registered user base is over 5.8 million as on 31 March 2008.

Tourist Cars—for smaller groups of travelers, IRCTC offers luxury tourist cars. These are air conditioned cars with all modern amenities providing the luxury of a hotel on wheels.

Train and Coach Charters—IRCTC organizes train and rail coach charters over Indian Railways for the convenience of tourists traveling in large groups.

Tour Packages—IRCTC provides tour packages all over India, covering a variety of tourist choices and preferences. These packages are primarily run on an all services inclusive of rail travel, road travel, hotel accommodation, sightseeing, hospitality, etc.

Budget Hotels—IRCTC's budget hotels at important railway stations across India provide quality accommodation with modern facilities for budget travelers.

Bharat Darshan Facility (special tourist trains for economy travelers)—These trains cater to the economy-class travelers and cover places of cultural, historical, and religious interest. The package includes travel by rail and road, boarding and lodging arrangements, sightseeing, and other associated facilities for customers.

Call Center—this feature provides train and tourism service-related information and bookings.

Help Guides—different help guides are also available on the web site for the convenience of online users to facilitate them to use the web services such as User Guide for Guest Booking, User Guide for Registered User Booking, User Guide for (Guest User) Cancelation, and User Guide for (Registered User) Cancelation.

Catering Services

IRCTC primarily establishes three catering facilities as follows:

- The stationary passenger stalls;
- Mobile units, which are the pantry cars attached to the trains;
- Base kitchens which supply food to trains.

Among several plans laid out by the corporation were the food plazas, which have now been set up at various railway stations. These multicuisine food plazas were started not with the motive of profit making or revenue earning but as an endeavor to facilitate and promote rail tourism. Passengers get the opportunity of having their favorite brand of fast food, as these food plazas are subcontracted to many private players.

7.3.5 Automation Points

The e-reservation web site http://www.irctc.co.in was inaugurated on 3 August 2002 and the software for the same was developed by CRIS. The Center for

Railway Information Systems (CRIS) is an autonomous department under the direct control of the Ministry of Railways. It is headed by a Managing Director. CRIS is primarily a project-oriented organization engaged in development of major computer and information systems on the Railways. CRIS has acquired the required knowledge and efficiency in the field of informatics. With such a rich practical experience, a dedicated team of professionals and its own R & D effort and facilities, CRIS aims to be a leader in this fast developing field. Indian Railways is one of the most advanced conglomerates in India, with an innovative and extensive IT environment.

- The software developed by CRIS consists of:
  - Complete interface software between the IRCTC front-end server and the back-end Alpha server.
  - Complete e-reservation and back end servers for inquiry mechanisms.
  - Ticket printing and cancelation facilities in existing clients.
  - Reports for IRCTC transactions.
- Infrastructure used to implement the reservation and ticketing systems:
  - HP's Alpha Server hardware
  - Operating System—OpenVMS 7.3-2
  - Routers to implement a network of five passenger reservation system centers over 2 MB leased DOT lines
  - Over 4,000 terminals connected to the 5 centers over DOT and leased lines
  - DecNet phase V/TCP-IP networking software

As part of its long-term strategy toward organizational reforms and restructuring, the Indian Railways has made serious attempts to induct professionalism into their stream and divest its noncore areas of operation connected to its core business of transport. In the marketing department, IRCTC is currently working on certain policies on accommodating private parties from the travel trade fraternity to participate in their joint ventures to promote tourism in the country. The IRCTC also announced their interest for working on JVs with the organized sector of the hospitality industry. This initiative came when the railway authorities decided to make their presence felt in the tourism and catering sectors as the largest passenger transport organization of the country.

With over 17 million passengers traveling by train everyday, IRCTC taps this burgeoning market by enabling customers to book their train tickets online. Instead of having to check different aspects of the booking separately, a single search provides users with train fares, schedules, and availability simultaneously. Moreover, users can instantly review fares from multiple classes, such as AC 2-Tier and AC 3-Tier, giving them the option to upgrade to a higher class of travel if they prefer. Exhaustive information is provided for each train including arrival and departure times, number of stops, and the train's route with all stops.

7.3.6 Strategic Initiatives Using E-Commerce Strategy

On Dec 10 2008, IRCTC launched online hotel bookings in collaboration with Cleartrip.com. They launched an online hotel model, where consumers can book rooms at 3,500 hotels across India via their official web site www.irctc.co.in. IRCTC then released an Expression of Interest (EOI) inviting all leading hotel consolidators in India to set up the hotel booking engine on both their web sites www.irctc.co.in and www.railtourismindia.com. They plan to offer a variety of hotels across the country at the most reasonable and competitive prices.

7.3.6.1 Inquiry Points on the Web Site

Trains between a pair of stations—this inquiry gives all the trains between the selected source and destination station.

Accommodation availability—this inquiry gives the latest seat availability position of the chosen class, date, train, and route.

PNR status inquiry—this inquiry gives the latest updated status of the passenger.

Train Schedule—this inquiry gives the complete path information of a particular train with the arrival and departure time at a station.

Rules—reservation rules, refund rules, break journey rules, luggage rule, change in name.

General Information—season tickets, circular journey, booking locations, concession forms for blind, orthopedically handicapped, mentally retarded and deaf and dumb persons, general reservation form, tele booking, tatkal booking.

Tourist Information—worldwide tourists' information, details of different travel agents, providing the facility.

Inquiries on cell phones through SMS are also made possible.

7.3.7 Decision/Need for Automation

On April 23 2003, the IRCTC selected the Oracle E-Business Suite to automate and streamline all its processes. The project was implemented by Tata Consultancy Services—an Oracle Certified Advantage Partner with the Oracle Partner Network, which used the Linux platform for its operations. This specific selection of software solution gave IRCTC the ability to control and run their country-wide operations in a cost-effective manner. With Oracle E-Business Suite, which was a fully integrated solution, IRCTC also saved the cost of integration.

The major decision of automating the processes came when IRCTC was on the verge of a major expansion across the country. They needed an efficient and robust system, which should also stand the test for scalability. That is when the IT implementation team at IRCTC decided that The Oracle E-Business Suite will meet all their present and future requirements.

That implementation helped IRCTC streamline its business processes and information flow across its country-wide operations. IRCTC gradually scaled up to a 7,000 employee, catering and tourism operation spread over 1,000 locations across India. IRCTC's operations included food courts at railway stations, in-train catering, refreshment rooms, special catering, and hospitality services for Indian Railway. As a result, IRCTC had to deal with multi-faceted operational challenges:

- Quality assurance
- The logistics associated with the management of existing food chains and catering vendors
- Cash flow monitoring
- Management of costs and human resources

For IRCTC, their employees and customers are key to their operations and the best processes are required to ensure effective functioning of their web site.

IRCTC worked on the Oracle E-Business Suite on Linux platform as this enabled IRCTC to realize additional cost savings and benefit due to greater efficiency. The Linux platform also provided a reliable, mature, and low-cost system for the Oracle applications that supported IRCTC's business operations.

7.3.8 Benefits of Automation

In the IRCTC web site, one can search for the train destination, day schedules, etc. There are so many advantages that the web site provides to its customers. Right from finding the train to online booking and easy payment options are available. The web site contains online rail ticket booking, and provision of checking the ticket reservation status. It also includes train schedules, availability of tickets, train fares, etc.

With an easier user-interface, it is convenient and fast to book tickets online for the railway journey. The official IRCTC railway reservation web site is informative and useful even for first-time online users—it is that comprehensive. For example, when the journey is selected, it gives the date of arrival, fare, and ticket availability on one screen; if the ticket is available, one can go ahead and book the train ticket. In case a wrong entry is made, it gives the facility to go back and edit the changes. One can make the reservation train ticket using credit card or debit card.

IRCTC also has a toll-free phone number for passengers traveling on Indian Railways, on which travelers can lodge their complaints about the quality, quantity, price, and even standard of the catering service.

Passengers traveling by any train at any point in time and present in any part of the country can register their complaints and the operator will make a note of the train/PNR number, etc. of the passenger and give them a complaint number for future reference. The complaints are sent directly to the IRCTC managing director, who then inspects the matter and fixes the problem accordingly. This makes the catering service staff accountable to the services provided, especially to provide better quality food.

7.3.9 Services Offered by IRCTC on the Internet

- Advance booking in any class for the journey between any two stations.
- Booking on payment of fare concession available to senior citizens in all stations.
- General inquiries regarding:
  - Accommodation available for a train/date combination
  - Current Status of reservation
  - Timetable
  - Train fare
  - Trains available between a pair of stations
- Courier delivery of tickets booked.
- Collection of tickets by customers from authentic and allocated collection centers.

7.3.10 Security Levels Maintained for Online Ticketing System

Servers are located at five centers fully owned by Indian Railways. Access to the server rooms is strictly restricted to the maintenance staff. The centers are manned/controlled by Railway personnel. All access points to the system are through highly secured terminals.

Use of proprietary Operating System (OS) and networking protocol, whose usage is limited, that makes it difficult for hackers and intruders to affect the system. Regular updates and patches are applied for the OS whenever they are released. *'Proprietary' and 'closed' features of the OS provide additional security.* Passwords are maintained at two levels—user level and terminal level. Limited User Accounts are created with privilege policy according to user specific needs. The protection privileges of the significant application programs have been defined, so that they can be run only from the specified user accounts. The operating system has extensive logging and auditing features, which can be enabled whenever required.

- Inquiry—only read access to the database
- Booking—write access for ticketing only
- Supervisory—updates on the database for implementing special functionalities

Hierarchical privileges at User/Terminal level:

7.3.11 Return on Investment Calculations

The purpose of the ROI calculation is to compare the costs of an investment with the value of its results. Every organization views ROI differently, and ROI is different for different types of projects undertaken.

IRCTC plans to automate the service for the following benefits:

- Customers can plan their itinerary themselves and online
  - Value to customer—Speed and 24 × 7 availability are most significant
  - Aligning with business trends that will reduce transaction costs
- Online payments will reduce credit issues and penalties
- Competitive value

Challenges

- Reliability and speed of transactions
- Integrating business process
- Dynamic linking and performance
- Holding partners' commitments

7.3.12 Cost Calculation

7.3.12.1 Initial Questions to Determine Costs of Automation:

How many software licenses are you purchasing?

What is the cost of hardware bought for the project?

What is the initial cost of implementing for the project?

How many complete hours will Information Technology staff spend on the project?

What is the average annual compensation and benefits given to the Information Technology staff?

How many Information Technology staff will be allocated for the continuous system maintenance? In addition to these, there will be costs associated with product license charges, product per-user charges, database expenses, operating system software, additional server software, additional network software, annual Maintenance Costs.

7.3.13 Benefits from E-Commerce Site

The benefits from the e-commerce web site are of two types—direct benefits and indirect benefits. Direct benefits include:

- Increased profits
- Increased revenues
- Reduced costs
- Reduced inefficiencies

- These are used to calculate direct benefits and can be quantified. The financial ratios that are used for these calculations are—net cash flow before taxes Net cash flow before taxes, net cash flow after taxes, net cash flow after taxes, annual ROI (direct benefits only ((Total Monetary Benefits—Total Cost)/Total Cost) multiplied by 100), Net Present Value (NPV), average annual cost of ownership, average annual cost of ownership, Internal rate of return (IRR).

These benefits can be measured directly and hence will contribute to the revenue directly. There are also indirect benefits, which cannot be counted directly, but will increase the strategic advantage of the organizations. These are

- Increased technology management
- Improved process management
- Reduced cost of errors and manual work
- Reduced logistics cost
- Reduced communication costs
- Improved accessibility
- Reduced customer care costs
- Increased customer hits
- Improved working capital

7.3.14 Competitive Advantage of IRCTC E-Commerce Web Site

Thus, IRCTC has enriched the life of travelers everyday and made traveling convenient by providing online ticket booking facilities and several other options through its comprehensive web site. Not only that, keeping in mind the vastness of our country, the rich heritage, the numerous tourist spots, and a large percentage of regularly traveling executives and economic travelers, it has become all the more easy to plan a holiday, plan a professional trip, book hotels, transport facilities, select cuisines, have customized menus, all through one and the same web site. Technology has made traveling more convenient. Now, it provides a full range of hospitality, travel, tourism, and catering services to rail passengers. IRCTC has now moved on to become the leader in e-commerce in India and records for more than one-third of the total e-commerce in the country providing more than 4 million tickets in a month and growing in recognition and appreciation with every passing day. Finally, one can conclude that the entire assortment of tourism products and services available for information as well as convenient booking on IRCTC's web site www.irctc.co.in and www.railtourismindia.com allows travelers to plan and book holiday travel while sitting in the comfort of one's home or office right in front of the computer.

7.3.15 Using E-Commerce as a Strategic Tool

Using e-commerce as a strategic tool, IRCTC can take customer satisfaction to new heights. It can plan to add the following features through its e-commerce portal and make the experience more than satisfying.

7.3.15.1 Movie Theater

In this fast moving world, time is scarce for all. Getting a business deal signed is easier than sparing time for a movie. Even to spend 3–4 h with one's family for an outing and movie is a big deal these days!!!

The plan is to start a movie theater where the latest movies will be played. It will help passengers to spend their time while traveling in leisure activity.

They plan to start an in-house theater for customers' convenience while they are on move. This will help in the following ways:

- Passengers need not take out extra time for the movie
- The latest movie will be played
- Limited number of seats
- Booking can be done while booking the ticket only over Internet
- Increased revenue for railways as it will attract crowd
- Increased revenues from advertisements played during movie as well as advertisement banners on the boogie
- Publicity on the whole would increase

7.3.15.2 Video Game

The plan also incorporates a video game parlor for children.

- To keep them busy
- Best time pass for youngsters
- Increased revenues for railways

7.3.15.3 Food Joint

Do away with the oily messy pantry food. Be ready to have highly hygienic, less calorific food at cheap prices.

- Low prices
- Less calories
- Items include burgers, patties, pizzas, instant coffee, and sandwiches
- Milk bottles, fresh milk for infants, cold drinks, juice bottles, water bottles

- Available 24 h
- Tie-up with nearest good restaurants for supplying packed food in train

When trains stop at stations, usually passengers in compartments at the extremes do not get anything to eat as most of the time the stalls are located in the middle of the platforms so, this will be beneficial for passengers traveling in such compartments.

7.3.15.4 Book Store

Books, novels, magazines would be available at low rent. Books will include weekly magazines, newspapers, and story books for children, and also motivational and inspirational books. Books will be available in different languages like English, Hindi, and also the regional language. Like suppose a train is moving toward Bengal then Bengali magazines and newspaper will also be available.

7.3.15.5 Store Room

Place will be provided where passengers can park their valuables and that too at a very low cost. The security of the valuables will be taken care of by the concerned authorities. This facility is available especially to those who go for the movie shows.

7.3.15.6 Marketing

It will be taken care by a brand as big as the railways itself. For easy availability of seats tickets will be available through the Internet by the IRCTC site, providing easy accessibility as everything available under one banner. This site will also help in promoting these services. Other official sites of the railways will also be used to communicate to the customers about the availability of services.

7.3.15.7 Financials

The revenue generators will be the tickets for the movies, sale of food from the food joints, the game parlor; however, the main source of revenue will be from the promotional activities. There will be advertisements outside the coach and also during the movie breaks. Further, the interior will be designed in such a way that hoardings can be placed which will act as a revenue generating source.

The application of funds will be mainly on the day-to-day operations like maintenance, salary of the employed, expenditure to procure the eatables, and so on. But the major chunk will be required for designing the coach and providing comforts like the seats, light, movie screen, and so on. This will be a one-time expenditure to be slowly written off during the lifetime.

7.4 Brand Equity Through E-Commerce

The power of a brand *name* justifies higher margins and builds influence over distribution channels. The brand power is built slowly, over time by investing in mass-media advertising (TV, print, radio, online banner advertisements, and transit advertisements such as billboards and bus shelter posters). The Internet is changing the meaning of a brand, the nature of brand loyalty, and the effectiveness of traditional branding investments made by marketers. Online branding approaches allow marketers to cut through past constraints of geography, timeliness, at reduced cost. Online advertising helps in creating a branding message that may be seen by millions of people in a single day. Access to online knowledge, especially through online marketplaces, provides a buyer with product choice. But most of the times, in a global business market, a potential customer who encounters your brand or product name first on the Internet may have no previous information to rely on. This lack of reliability is because the prospects have not seen the TV advertisement or they have not read product reviews. Because of these factors, brands on the Web must be equipped with all possible details so that prospects would be ready to acquire a new product.

7.4.1 Framework for Assessing Readiness of Existing Brands

The first step is a thoughtful assessment of the readiness of the existing brand for online marketing. To make this more than just a guess, it is useful to have a scorecard to guide the process. The following scorecard is based on the experience of market leaders and factors in several dimensions that make a real difference when moving a brand online (Please refer Fig. 7.1).

The products to be the first in e-commerce have the advantage that they are on the top of mind recall for everybody. The disadvantage is that there could be risks associated with the acceptance of the products and hence they might be ahead of their time. This might lead to rejection from prospects. This can be assed from assessment of prospects readiness for being Internet savvy. Do the prospects rely on the Web? Some prospects have no problem being drawn to e-commerce channels. Buyers who deal with computer manufacturers such as Apple, Dell, and IBM tend to be more familiar with computer-enabled transactions. Others, say, prospects of Big Bazaar or Tesco, maybe less adventurous technically or have fewer opportunities to use e-commerce media.

Brand equity for e-commerce will also depend on the reputation of the company as an innovator. If the company enjoys a reputation for marketing innovation and

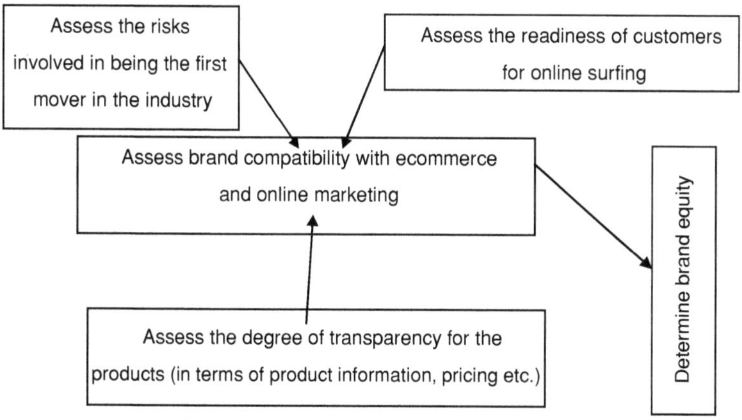

Fig. 7.1 Framework for determining brand equity in e-commerce

creativity, then e-commerce branding will be easier and faster. This also depends on information richness viz. does the product offer high information value through e-commerce web site? The Web's search and interactive possibilities are ideal for setting data-heavy purchase decisions, such as financial services and travel planning, and for digitally rich products, such as software, music, books, and timely news. The brand readiness also determines whether the prospects are adaptable to an e-commerce channel. The products such as catalog retailers help prospects with high degree of self-service in product selection and purchase options. This makes the entire purchase process quite an involved one. These types of products will make the brand equity higher through e-commerce marketing. Amazon.com's success through e-commerce marketing has increased its brand equity.

Organizations need to consider domain readiness issues, such as registering all variations of trademarked names into e-commerce web sites. Companies like Maruti Suzuki, Hyundai have created domain names such as Swift and i10, respectively, and offer discounts if the products are purchased through web sites.

7.4.2 E-Commerce Alignment with Changing Customer Behavior

Good branding on the Web should not be an accident. E-commerce strategists should not think customers that would behave the same way in online channels as they do in the physical world. They assume that the tried-and-true media would work just as well to get the message across to online customers. The simple analysis of how customers find web sites illustrates an important point. Traditional marketing advertisement media, such as television advertising, print ads, bus shelter, and billboard blitzes—are often less effective in building long-term visibility and brand equity over the Web. It has been found that Web users have a better chance of finding a web site "by search engine" than by TV, print, and radio. Web banner ads on the most heavily visited Web pages of Yahoo and AOL, create the initial brand awareness. These advertisers also keep on changing their banner ads as the products move in their life cycle. The change takes care of changing customer behavior which goes in line with product maturity. For example, e-commerce web sites for automobiles have been changing their advertisement based on the maturity of the cars. When Swift was launched, it started advertising on the experience of driving the Swift car, but as the product became a success but had a number of competitors; it started advertising on the value for money concept in its e-commerce web site.

Good e-commerce web sites require an online environment that encourages customer-to-customer communications. For consumer companies, e-commerce capabilities can be built into the online sales engine—for example, allowing users who have just completed a purchase to either post their opinions of the experience, or forward information about their experience to an e-mail network of family and friends. Other methods to encourage passing along information to others include online wedding, baby, or gift registries, making gift certificates available electronically, and hosting issue-oriented bulletin boards or chat rooms. When creating e-commerce portals, the right motivating trigger points might evolve out of research into the most frequently asked customer questions, e-mail responses, and customer complaints. This can also encourage customers more likely to actively share information.

7.5 Summary

E-commerce web sites can thrive through repeat visits by customers. The previous focus on building brands fast and gaining new customers quickly often meant that important technology tools and interactive techniques for customer retention, such as personalized product offerings and automated customer care, were given less emphasis. Smart marketers have learned that service, relevance, and reliability are highly important to online brands. Brand response will not only permit marketers to measure and modulate brand impact; it will enable them to capitalize on the emotive aspect of the brand with unprecedented efficiency. Consider point-and-click television, which will make it possible to translate consumers' emotional reaction to an ad into an immediate purchase response through TV-commerce. The next generation of TV product placement, for example, is likely to allow viewers to freeze frame during an episode *of Friends,* learn details about Jennifer Aniston's wardrobe, and then buy a copy of her blouse directly from Calvin Klein. This sort of "emotional interactivity" will epitomize future branding strategies, drive profits, and garner customer loyalty. Traditional marketers must totally rethink branding strategies and investments if they want to remain relevant to customers that attend to new media.

7.6 Review Questions

1. What is the need for developing brand equity for e-commerce?
2. How can we build brand equity through e-commerce?
3. What are the steps needed for building bran equity in e-commerce?
4. How do you align changing customer behavior with e-commerce?
5. Please refer to the case IRCTC. How has IRCTC created competitive advantage through e-commerce?

Chapter 8
Channels in E-Commerce

8.1 Learning Objectives

At the end of the chapter, readers would learn

- Different channels that are available for e-commerce
- How to manage multiple sales in e-commerce
- How to blend channels for growth and profitability

8.2 Introduction

In today's business scenarios, product and service selling happens through a combination of field sales, retail, business partners, direct marketing, call center, and electronic media. Using a mix selling channels is already common in the high technology, retail, and financial services industries. It is fast becoming a fact of life in mainstream businesses. Any business that expects to grow profitably and effectively will have to master the art of selling through a coordinated mix of multiple channels. This is because when sales and marketing resources work well together, the result is usually lower selling costs, happier customers, and more reliable results. When channels are not managed properly, sales opportunities tend to slip through the cracks, and sales and marketing costs get out of control. In order to make these different online and offline selling channels work in a unified way, sales and marketing managers will require a new game plan for planning, measuring, and coordinating their sales and marketing resources.

S. Mohapatra, *E-Commerce Strategy*, Springer Texts in Business and Economics,
DOI: 10.1007/978-1-4614-4142-7_8,

8.3 Airtel: Getting Selling Channels to Work Together

Airtel has tried to reach out to its partners and customers through greater control to improve its market share in Indian mobile industry. It has used e-commerce portals to coordinate the efforts of 100s of selling partners with call centers and online marketing programs. Airtel sells high speed Internet and data services over standard mobile and landline (fixed) phone lines. The segments that Airtel cater to are the small and medium sized business markets, large business houses (broadband connections), retail customers (individual connections).

Airtel sells these services through a multichannel selling system that is made up of a combination of third-party business partners, such as stationary shop owners who their own office space to sell 'recharge vouchers' to individuals and its own key customer account sales forces. They also use the banner advertisements in different Internet web sites and call center channels to generate demand and support business partners. Though in a competitive market, it has enjoyed sustainable growth rate from 2005 till now (year 2011) and has the highest market share in the market (in the year 2011). With more than 300,000 subscribers it is one of the top ten broadband suppliers in India, competing head to head with state owned BSNL and Vodafone. In order to acquire more market share quickly in the new and highly competitive market, where there is heavy pressure on the margin, Airtel knew it had to get its combination of resellers, field salespeople, call centers, and Internet channels to work together.

At first, the strategy did not run very smoothly. For example, to acquire new customers Airtel invested heavily in direct marketing and advertising programs to generate leads for its call centers to qualify and its business partners to close. These included print, online and radio ads convincing homeowners, individuals, and corporate to switch over to DSL from regular dial up modems so as to access faster Internet. While these campaigns were successful in pulling in between 200 and 500 leads per day to the call center, it was discovered that most of the ISP business partners were not following up these leads, because they felt the leads were of poor quality and the hit rate (the rate at which prospects are converted to actual customers) is quite low.

Airtel had to start getting these different sales and marketing resources playing like a team. To get online leads quickly into the hands of the regional or local partners, who were nearest to the customers place and were best positioned to close the calls, it added an automated customer tool and an online reseller locator to its e-commerce portal. To improve the process of qualifying leads and following up on them quickly, it invested in a work flow management system for internal use where each and every lead that failed was analyzed and lessons learned. These lessons were then shared with its selling teams so that they do not repeat these mistakes. The software was linked to a centralized call center and an interaction points and streamlined the passing along of relevant information to business partners. These technology tools made it easier for the call center and Web channels to coordinate their efforts with the retailers and sales force.

The software also allowed Airtel to measure the performance of each business partner in following up leads. Though its partners were widespread throughout the country, Airtel was able to have control of the early part of the selling process. They established business rules and goals for the sales force, business partners and retailers regarding response time, location, awareness about new products, and other key management criteria. An immediate result of this new scorecard was that Airtel was able to convert a higher percentage of the prospects into new customers than before. Also, when the same business partners started dealing with many ISPs (who were Airtel's competitors), Airtel was able to monitor and measure the effectiveness its business partners. It helped Airtel to survive and grow whereas many of its competitors struggled to reduce their operational cost.

8.4 Importance of E-Commerce in Multichannel Marketing

The Airtel case shows the need to have e-commerce channel in multichannel situation. In order to gain rapid and effective market share and still be able to 'learn' from its past mistakes, e-commerce portals need to track each and every sale and collect data for these sales. Using these data, meaningful information is generated so that proper managerial decision can be taken. These decisions help in improving sales for the organization. Thus, e-commerce can help to make multichannels work together. Managing channels is important because customers and cost pressures will force organizations to sell through more channels in the future.

8.4.1 Understanding Channels

The literary meaning of channel (as per Oxford dictionary) is the path or the way to deliver goods or services. In business, it implies the route or the different ways companies reach out to customers. Channels that are used by business houses are different viz. sales teams, distributors, newspapers, the Internet, and business partners that allow organizations to reach, sell, and provide after-sales service to their customers. Broadly defined, channels can include anything that can interact with a customer and conduct business.

Channels come in many different types and roles. For instance, the role of a sales channel is to generate revenues while an advertising and marketing channel is responsible for generating leads and awareness. Service channels are meant to deliver technical support, field service, or customer service. However, these channels are not free and require investment. These channels are also important resources for the organizations. It is important to remember that these channels that are resources, cost money and must get results. A "sales channel" has a discreet revenue objective and set of costs associated with it. For example, a telesales channel might be expected to get 120 % return on investment. It is also useful to think of channels as "pipes" that carry goods and services as well as handle customer complaints.

Over the last several years, marketing and sales departments have found it increasingly difficult to achieve rapid growth cost-effectively using traditional brick and mortar route. For example, it is not as profitable to sell personal computers using direct marketing as it was done in earlier days. For direct marketing, taking an appointment with a prospective and then meeting him personally for direct marketing can cost a lot. The cost can be prohibitive sometimes as we factor in time and effort required to get an appointment and convert that into actual sale. If finally the personal meeting yields the sale of a desktop personal computer, the cost of the appointment can be many items more than the gross margins made on the computer itself.

8.4.2 Role of E-Commerce in Multichannels

In the knowledge era, lower cost-selling channel alternatives such as Internet and telephone have proven to be easier to adopt, less expensive, effective, and more profitable. These channels also have convenience factors in selling; the prospects can decide when to watch an e-mail based advertisement (based on his convenience) and when to see the details of a short message service (SMS in mobile phones) based promotions. Traditional approach such as a direct conversation between a prospect and sales representative might cost INR 3,000 (three thousand rupees approximately), while an e-commerce based marketing initiative can cost as little as INR 300 only (approx, may vary depending on type of product. This approximate cost is for consumer white goods). This means if the selling organization can use e-commerce portals to chose their target customers and send promotions (through automated mailers, SMS, telephone calls, etc.), then the organization will have a better chance to show profit. Through live chats, if customer complaints can be answered online instead of on the phone, more money is saved and the call center agent is free to answer another call. This increases productivity of the sales department as well. Further, if customer questions can be routed to an e-commerce web site and answered by e-mail, instead of on the phone, more money is saved and the call center agent is free to spend more time on sales calls.

Customers are more demanding now than before. They are becoming increasingly tech savvy, demanding the advantage of buying through multiple channels, and the choice to freely migrate between channels during different phases of the selling process. It has been observed that 50 % of online purchases were checked out first in a retail store and then ordered through e-commerce portals. A range of goods involved in these online purchases varied from apparels to electronic items. These cost and customer pressure are forcing larger enterprises to combine these call center and electronic channels with traditional field sales, retail, and distribution partners into multichannel selling systems. In the year 2000, most organizations were selling through about three channels (an average of 2.75 per company) according to a survey by IMT Strategies of 50 Global 2000 organizations. The study went on to show that at that time, traditional channels remained by far the largest portion of the revenue stream, with electronic channels representing less than 5 %. This trend has totally changed now. The greatest expansion of effort centers on retooling telephone (tele-rep) call center operations and e-commerce. This was expected with Internet penetration and consumers becoming more tech savvy. The penchant for e-commerce channel is not surprising, as these can support both direct selling and indirect selling (for example business partner networks or Web affiliate networks). In many cases, in industries such as computers and electronic goods, banking and personal insurance, the direct marketing approach would be too expensive to adapt. As a result, alternatives to face to face and partner selling channels are being used. Thus, e-commerce channel is able to use available resources to create value for these customers.

8.4.3 Advantages of E-Commerce in Multichannel

Coordination and teamwork require a well trained set of discipline professionals, passing the information to all relevant players so that a coordinated decision can be taken. This decision will help achieve an optimum result for the organization. HP is working hard to build a "Multichannel sales and marketing system" that would give it a higher market share in India. Unlike Dell, which thrusts its marketing only on e-commerce, HP has decided to use multichannel marketing so as to get maximum market share in personal computer industry. It has e-commerce portal, where the customer can chose among different varieties of products and decide the best one for him. The customer is also allowed to configure according to his needs. In addition to this channel, HP uses dealers to sell its products. It also uses his sales team to approach institutions for bulk purchases. HP's strategy is to use different channels to cater to all segments of the market. They also use low-cost tele and electronic channels for maximum business impact. One of their more successful pilot programs demonstrates how effective this strategy can be when it works well. HP consolidates leads generated from a variety of marketing programs in a special e-commerce web portal responsible for lead qualification. This provides HP the ability to control, manage, and measure the performance of these marketing campaigns and optimize the distribution of these leads. In this portal, marketers use a CRM software application to access customer data necessary to qualify the inbound leads. The best leads are enhanced with useful customer information and customized promotions to make it easier for business partners to make the sale. Once a lead is qualified by the web portal, it is passed to the right business partner using an electronic channel, for follow-up. Within a year, it was found that leads that went through this "hybrid" process had a 50 % close rate and market share increasing by 7 %.

The above example from HP, it is clear that using e-commerce portal in a multichannel system is effective and increases business potential. In the past, we have had many examples where because of presence of multichannel system, there have been conflicts between selling channels, lost sales leads that fall through the cracks, and gaps in market coverage where potential customers are not serviced. In such multichannel system, executives responsible for managing more than two selling channels first need to shift their focus from building channels to integrate channels. Instead of prioritizing opening new stores, the focus should be on the strategy to integrating channels. Any business that starts to sell through many channels can expect certain problems will arise:

1. Salespeople in different channels will compete for the same business;
2. Leads might not be followed up for converting them to customers;
3. Inconsistencies in customer relationship management;
4. Ineffective integration of channels because of which there could be revenue leaks.

For channel integration to be productive and be able to produce results, a clear cut demarcation of accountability should be well defined. Service Level Agreements (SLA) for each channel needs to be defined and communicated to all channel partners. These SLAs should demarcate the boundaries that are acceptable to staff so as to manage and mitigate the conflicts that can arise. Ultimately, senior management must explore new incentive plans that encourage people in different channels to work together. This will ensure that (1) strategizing the entire potential market with a coverage that will articulate effective market coverage through all the channels, (2) defining new rules and channel policies that encourage cooperation and speed up channel integration and (3) clear cut SLAs for the complete covering the entire market. E-commerce helps to develop a unified, clear picture of the playing field. This means that everyone on the selling "team" has an understanding of what products are to be sold through which channel to which specific customer segments. In many cases, a "market coverage model" can be an actual picture or graphic rendition that shows who and what goes where.

8.5 Automation in E-Commerce Portals

In e-commerce sites, different tools such as business analytics and reporting tools can be used to generate more detailed sales performance measurements to manage sales performance and calculate incentives across channels. Using work flow management systems that automate, track, and intelligently route leads based on business logic and dynamic market conditions, the organization can improve its rate of converting prospects to customers. The portal also should have analysis and reporting methods that can measure system wide performance. This work flow management system can be automated to integrate campaign development, management, and measurement into the overall selling process. Using Customer Relationship Management (CRM) tools, the e-commerce portal can help integrate lead flow management, partner relationship management (PRM), and integrated business process performance data marts and measurement systems.

8.6 Using E-Commerce for Order Fulfilling in Supply Chain Management: An Example

Supply chain management involves getting the right product in the right quantity, to the right place at the right time and at the right cost. In today's complex business environment, superior management of the supply chain provides organizations with a competitive advantage.

In recent times, organizations have focused on delivering enterprise solutions that integrate systems within an enterprise. This is simply not enough. To effectively distribute product through the supply chain, an organization has to build partnerships with its vendors, subcontractors, logistics providers as well as its customers. This integrated environment in which the partner solutions coexist is called the extended enterprise.

To effectively manage information within the integrated supply chain, solutions must integrate with the enterprise and the extended enterprise systems. Understanding the challenges of an integrated supply chain and addressing them through technology solutions is a core competency through e-fulfilling server. The e-commerce based fulfilling server helps its stakeholders in increasing their productivity. As a result, a long-term business strategic partnership is developed. The relationship helps in improving supply chain efficiencies. As business partners, they work closely with them for defining future technology and functional directions of their business models. This portal also helps in providing round the clock support with different degree of customization to suit their specific requirements. The customers are offered a choice of different levels of support to suit their specific requirements.

This also help in fostering alliances with leading industry vendors of business systems, hardware, peripherals, special equipment and third-party service providers to offer a cost-effective and integrated solution to the customers. In the portal, project management tools have been installed to help manage projects for the customers. Project management tools help to provide a detailed plan and schedule for the implementation program. Well-defined mile stones and regular status reports keep the customers in control of their project implementation process.

The e-commerce portal also helps to provide required training and skills to their partners and customers. The technical personnel manning the portal are highly skilled and ensure a smooth transition to a new channel. These methodologies are continuously fine-tuned to enhance their utility. The portal can also be used to impart online training modules to their partners. Specially trained staff can conduct these programs. These programs are arranged online or through web conferencing to reduce time involved in logistics.

8.6.1 Inventory Management Through the Portal

Inventory in the Distribution Center (DC) must be accurately tracked to provide up-to-date information about stock quantities and location. This is essential for cost and operational efficiency in the DC. The operations involved in tracking inventory in the DC are part of the portal.

Inventory management functions will enable to inquire into the location of SKU and License Plate Numbers or cases (LPN), inquire into specific LPN's, view audit records of inventory transactions, adjust inventory for irregularities, adjust inventory inside or outside accounting bin locations, or without uploading to the host system, dedicate locations to specific SKU's, dedicate areas to specific SKU's, storage types, quality status or product classes and modify LPN and SKU numbers, etc.

8.6.2 The Inbound Planning Process

The goods receiving process can be executed efficiently through the portal. It requires that the portal should organize warehouse resources appropriately prior to receiving SKU's (stock keeping units or the basic product unit). Some decisions such as where to unload containers, and how to put away the SKU's, if SKU's need to be diverted for quality control (QC), packaging and other operations should be taken and these business rules should be fed into the portal. This helps in increasing the productivity of the channel. Using this information as well as on future expected receipts (based on the orders placed with the supply partners), warehouse resources need to be planned and space needs to be earmarked for receiving the goods. This process is called inbound planning.

Inbound Planning provides functions that enable the executives to

- IInquire into expected receipts against purchase orders or Advance Shipment Notices (ASN's)
- (Re) print receiving worksheets for an ASN using the Receipts Planning (01024) function—in warehouses that do not use radio frequency (RF) equipment for receiving and other operations, the printed receiving worksheet can be used to record receipts
- Create or modify advance shipment notices (ASN)
- Create LPN's (License Plate Numbers)—bar-coded ID's for cartons or cases; you can inquire into and create LPN's
- Schedule docks and workers for unloading
- Enter, modify or change the status of ASN's

8.6.3 Consolidating Orders Through the Portal

Consolidated orders can be prepared for optimizing the utilization of trailer space. This is usually done through Load Planning Module (LPM) tools. Through these the executives can specify the shipment modes that can be sent to the LPM. The LPM considers trailer availability, customer and SKU loading constraints to plan loads. A load is accordingly created. An SCAC is assigned to the load based on the shipment mode and destination of the shipment, and customer preference. Warehouse level inventory allocation is done for the load. If the entire inventory required for the load is available, the load can be directly confirmed into a shipment. If sufficient inventory for the load is not available, the system can be set up to retain the load, or return it to the order pool for consolidation again.

Shipments can be grouped based on certain criteria. For example, shipments for the same customer can be consolidated into a master shipment. Instead of shipping multiple LTL's (less than a truckload), the master load can be shipped as a TL (full truckload), thus reducing the shipping costs. The shipment consolidation (task/untask load) rule defines the criteria for consolidating shipments.

Consolidated orders can be sent to a Load Planning Module (LPM) for load planning to optimize the utilization of trailer space. You can specify the shipment modes that can be sent to the LPM. The LPM considers trailer availability, customer and SKU loading constraints to plan loads. A load is accordingly created. A SCAC is assigned to the load based on the shipment mode and destination of the shipment, and customer preference. Warehouse level inventory allocation is done for the load. If the entire inventory required for the load is available, the load can be directly confirmed into a shipment. If sufficient inventory for the load is not available, the system can be set up to retain the load, or return it to the order pool for consolidation again.

Shipments can be grouped based on certain criteria. For example, shipments for the same customer can be consolidated into a master shipment. Instead of shipping multiple LTL's (less than a truckload), the master load can be shipped as a TL (full truckload), thus reducing the shipping costs. The shipment consolidation (task/untask load) rule defines the criteria for consolidating shipments.

8.6.4 Benefits and Usefulness of E-Commerce Portal in Supply Chain

Through a long-term commitment the portal helps to

- Builds long-term strategic relationships with all the business partners including customers.
- Recognizes and rewards team efforts above individual actions in multichannel situation.

- *Easy to use and implement.* Continuous user feedback is obtained to provide a friendly and intuitive interface for process improvement. Thus, processes get continuously enhanced with richer functionalities and better practices. These are converted to better implementation methodology and training material to reduce implementation times for the customers.
- *Flexible, modular and scalable.* All the business rules are based in the portal and also change from time to time. This helps to be agile and be able to change the business processes at a rapid rate. Sine the portal is completely rules-based, they are quite flexible. This allows it to be highly scalable to support business growth and can be configured to run on one or more servers.
- *Open systems, client/server.* The portals, nowadays are based on open systems, client/server. Opens systems approach offers a choice of reputed open systems hardware vendors to customers. The client/server architecture makes the system truly scalable. This helps to support global distribution networks. This supports global companies with subsidiaries in multiple locations with own and third-party warehouses and vendors in several countries, and operating in multi-lingual environments and multiple time zones. Since, these are based on open system architecture, integration with different systems become easier. Thus, they are easier to inter-operate with third-party business systems within the extended enterprise. This helps the customers and business partners to use an integrated solution encompassing their enterprise and supply chain.
- *Cost-effective.* The approach of integrating channels through e-commerce is cost-effective as they provide rich functionality to meet the needs of their target customers. By constantly identifying best practices and incorporating these into the system helps improve stakeholders' satisfaction and increase productivity.

8.7 Case: Carwale.Com and Cardekho.Com—A New Business Mode for Buying and Selling Cars

Bharati wanted to buy a car which a view to upgrade the present car. She wanted to exchange the present car within a budget. Her daughter Shrestha came up with many web sites. Shrestha then narrowed down to two sites: CarWale.com and cardekho.com. She has furnished the site with information such as her age, budget, presently owned car, her choice of models, when she plans to buy, her safety needs, looks and feature requirements in the new car. She also mentioned the color that she prefers to have and the make (make means the name of the manufacturer). On receiving these information, the site starts shows available models, listed in order of potential appeal. Her list starts with the Ford Figo, an inexpensive compact, and ends with the Ford Behemoth, a 22-foot vehicle that can transport an entire soccer team. She clicks on the Figo, and looks at a range of options.

Since she had mentioned her hobby as traveling by car, the site displays roof rack specially configured as accessories which can accommodate her extra luggage. She selects it without hesitation. The site also mentions the need for navigation system and music system for long drives. Most of the time she drives short distances, but during vacations, she travels long distances. She decides the color, place of delivery, choice of number plate (where she chooses a lucky number for her number plate) and finally clicks to get the final price on her custom-configured car. The site adds the applicable road taxes, and shows the final price. After confirmation that she intends to purchase, a list of dealers in her town, who could offer a test drive, comes up on the screen. Based on her availability she chooses a time and place for test drive. The appointment is confirmed and she gets a Short Message Service (SMS) that the appointment is fixed.

Once she decided for the purchase, the site offers options for financing the purchase. She is given a wide range of options for financing the deal. Before clicking on the "Finance Your Purchase" button, the site saves her vehicle configuration with her details. These details were given by her with her registered login id (when she registered in the e-commerce web site for the first time). The site also offers different accessories such seat cover, steering cover, wheel cover, floor mat in different colors. She does not have to be worried about the size as the web site offers accessories that can fit her model. She also orders for a music (car sound system) system to be fitted before the delivery.

Before making final deal, she decides to look at the review section, where present and previous owners have narrated their experience about the same model. She sees a number of users have given good feedback, while others, who were not happy, have voiced their concerns. These unhappy customers have voiced concerns about the performance in terms of mileage, engine sound, dealer service, etc. Looking at the feedback, she decides not to buy the vehicle from the dealers, who have not been able to service customers well. She also looked at the customers feedback about the warranty offered by the manufacturers and decided to pose a question or two to the e-commerce web site users. These questions were answered within some hours and by the end of 2 days, she had answers for her questions from the customers. At that point of time, she noticed that the web site also offers expert advice and so she asks the same questions to the experts in the web sites. After being totally satisfied with the answers, she decides to go ahead and make the final payment.

The e-commerce web site also is connected to secured payment site through which she can make her payment using secured (digitally secured) web sites. Bharati was wondering how fast the entire research, selection, customization, financing, test drive, and final payment has taken place. In contrast, her father Hrishikesh spent days or weeks looking for new cars, and still not end up with one he really wanted.

How likely is the above scenario? What would need to be done, when, by whom? Who would gain and who would lose?

In this case, we describe a preliminary exploration of these issues. We argue that the Internet-mediated scenario described above will come about only if several other major changes in the auto industry occur as well. That is, in order to be able to buy a car through e-commerce channel, the car manufacturers have to provide relevant information to the web site. Even, before they declare the arrival of new models to the media, these manufacturers would have listed the forthcoming models under the section 'New Arrivals'. Customers who would like to own for certain features which are not available in the present models, can check in the section 'new arrivals' to know about the forthcoming models.

In order to be able to use full potential of e-commerce, the organizations need to put in place a proper strategy in collaboration with partners. This case exemplifies that. The web site carwale.com and cardekho.com are e-commerce sites where different manufacturers have tied up with the web sites to provide information so that the consumers get one stop solution. Different manufacturers have come up with different financing options which are shared with the consumers through these web sites. The test drive schedule, delivery of the accessories and final delivery are all aligned with the e-commerce strategy. In a way, these two sites are similar to the way we buy a computer today (online, with the consumer specifying components, software, and services provided by different firms). Corresponding to the customized requirements the production systems need to be flexible and tuned to the customer requirements. If in future the cars need to be "built to order" as personal computers are today, then it would require large changes in product development (a more modular product architecture, with more standardized or common parts across models). In the supply chain the suppliers will have larger role in designing, building, delivering, and possibly even installing modular parts. The e-commerce web sited that would serve as a conduit of information between consumers, designers, and assembly plants, would derive revenues primarily from the provision of services rather than from vehicle sales.

In India, given the present condition where mass marketing of automobiles is the business model, this is a daunting prospect. This will require overcoming the infinitely greater complexity of automotive product designs, customizing and inducing flexibility in production processes, and supply chains. It would also require change in attitude for the customers, who would like to select everything (starting from color of the vehicle to accessories and finance options) online rather than traditional face-to-face discussion mode. In India, where the customers always look for value for money, this can be possible only if the web site based sales can provide discounts compared to direct sales.

E-commerce will still have a very large impact on the auto industry even if the "build-to order" vision is not realized. At a conceptual level, the e-commerce is a powerful tool for promoting fast, asynchronous communication among large groups of people, without a need to invest in physical assets. Even in the present case, the automobile manufacturers have not spent anything for developing or maintaining the web site. The only investment has been in that of partnering with e=commerce web sites. This strategy of partnering with e-commerce web sites is seen as having two types of impacts: (1) aggregation of buyers and suppliers; and (2) facilitation of information exchange (The Economist, March 2000). Since the automotive market in India is already so large and still expanding, the aggregation benefits of the e-commerce will be high in this industry.

Ultimately, the challenge for automakers will be to provide configuration choices without increasing complexity which while providing the customers the necessary ability to choose what is really important to them will not increase the cost of production. With an early proliferation of B2C automotive buying services on the Web, many observers argued that removing dealers would be the strategy for vehicle manufacturers (similar to Dell, where it ships final products directly to customers). But it appears that supply chain through dealers will continue to exist but slowly more and more information will be shared in e-commerce web sites. Even with advancement of technology, seeing, touching, and driving the product are still crucial to the decisions for purchase. As the industry is in buyers market, margins on vehicle sales are being eroded. The differentiation factor between manufacturers lies not in features of the vehicles rather at service levels of service provided to the customers. In the process the entire chain of delivery needs to be tuned toward servicing the customers. This approach can be made easier through web sites (e-commerce sites) by defining service level agreements well in advance. Thus, in the scenario, the dealership becomes the place to initiate or reinforce the customer relationship, not the focal point of the purchase transaction as it was earlier. With such a major shift in the roles of dealers, their ability to link a customer's order with a production process and then providing the required customer support will make customers loyal to the manufacturers.

To make the automobile industry completely dependent on e-commerce sites, the manufacturers have to adopt modular product design as enabler of "Built-to-Order". Similar to the approach adopted by "Dell Direct", this e-commerce oriented strategy would standardize modules. These module oriented manufacturing will result in reduction in manufacturing cost while increasing productivity. The manufacturers of these modules will innovate new modular products with high-end functionality. However, it is not that easy to comprehend such a situation in India given the investments already made by ancillary OEM units.

Review Questions

1. What are the differences between traditional and e-commerce based car sale?
2. How can one do research on available car models using technology?
3. What are the limitations of e-commerce web site in automobile industries?
4. Discuss, if in future, e-commerce can make 'build-to-order' cars in India.

8.8 Case: Cafe Coffee Day

Amalgamated Bean Coffee Trading Company Ltd sells coffee through a retail division known as Cafe Coffee Day (CCD). The turnover of CCD is more than INR 350 crore and has been awarded ISO 9002 for its process orientation. It exports coffee to USA, Europe, and Japan and has plans to expand further and uses coffee produced from coffee estates mostly owned by itself. It has different divisions such as Coffe Day fresh and ground, coffee day express, coffee day take away, coffee day exports and coffee day perfect. From six outlets in initial 5 years, it has grown aggressively by using technology. Using its e-commerce web sites, it wants to become a fast food leader (quick service restaurants) and to take Barista head on. As it opens new franchises all over the places, the challenge will be to retain the flavor of 'meeting place'; this CCD plans to achieve through technology.

On a given day, customers at a Cafe Coffee Day outlet can enjoy their espressos and cappuccinos even as they access the Internet from their laptop computers, without having to attach a telephone line. Using wi-fi technology, the customers can carry their business as if they are in a cyber cafe while sipping hot stimulating coffee. Bangalore's first cyber cafe—circa 1996—is now India's first wireless cyber hotspot for the general public. The catch line is 'you surf, as you slurp'. Waiters in these outlets take orders using smart handheld machines, which connects to the web site that has details of available food items, cost, etc. The machine, when connected to the e-commerce site, also tells him approximate time that it would take to complete the order. Once the order is discussed, he just sends the signal to the site that immediately transfers the order to the kitchen. Simultaneously, as the order is being placed on the table, the web site also calculates total cost of the order and prepares an itemized bill for the customer. At the end, when the customer is ready to pay the bill, the invoice is presented at the table. This system reduced total ordering time compared to traditional approach. Prior to integrating the hand held devices to the e-commerce site, a waiter had to move several times (sometimes even up to six times) to complete the ordering process.

As the order gets placed, the web site also does inventory management, where the quantity sold is removed from the available quantity. Depending on the re-order level, the web site orders for replenishment. The replenishment is done through the central server, where all such replenishment orders are aggregated. If the order needs to be ordered from a particular vendor, then a purchase order is prepared and the same is transmitted to the vendor. This helps in bulk ordering from the vendors. Bulk ordering has advantage that CD can negotiate better terms and conditions from the vendors. Once ordered and confirmed by the vendors, the central web site, triggers its logistic module to transport the consignment to different locations.

Intel, the world's leading chip maker, chose the ambience of the Lavelle Road Coffee Day for the South India launch. Using its "Centrino technology", the combo of mobile processor, associated chip set and the Wireless Network connection, approach to 'coffee experience' has been changed in CCD. As a result, waiters can hold small, wireless devices which increase productivity. Major notebook makers including IBM, Acer, Toshiba, and HP now offer Centrino-powered wireless LAN enabled notebooks. Wipro became the first Indian company to launch a Centrino-based portable PC—its 'Little Genius C Series'. All of them offer the technology at different locations in CCD.

To increase its customer loyalty, CCD has introduced smart cards with magnetic strips. These cards stores all the past records related to a particular customer. During visit to the CCD outlet, if customer offers this card to the waiter, then the staff at the outlet swipes on the hand held device and comes to know about the preferences of the customer. Points are accumulated for each order and credited to the customer's account. Customer can redeem these points against purchase of merchandise from the stores. Also, customer feedback (both complaints and appreciations) are stored in the card. These are available to the front staff while serving the customers. These feedbacks come in handy for customer care department which would act on different feedback received from the customers.

In Feb 2011, Cafe Coffee Day launched an integrated initiative with social networking sites to increase customer loyalty. Loyal customers can register in social network site 'Foursquare' and get discounts in CCD. A customer can visit 'Foursquare' and he can get a 15 % discount on your 3rd check-in. With this offer,*Cafe Coffee Day is the first Indian Brand on foursquare to have its own Brand Page*—http://foursquare.com/CafeCoffeeDay! Using e-commerce site, CCD stores location of residence for its customers. CCD had tied up with Nokia last year for a 2-month long location-based advertising campaign where it was targeting consumers based on their location and then prompting them to drive to the nearest CCD outlet. Nokia users with models like N97 and above were served CCD ads on the weather or events page. Clicking on the ad gave users two options—click2web which took them to CCD's social networking site page and click2route which directed users to the nearest CCD. Now with sites like four-square which keep a tab on customer's location, CCD e-commerce capabilities leverage these to serve ads or promotional offers at any particular location. Even though the user base is not huge as of now and audience type is quite niche but this definitely seems to be one of the interesting newer ways to reach out to the consumers on the move. CCD hopes that this niche will actually increase its loyalty base. In future, CCD plans to integrate with other promotion triggers from different brands and offer its customers more options to redeem their loyalty points. All these promotions are available to its customers on its web site. Also, with acceptability of more similar services like 'location based advertise-ments' customers will be attracted toward the site more often.

Review Questions

1. Describe CCD's business model? What is unique about its strategy?
2. What are the approaches that CCD has undertaken to implement the strategy?
3. How e-commerce based approach has benefitted the customers?
4. Can e-commerce be used to consolidate its business and still be able to expand?
5. CCD wants to provide a 'local coffee' ambience in all the outlets without variation. Can it achieve this principle? Explain.
6. What is target audience for CCD and how does CCD want to increase the loyalty?

8.9 Summary

In this chapter, we discussed about role of e-commerce in a multichannel systems. Even though many organizations are moving toward e-commerce for better return on investments, still some industries will require staying put with multichannels. Hence, the role of e-commerce in the multichannel system is critical to improve effective conversion rate and also to make sure that no lead or information falls through cracks. E-commerce can use different tools to automate the integration process. By automating, e-commerce can help in improving predictability, sustainability and accuracy of results. By having the best channel resource at every step of the selling cycle the average cost of sales can drop from that witnessed in traditional multichannel system.

8.10 Review Questions

1. What do you understand by multichannel system?
2. How can you use e-commerce for effective integration of multichannels?
3. What are the benefits of e-commerce in multichannel system?
4. What are the tools that can be used while automating e-commerce portals?

Chapter 9
E-Commerce Portal Design Strategy

9.1 Learning Objectives

At the end of the chapter, the students would learn

- The need to design e-commerce portal
- A framework to design the portal for effective channel management
- Implementation strategy for the portal.

9.2 Need for E-Commerce Portal

Traditionally, the USA has been at the forefront for adopting technology. Be it in the field of healthcare, aviation, education, etc., the USA has been the first to recognize the need for implementing technology and automating their business processes. For e-commerce, the USA almost started the revolution, and is a pioneer in e-commerce portal design, implementation and providing services. Many of these initiatives have given big benefits while many have not. On one hand, there have been good success stories while there have been failures. Hence, we need to understand the success mantra and then use the failures to fine-tune our approach. While there is no doubt about the benefits of e-commerce, still the need needs to be assessed properly. The assessment should lead to business alignment which will make them sustainable.

During the period of dot-com bust e-commerce was at its growth phase. E-commerce concept started in the mid-nineties, gaining acceptance rapidly through 1999. The stock exchanges reacted favorably for e-commerce developers, venture capitalists were ready to fund the entrepreneurs, shares traded at high levels, which made market capitalization for these organizations very high. However, the bubble burst in early 2000 and the prices of shares tumbled to a fraction of their previous

S. Mohapatra, *E-Commerce Strategy*, Springer Texts in Business and Economics,
DOI: 10.1007/978-1-4614-4142-7_9,

values and funding ended. During a period of 18 months from early 2000 till late 2001 were tough for the entire business community and all including e-marketers, investors or financial institutions were troubled by the US recession. In the year 2000, an estimated 7,000–10,000 companies engaged in e-commerce activities received funds; but most of them (almost more than 500) companies were shut down within a year. Out of the rest e-commerce sites that were funded, more than 1,000 companies were taken over by conglomerates at cheap rates. But still, the concept of e-commerce survived and went on making waves.

The e-commerce channel became a good source of revenue and increased market share for many organizations (who adopted the channel). Gradually, in one group or another, it became apparent e-commerce was surviving and growing every year. During the same period, the terrorist attack on twin towers (a phenomenon known as 7/11). This attack on twin towers made many companies to close their business for quite sometime and some never recovered. Those who were housed in the tower and could recover were largely Internet based organizations that had planned and executed their disaster recovery plan. Particularly, it was easy for the organizations that had e-commerce portal as part of their channel strategy. These companies could not only withstand the attack and subsequent disaster, but also regrouped faster. It was also found that these companies could comply with different statutory requirements easily and were quite at ease while adopting changes in the regulations as well. They were also least affected during corporate accounting scandals. The e-commerce recovery continued, with better results in the business to customer sector. The hype of dot-com bust is over, but e-commerce remains an essential and growing part of the organizations. The Forrester prediction of worldwide online revenues amounting to $3.2 trillion by 2004, was based on heady prospects in 1999, and has since been revised to $217.8 billion by 2007 and in 2003 to $105 billion by Jupiter research.

9.3 Lessons Learned

E-companies successful today fall into several categories. There are those who became market leaders—Amazon, eBay—by starting big at the right time, and by continuing to invest heavily in technology. There are those with forward-looking managements that have integrated Intranets, e-commerce portals, customer relationship management (CRM), and enterprise resource planning (ERP). These portals not only provide with far reaching one-stop solution for logistics as well as complete buying experience; they also help the customers to choose their products based on their past buying history. Thus, it is important that the e-commerce portal is designed to give optimum benefits to all the players and should be aligned with business model. Design of e-commerce portals should be done keeping these things in mind. The portal should deliver value to all its stakeholders.

9.4 Delivering Value Through E-Commerce Portal

From the year 2005, e-commerce portals became popular as a way to consolidate IT infrastructure and reduce costs in maintaining them while being able to meet all the requirements. There are many organizations that have numbers of portals, each catering to different need of the business such as human resource (HR) portal, finance portal, marketing portal, etc. Most often, portals were designed to be used by Internal employees only viz. for accessing HR benefits information, IT help desks, corporate communications, collaborative workspaces, and departmental information, etc. Now, companies face difficulty justifying further investments in these internal projects as tech-wary businesses question the value of "better access to information."

However, the chief information officer (CIO) has to deliver the required return on investment for each and every portal that is maintained by the organization. He (the CIO) is asked to justify existence of each portal and provide the value to the stakeholders. In such a situation a focused portal strategy helps companies build consensus among business stakeholders, ensure downstream adoption of portal applications, and ultimately avoid overspending on portal implementations. The approach should be able to align the business model with technology investment and thus ensure that the investment gives the desired result. For this to happen it is wiser to prepare an e-commerce portal strategy first and then implement it. Successful e-commerce portals invest more in upfront portal strategy and focus business cases on high-value opportunities. The strategy should look at the different aspects of the business model such as fostering closer relationships with partners, reducing costs to serve existing customers, and opening up new potential revenue streams before taking decision on technology.

9.5 Aligning Business Model with Portal Strategy

As the recession hit industry is slowly looking up, new avenues are unfolding. It is predicted that there could be 30 % growth rate for most organizations (in retail industry) and many of them are looking at the e-commerce portal strategy to increase their market strategy. These companies will either buy new software or upgrade existing software to match the business model. The risk of adopting this strategy will be resistance to acceptance by existing employees, long gestation period, etc. However, companies purchasing or upgrading portals cannot afford the high implementation costs, low employee adoption rates, and questionable business cases. This requires a proper risk management plan, and an effective change management strategy needs to be adopted. It also requires selecting the right program leader, understanding the business context in which the portal operates, and taking a balanced approach to prioritization and change management. The following sections give an approach for designing successful e-commerce portal.

9.5.1 Creating a Steering Committee

CIOs are now responsible for success of new portals and they need to provide justification for the investments. They (CIOs) must consider business users as his partners rather than just end-users of the portals. This thought process will make it sure that the CIO designs the portal with end-users as partners. This implies that the portals are no longer solely the domain of the IT department. Thus, the portal designing steering body should be represented from different functions and steering committees should be empowered to take decisions on behalf of the management.

9.5.2 Allocate a Leader for the Committee

A heavyweight program manager, preferably CIO, with cross-functional knowledge should head the committee. He should also have good communication skills, interpersonal skills and leadership qualities so that he can keep the team together. He should be able to set priorities, ensuring ongoing sponsorship, and remove organizational road blocks. However, portal programs must find a "heavyweight" program manager with cross-functional knowledge to help catalyze change effectively. This heavyweight manager must drive not only the thinking but also help define the process. The best leader is the one who would have experience working in one or more business lines, general portal technology knowledge, and a trusted relationship with the IT team responsible for the portal.

9.5.3 Alignment with Business Goal

The steering committee should focus on the strategic objective of the portal and align with the business goal. The strategic goals should be defined in terms of achievable, measurable business goals such as increase in productivity because of usage of the portal, reduction in delivery time to the customer by 7 %, etc. By this the members of the committee are challenged with finding the right definition of strategic goals that would feasible and also technically possible. The committee should also have time bound goals to achieve which will instill confidence among the stakeholders. When companies put excessive focus on the committee, decision making becomes overly bureaucratic and slows the program's progress. The members of the steering committee can include personnel from strategic direction to feature design, systems architecture, user interface design, and rollout planning. A central committee can realistically engage in and add value to all of the decisions necessary during the course of a portal program. This approach will result in success even if the members are not from the same department with direct reporting relationship.

9.5.4 Senior Management Commitment

The steering committee can provide much needed visibility and influence across the company. When time comes to marshal resources for managing portal content, senior committee members should facilitate resources such as money (budget support), availability of dedicated persons and availability of other infrastructure. Also, if required, they should facilitate important personal connections between the portal team and the rest of the company. They also need to review the progress and communicate time and again to the rest of the organization that they are solidly behind the committee and wish the committee to be successful.

The senior management also should limit changing the membership of the steering committee too often. "In the course of a 5-year period, 6 senior leadership members rotated through the portal steering committee," an IT manager recently told Forrester. Frequent portal leadership changes lead to widely differing views on the strategic direction of the program. Personalities and individual likes and dislikes have a habit of overshadowing sound business analysis. In addition, portal program members waste valuable time getting new committee members up to speed on prior decisions. To maintain consistency of vision and strategic direction, organizations should try to limit committee membership change to special circumstances—such as employee departures or major reorganizations.

9.5.5 Define Road Map

The design and implementation of e-commerce portals take 2–3 years to design and implement. The senior management in the companies should look at a 2–3-year minimum tenure for steering committee members. This allows time for upfront portal business cases to be developed, tested, and measured against real outcomes that can be used to improve the portal implementation over time. This also helps in maintaining consistencies in decision making process. The project should be broken into different milestones and deliverables at each milestone should be clearly identified and accounted for. The milestones should be reviewed by senior management so that they can track progress of the project. The milestones in the road map are essential as at these points critical decisions can be taken. These critical decisions, such as extra resource requirements, extra budget sanction, etc., can be decided so that the project schedule is adhered to. At these points also decisions on risk mitigations should be made so that they can effectively be deployed.

9.5.6 Understand As-Is and To-Be Processes

The portal team should understand both present practices and the state of affairs they want to be. To understand the desired state of affairs (which is also known as To-be process), the team needs to understand macro-level issues such as the desired business model, market potential, factors that affect market conditions, and competitive factors. The team also needs to understand the competencies of the organization at present, its weaknesses and which departments require access to which applications and the types of content that will drive the department toward the desired stage. Strategizing for the portal will require balancing between the desired stage and present capabilities. It should be clear, who are the end-users of the portal and what are their expectations. What are their business processes and how can the new portal help them to carry out their daily transactions. These basic questions start to tease apart who are the primary constituent groups that the portal will serve. The answers should drive decisions regarding how content and features get targeted to each group and which groups will be likely portal adopters.

While deciding the to be process, the team should understand the company's strategic business objectives such as where the company want to position itself, who would be the competitors, will there be a need for new infrastructure for using the portal. It should also address issues such as prioritization of business processes in the new scenario, new work flow that might be required to be developed. Other points such as what core functions and processes are likely to deliver value if offered through a portal, and how will these change in importance over time? The team must recognize which initiatives will generate the optimum value to the stakeholders and which will delay achieving the stated business goals. For example, for a telecom operator in India, an e-commerce portal designed for call center executives will save few seconds in handling calls. This will improve customer satisfaction, and also can increase the potential of selling more "value added products" to the customers. This could translate into millions in savings as well as remarkable improvement in revenue.

9.5.7 Define Stakeholders Expectations

Before the start of the e-commerce portal, all the stakeholders should be identified. The detailed identification of stakeholders will help in increasing their involvement at the design stage which will reduce rework later on. This involvement also expedites change management efforts and smoothes negotiations between different players. Thus, it can be seen that the portal initiatives are less about technology and more about change management. In contrast, an IT initiative will target a specific function and features (e.g., financial systems) and will not worry about stakeholders' involvement. Designing and implementing e-commerce portals will impact multiple business units and/or functional groups and will involve change management. Managing change means meeting expectations of the stakeholders, iteratively problem solving their issues, and introducing change incrementally.

9.5.8 Define Measurement Systems

Measurements are quite necessary to quantitatively determine the success of the design of e-commerce portal. It will be advisable to determine and define these metrics before the start of design activities. The definition of these metrics needs to be accepted by all stakeholders. Examples are e-commerce usage metrics, ease of use, number of transactions per hour, number of hits per day, number of registered users, etc. Some e-commerce sites also use metrics such as demographic profile of the users, amount spent during each visit, amount of time spent per visit to the site, etc. These will all yield insights that can drive portal design. Metrics also provide objective, powerful insights that can help change entrenched assumptions about how users behave and interact with the company's portal. These metrics will help to set the expectations from each stakeholder.

9.5.9 Maintainability

These include everything from bug fixes, incremental technology enhancements, and software upgrades to new types of content and transactional service improvements. Enhancements such as enabling single sign-on and improving ease of navigation from one window to another. A focus on high visibility quick-wins, such as look-and-feel upgrades, will add incremental value for end-users and act as the cash cow of continued executive sponsorship. The choice of platform, software and system integration should be such that the total cost of ownership (TCO) will be the least. TCO is the cost involved in purchasing hardware, software now along with training cost, upgrade cost, etc. Thus, the team while strategizing for the portal needs to look at the cost factor for future and decide on technology and system integration. They also need to look at the savings made because of reducing call center volume by deploying self-service access to customers and cutting accounts receivable cycles by introducing transactional bill-payment and remittance services through the customer portal. Successful e-commerce portals should look at the cost involved while developing these applications for the portal versus savings in the future.

The design team should also look at designing new capabilities that could be offered through the portal. Using standard third-party software (which can be integrated to the portal), common features such as self account, content and document management capabilities will help customers to manage their own account. This will free up valuable portal maintenance resources to focus on other high priorities.

9.5.10 Cross-Functional Integration for Future

The portal design should consider this as a system integration approach rather than stand alone feature for online transaction only. The design should be able to integrate portal technology, enterprise search, content management, asynchronous collaboration, process management, and work flow management systems. For example, the team can design the portal only for sales department. This will limit the capability and the organization will still require information to flow among different departments using other available means. During the design of the portal, this thoughtful approach will help to integrate different functions and will help in data integrity and simultaneous publication of information for all concerned stakeholders. The design should be such that if required, external partners are also involved (such as logistics, suppliers, etc.) can be given access to the portal through extranet. At the time of design, complex composite applications for several functions can be developed that can integrate several back-end systems. The IT industry and portal technology has reached a state in which the portal can accommodate virtually any integration, feature set, or user interface convention.

9.5.11 Business Versus Technology

The approach mentioned in this chapter for designing portal strategy has been more of a business approach than that of technology. The present and future e-commerce portals would provide business solutions and not technology solutions. Hence, the portal design strategy should focus on the business processes rather than worry about technology. This approach will avoid common portal pitfalls. Aligning all constituents involved in a portal initiative against a common set of goals requires strong executive leadership as well as pragmatic program management. The team needs to understand business priorities and expend resources to develop portal for those business processes that would provide immediate returns. These business processes, when executed through e-commerce portals, will provide quantifiable savings, revenue opportunities, and/or strategic importance to the company. This also will increase portal usage after implementation.

9.6 Role of CIO in Portal Design

In the new economy, a new job title has been prominent in many “forward looking” organizations. These organizations take lot of initiatives in IT infrastructure and use IT to support business goals and objectives. To derive maximum benefits from IT investment and align IT goals with vision and mission of he organization, all these initiatives and investment decisions are centralized. The role that heads this centralized IT department is known as CIO. CIO is a job title given to the person in an organization responsible for the information technology and computer systems that support organization goals. As IT has become the strategic tool for business models in new economy, the CIO is viewed as the key contributors to formulating strategic goals. Usually, a CIO proposes the information technology an enterprise will need to achieve its goals and then works within a budget to implement the plan. Typically, a CIO is involved with analyzing and reworking existing business processes, with identifying and developing the capability to use new tools, with reshaping the enterprise's physical infrastructure and network access, and with identifying and exploiting the enterprise's knowledge resources. Many CIOs head the enterprise's efforts to integrate the Internet and the World Wide Web into both its long-term strategy and its immediate business plans. These CIOs head the initiatives to integrate Internet and the World Wide Web into both its long term strategy and long term business plans.

The managing strategy implementation is as important as strategy design. It involves guiding, organizing, driving, leading and adjusting. The principles to implement other business strategies and portal strategy are the same. The portal strategy roll-out is not the job of CIO alone but it is organization's responsibility. The top management team must own it and support. The top management should endorse and participate in using the system. The roll-out of portal strategy is like effecting any organizational change. It needs good planning and careful steps. Enabling people and putting organization structure in place is the first step in implementation. Knowing well the behavior of people that they resist the changes being proposed by others, where as demand for change to break monotony and make progress, managers must create a strategy of people driven change. And this is achieved through their participation in decision making. The management team including CIO must plan to face certain unfavourable situations while implementation. For this to be successful, an effective risk management plan should be in place before implementation. This can impact portal service strategy as well.

Every portal strategy implementation has its inherent risks, which can surprise, at times. These risks can be from the area of business, business drivers and priorities, people including skills, technology and implementation approach and infrastructure. Sometimes they are so severe that they change the direction itself. Merger and acquisition, financial crisis like the one in 2008, invasive and compelling technologies like remote IT services and outsourcing after Internet technology maturity are the few examples. No one had thought about financial meltdown in 2008, which impacted most of the strategies and changed the direction altogether for many. Therefore, a risk management strategy must go hand-in-hand with implementation, where by they are regularly watched and actions to mitigate are initiated in timely manner.

Portal strategy is for certain purpose. It is in the interest of the organization that they identify the goals in measurable form for different stage/phase and time blocs. This provides a sense of direction, helps in identifying deviation, and maintains alignment. Some could be IT internal, which CIO can review but some are external to IT functional area, where business managers must be involved. This also includes economic value and ROI from IT.

Recent data shows that portal projects have failed because of weak alignment with business goals, improper budget justification, and more stress on choice of technology rather than on business processes. Most portal projects get dumped entirely as responsibility of IT department alone and, as a result, suffer from misalignment with business needs, and low adoption. It also results in portals that have lot of features which are mostly unutilized. To avoid this chaotic end state, large firms must make portals a priority for the whole business, not just IT. The role of steering committee drawn from different functions is quite important here.

The role of CIO leaders is quite challenging. To be successful, these CIOs should have combined role of enterprise architects, project managers, and business analysts. These jobs depend on communication skills, business process knowledge, and project management expertise, all of which depend on education and training. No matter how good the technology implementation may be, the biggest challenge in using e-commerce portals from traditional brick and mortar approach is a matter of change of culture. The CIOs should be able to anticipate resistance to process change and deal with it through various methods, including communications, meetings, and focus groups.

9.7 Cloud Computing and E-Commerce Portal Design

Today, the world is moving toward cloud computing, where resources are available either on a private or public cloud and the organization needs to use it as per its convenience and business requirements. In such a scenario, the design approach for e-commerce portals will undergo some changes. No longer the organization would require spending time and efforts for designing the portal, rather they will adopt best practices, tools that are already available in the portal. This approach has made several impacts on the e-commerce portals. One of the biggest effects that these cloud computing based e-commerce portals have had on business is in forcing adaptation of best practices, global standardization of tools and procedures. An organization can create a portal easier and faster than before, and use it faster too. A thriving organization in retail sector can link its business processes with several other partners in other countries. Thus, these firms can immediately adopt most standard business functions, allowing entrepreneurs to concentrate on their core strengths.

Because of cloud computing, e-commerce business isn't just more globalized, but more open to newcomers. New enterprises spring up who are using e-commerce channel more often than before and want to capitalize on niches in human nature that can now be tapped thanks to new technology advances. Since many decisions by then will be automated, using data mines and artificial intelligence analysis to spot market potential, the e-commerce strategists will have to provide enough business logic to these portals so that automated decisions can be as accurate as possible. This is a natural consequence of the emergence of the information economy, where the strategists will be moving to next orbit rather than get bogged down by technology issues.

The trend that we notice today will also standardize the funding and resource holders. Advanced materials will be of high value, but their development is often expensive, requiring large R&D establishments and often the use of exotic raw materials. These standardization will force the strategists to look beyond operational aspects and strategize on business processes, business models that can be supported by the cloud based e-commerce portals. Still some of the new industries will lend themselves to customized business practices, but most, who want to be agile, will rather embrace cloud e-commerce portals. These enterprises will be best suited to market niches, where small-volume manufacturing or niche talent and skills pay off. But for global industry and services, cloud based global resources will be needed—the huge server farms, big factories, mines and shipping fleets.

9.8 Case: Walmart.com—Not Always Rosy

This case deals with failure of e-commerce in retail space. Wal-Mart is well known for its traditional retail business. But still Wal-Mart's online experience is proof that to be successful in e-commerce, different strategy needs to be adopted. Even though Wal-Mart is successful in the brick and mortar world, it doesn't guarantee corresponding success in e-commerce. Traditionally, Wal-Mart is a known as a giant, the world's largest retailer, which has weathered many economic downturns. It has more than 3,300 stores in US and it employs more than 1 million workers, which means about 1 out of every 300 Americans is a Wal-Mart employee.

"It's a real category killer," claims Gartner research director Geri Spieler, who says that that Wal-Mart's success is "what everyone is trying to compare to." It has become a benchmark in retail business and any company that wants to be a supplier has started using the Wal-Mart EDI (electronic data interface). So Wal-Mart can replenish its stock—straight from wholesalers—faster than you can say "discount retail." Wal-Mart is still expanding its product line as well has started opening in geographies outside USA. Its new stores will augment its capacity to offer more products to the customers. This will increase its consumer base. Wal-Mart has opened 14 stores in India (as of December 2011).

E-Commerce in Wal-Mart

When it ventured into e-commerce, Wal-Mart's dominant place in traditional retail was expected to provide it success with e-commerce. But analysts say Walmart.com is distinctly back of the pack in terms of total online sales, as suggested by different industry figures. The reason for such failure is Wal-Mart's offline retail success isn't replicated online. In 2010, Wal-Mart consolidated its e-commerce activities around the world in a Global e-commerce Division. This division has 3 goals: 1) develop and execute a global e-commerce strategy; 2) accelerate global online channel growth; and 3) create technology platforms and applications for every Wal-mart market.

Wal-Mart offered e-commerce sales through dedicated online platforms in 7 countries, with the most significant being Walmart.com in the US. ASDA.com, our

UK grocery home shopping network, is now a doing well in online business, serving 97 % of all UK customers. The investments made in these platforms are helping to accelerate growth in other markets, including Brazil and China. The factors that drive shopping behavior were considered to be price, assortment, customer experience, and trust. These attributes are as relevant for e-commerce as they were for brick and mortar industry. However, Wal-Mart could not use the technology that enables and shapes the online transactions. The challenges were to change the strategy for logistics and pricing, changing the mindset of the employees (most of the employees were transferred from physical format retail store to e-commerce business) and using the correct technology to the business partners. Most of the partners were using technologies that were not in synch with that of Wal-Mart; these partners were not willing to invest in new technology (Wal-Mart used technology that had proprietary applications and were expensive). This had impact on mobile based transactions and location based services. Its competitors were able to use technologies to provide a variety of customized services to the online customers.

One of the differences in traditional and online shopping at Wal-Mart was that customers who shop at Wal-Mart would go to the store with families. The stores at Wal-Mart cater more to people with large families and people who aren't in much of a hurry. In contrast, an average online shopper wants to save time through online shopping and will not mind paying more prices for a quality product. He would rather have choices that would allow him to pick up consignments without having to spend more time in front of the screen. These shoppers usually expect the items shown to him based on his tastes and thus spend less time in surfing the site.

In addition to this, many employees who were appointed in e-commerce venture could not take decisions as to which merchandize need to be put in the store (http://247wallst.com/2012/01/17/walmarts-e-commerce-woes-cannot-be-solved-by-a-new-online-ceo/). The pricing strategy for online shopping at Wal-Mart was never advantageous compared to Target and Amazon. Also, as per many analysts, the members of the online retail segment are "technology laggards." Wrong choice of technology made integration with business partners difficult. Also, customers could not get a user friendly site compared to other e-commerce sites.

In the 1999 holiday season, it had to warn consumers that it could not guarantee delivery of orders placed after December 14—unusual for a retailer with such well-developed infrastructure. Wal-Mart, created a separate company called Walmart.com with Accel Ventures (as technical partner) in January 2000. This was meant to remain focused on online marketing and gain market share in online retail business. But, in what was widely seen as an unusual tactic, Walmart.com shut down for a month in the fall of 2000 maintenance activities. This was a shock to its customers, who would have liked to visit the site regularly for availing different offers during peak holiday sale period. This was unusual and drew a lot of flak from consumers; shutting down the site clearly indicated that the e-commerce site was not ready technically for the peak holiday season which undermined web site's credibility. That a major e-tailer would shut down its site in a holiday ramp-up period, instead of readying a platform beforehand, left some industry observers puzzled.

In 2001, Wal-Mart bought back Accel's minority stake, so Walmart.com is once again a wholly owned subsidiary of Wal-Mart. Gartner's Spieler is of the opinion that Accel wasn't doing a good job with it. But, whatever the reason, Walmart.com, with or without outside help, does not appear to have a strategy for moving the site forward.

Lack of Channel Strategy

Based on performance of the e-commerce site (Walmart.com), where there were shut downs periodically, it is clear that the site does not have a good channel strategy for online business. The technology is not stable and cannot take many hits (one visit to the site by a customer is considered as a hit) and will be difficult to scale up the operations. Compared to other competitors (such as Amazon.com), the site still lacks the customer personalization features.

Walmart.com recently launched a Netflix-style DVD rental plan. Users order DVDs through the site and receive them in the mail, keeping them as long they want with no late fees. Considering that Netflix itself has yet to make turn a profit (as of 2010), Walmart.com's new venture cannot be described as a successful forward looking. Here again pricing strategy is different. Instead of deciding on effective pricing strategy, Walmart.com slashes price of everything and anything that it sells through the site. For DVD rentals, Walmart.com is undercutting Netflix's price by about a dollar and also offers service for Internet access. For $9.94 a month, one can buy unlimited dial-up service through Wal-Mart Connect, which is AOL service offered with the Wal-Mart brand. The strategy has been to slash "Internet access" cost by half while offering AOL ISP.

Integration of Online Store with Physical Store

The pricing strategy shows that Walmart.com has made similar pricing strategy of its physical format of selling in stores. It also offers integration of physical store with online business. A customer can choose to replace tires at Walmart.com and have them installed at a local Wal-Mart. The site's pharmacy section lets you place an order to be picked up from a local store. The site also offers customers to see their prescription history online and set up reminders for refills. The site's vision center offers a similar service for contact lenses. Also, on can give photo reels at a local store for developing photos see the finished prints at Walmart.com. Thus, any item can be purchased through online and exchanged at a local store.

With the power of this integration, it has provided unique opportunity to leverage its physical presence to compliment its e-commerce operation. However, it has still a long way to catch its competitors in terms of e-commerce business.

Review Questions?

1. Contrast pricing strategy for Walmart.com with Amazon.com. Also bring out differences in customization strategy for both the sites.
2. What are the lessons learned from Walmart.com strategy?
3. If you were given the responsibility to turn around Walmart.com, what would be your strategy?
4. Is integration of physical and online stores is a good strategy? Please support your answer with reasons.

9.9 Case: FutureBazaar.com

India has topped AT Kearney's annual Global Retail Development Index (GRDI) for the third consecutive year, maintaining its position as the most attractive market for retail investment. The Indian retail market, which is the fifth largest retail destination globally, according to industry estimates is estimated to grow from $330 billion in 2007 to $427 billion by 2010 and $637 billion by 2015. Simultaneously, organized retail which presently accounts for 4 % of the total market is likely to increase its share to 22 % by 2010.

India has one of the largest numbers of retail outlets in the world. Of the 12 million retail outlets present in the country, nearly 5 million sell food and related products. However, organized retail accounts for only 4 % of the total market, offering huge growth potential in this segment.

9.10 Context Overview

With the growing Internet penetration, retailing in India had moved beyond the traditional walls of malls and mom and pop stores to the graphical world of "e-retailing". The traditional brick and mortar model is being replaced by brick and click model and more and more corporate houses are venturing into it. Kishore Biyani's Pantaloons Group has entered this with www.futurebazaar.com. However, the e-retailing business along with the problems faced by traditional retailers brings in additional set of worries about doing business online and with IT being the backbone of this phenomenon; we attempt to seek a remedy by proposing an e-retailing model along with an internationalization strategy for futurebazaar.com

9.11 Introduction

Internet has definitely changed the consumer behavior. The first wave of e-commerce introduced the novel concept of generating business from mouse clicks. Futurebazaar.com also forayed into this business in January 2007 with the aim that it would provide "E-tailing like never done before". The company presently caters to Business-to-Consumers segment and has already clocked a revenue of Rs. 200 million in March 2008. The web site was awarded as "Best Designed Shopping Site" award in 2008 and it has recently added Big Bazaar Unlimited for browsing catalog and placing order over the Internet.

9.12 Stakeholders

Stakeholder	Objectives
Logistic Partner	Delivery from Warehouses to customers (Gati, Bluedart)
Technology Partner	Design, construct, implement state of art technologies (Wipro)
Customer	Quick delivery, low prices, wide variety, user friendly interfaces
Employees	Challenging work, work-life balance
Shareholders	Maximize Return on Investment
Suppliers	Long Term Relationships, High Profitability, Quality product
Government	E-governance, e-banking incentives, Information Technology Act
Financial Institutions/Banks	Incentivize online banking, promote credit card usage

9.12.1 Organization Structure

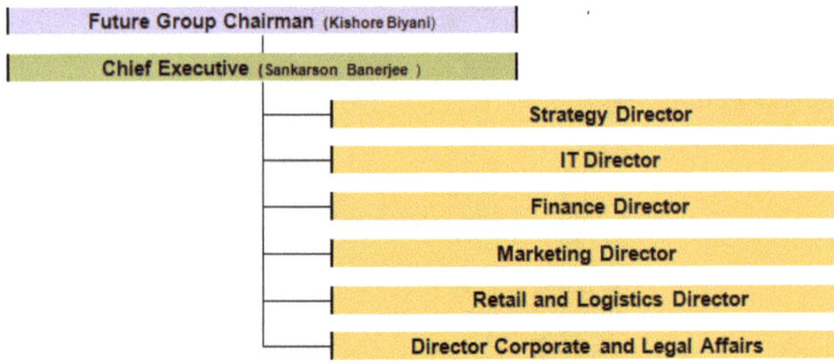

9.13 Vision

To serve our customers and stakeholders by creating and executing future scenarios in the consumption space leading to economic development

9.14 Mission

- To be the trendsetters in evolving delivery formats, creating retail realty, making consumption affordable for all customer segments–for classes and for masses
- To infuse Indian brands with confidence and renewed ambition
- To be efficient, cost-conscious and committed to quality in whatever we do
- To ensure that our positive attitude, sincerity, humility and united determination shall be the driving force to make us successful.

9.15 Industry Analysis

Before commenting about the challenges and opportunities, we decided to do an industry analysis to determine the attractiveness of e-retail industry in India. Porter's five forces framework was used for this along with the RFM analysis as online retailing as a concept started around 2000 and is a recent industry in India. Based on the five forces that determine industry attractiveness, we found the following score

Force	Impact on Business
Supplier Power	Moderate
Customer Power	High
Intensity of Competitive rivalry	Moderate
Threat of New Entrants	Moderate
Threat of Substitutes	High

Forces	Components	Rating	Overall
Supplier Power	Supplier switching costs	High	**Moderate**
	Degree of differentiation of inputs	Moderate	
	Presence of substitute inputs	High	
	Supplier concentration to firm concentration ratio	Moderate	
	Threat of forward integration	Low	
	Cost of inputs relative to selling price of the product	Low	
Customer Power	Buyer concentration to firm concentration ratio	High	**High**
	Bargaining leverage	Moderate	
	Buyer volume	High	
	Buyer switching costs relative to firm switching costs	Moderate	
	Buyer information availability	Moderate	
	Ability to backward integrate	Low	
	Availability of existing substitute products	High	
	Buyer price sensitivity	High	
	RFM Analysis		
	Recency	New	
	Frequency	Moderate	
	Monetary Value	Moderate	
Intensity of Competitive Rivalry	Number of competitors (Limited)	Less	**Moderate**
	Rate of industry growth	High	
	Exit barriers (Cost involved)	Low	
	Diversity of competitors	Moderate	
	Informational complexity and asymmetry	Moderate	
	Level of advertising expense (print, media)	Low	
	Sustainable competitive advantage through improvisation	High	
Threat of New Entrants	Existence of barriers to entry (regulations etc.)	Low	**Moderate**
	Brand equity	Low	
	Switching costs or sunk costs	Moderate	
	Capital requirements	Low	
	Learning curve advantages	High	
	Expected retaliation by incumbents	Moderate	
	Government policies	Low	
Threat of Substitutes	Buyer propensity to substitute	High	**High**
	Relative price performance of substitutes	High	
	Buyer switching costs	Low	
	Perceived level of product differentiation	Moderate	
Industry is "Attractive"			

9.15.1 SWOT Analysis

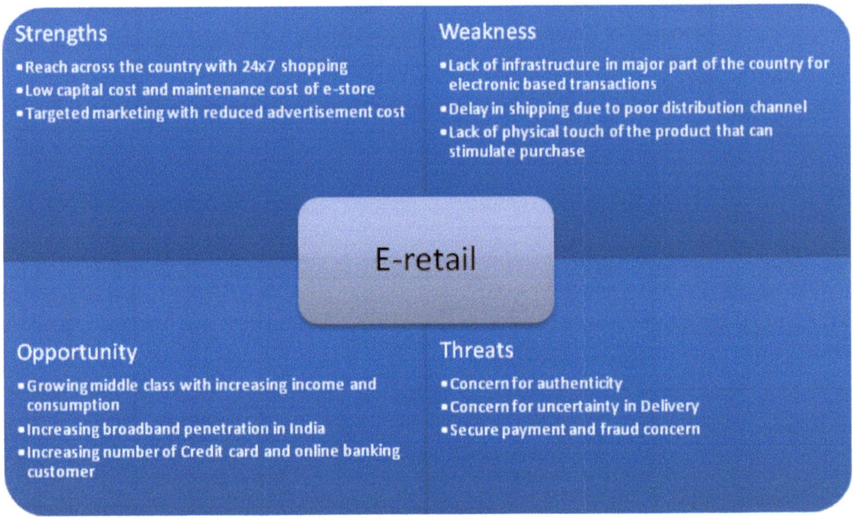

9.16 Corporate Strategy

Based on the analysis, we came up with the some of the corporate level strategy that the firm must target:

- Increasing competition, reducing margins, increasing need for good customer service and continuous operational efficiency improvement
- Customer now looking beyond price and brand and is more demanding
- Strategy to counter issues related to payment security, interactivity and special offer
- Mechanism for proper delivery of products and after sales service

9.17 E-Retailing Model

9.17.1 Developing a Dynamic and Robust E-Retail Supply Chain

For e-retailing to be successful, we need to have an efficient supply chain backbone to serve customers. The e-retailing supply chain proposed in figure will target to combat the challenges seen in the e-retail business.

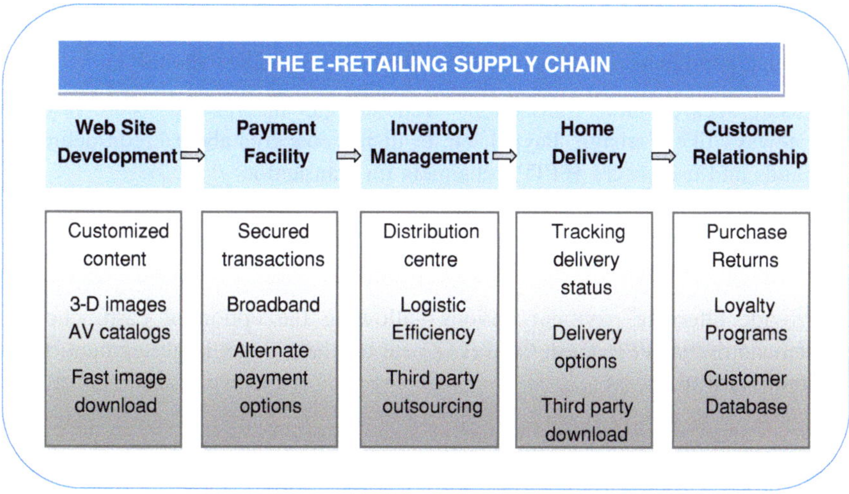

9.17.1.1 Customer Centric Web Design

To increase number of successful web transaction, we should aim at:

1. Simple Navigation structure—minimal step for buying process with facility to resume broken Internet connection link.
2. Light content—web page content should be light to ensure faster download of images at customer's terminal and also in mobiles, PDA's.
3. Customized content with tracking—the site should track past purchases and generate customized discounts or promotions for customers.
4. Detailed product description—detailed product description along with 3D product views will enhance customer satisfaction. Audio visual catalogs for high involvement products will be a stimus to retain customer and remedy the "abandoned card syndrome".

Best e-retail sites w.r.t parameter

Customer need – www.amazon.com

Good Value – www.tesco.com

Engaging – www.adidas.com

Trust – www.ebay.com

Source – UK website reviews

9.17.1.2 Enhancing Payment Facilities

To reduce apprehensions toward online payment, e-retailers should:

1. Ensure secure online transactions—retailers can incorporate secure payment gateways like Verisign, Paypal, etc to dispel concerns about credit/debit card frauds and use secure HTTPS channels for transaction.

E-payment fraud grew 16% in 2007 to $3.6 billion—1.4% of online sales

2. Provide alternate payment options—allowing the option of cash, cheques, demand drafts, VPP, Cash Card (ITZ) etc can help target large segment of non credit card users.

9.17.1.3 Efficient Inventory Management

There is an inherent tradeoff between reach of distribution and logistics efficiency. Big retailers operating on thin margins cannot afford to be on the wrong side of efficiency. Consequently it would be convenient for them to start with cities where they have physical presence.

A pure-play retailer can improve its efficiencies by tying up with a logistics company to avail its warehouses and staff. Collaborating with the right stakeholders would control upfront costs. i.e., futurebazaar.com has it own logistics Future Logistics to take care of logistic requirement.

9.17.1.4 Prompt Customer Delivery

Delivering the product on time and in perfect shape is a challenge for e-retailers. Economies of scale allow bigger retailers to maintain an extensive fleet of vehicles. E-retailers should offer purchase-return options, track delivery status and deliver at predetermined time-slots as desired by customers.

9.17.1.5 Developing Customer Relationships

For ensuring better customer response, following can be done:

1. Prompt conflict resolution—customers would appreciate better service to address their complaints and other concerns.
2. Formulate Loyalty programs—introducing reward schemes for regular customers based on their expenditure.

3. Maintain customer database—a comprehensive database for tracking the purchase behavior and personal details of each customer would give enriching results to the retailer.
4. Contact number and name of person in charge—name of person to contact in case of grievance along with his telephone number will add to the trust and confidence of customers.

9.17.2 Turning Visitors to Customer

One important aspect is to convert a visitor into a customer. Often a customer checks a product and places it on the cart but later discontinues the purchase and leaves the site. This phenomenon known as "abandoned cart syndrome" can be addressed by

- Improving site navigation
- Supplying relevant merchandise information as needed
- Incorporation of help link and interactive facility to stimulate interest
- Improved guarantees (delivery, data security and money back offers)
- Providing offline contact details preferably with name and phone numbers

To generate repeat purchase, e-retailer should inculcate a feeling of confidence and loyalty in its products and offerings. The failure to meet customer expectations can be devastating to e-retailers business and hence need to be addressed by:

- Providing information to granular levels about the product offerings with variety, color, size, etc.
- Payment and settlement issues addressed with high priority and confidentiality of customer information
- Tracking of the delivery of product to know the status of the order in transit
- Using the hybrid retailer model
- Multi channel retailers are making most of the current e-retailing market
- One size fit all strategy for e-retailers will not work

9.17.3 Developing Right IT strategy

Technology has been the backbone of e-commerce and for a sustainable e-retailing model, an IT strategy need to be formed. Although there will be specific strategy for each of the e-tailing firms, we try to bring a snapshot of some of the strategy that will cut across firms and will help in building business and fueling growth.

9.17.3.1 IT Strategy for E-Retailers

- Enhance the web site for better customer experience
  - Maintain consistent user interfaces for all suppliers and customers across geographies
  - Introduce online auctions
  - Flexible payment options by tying up with banks
  - Establish online customer support services with quick SLA
  - Special provisions for large corporate clients

> *E-retailing Best Practices*
>
> www.amazon.com
>
> The biggest Clicks-and-mortar employs **CRM system** to advice customers about new books of likely interest
>
> www.dell.com
>
> Has investment heavily in **staff training** and **customer service** to provide customers with a unique service experience

- Aligning the IT dept with the organization structure
  - Ensure IT Department has appropriate information flow with marketing, sales, operation division
  - Coordinate with finance Department for IT Budget
  - Collaborate with 3PL and achieve seamless integration between their IT systems
  - Integrate IT systems with suppliers
  - Implement CRM and systems for cross-selling products
  - Online advertising and buzz campaign
  - Train employees for making use of IT resources
  - Setting up of Kiosks in popular outlets and shopping joints
  - Maintain disaster recovery and business continuity plan
  - Benchmark IT processes and apply for international quality certifications
  - Implement knowledge management systems
  - Foray into mobile commerce
  - Net-centric model for information sharing environment
  - Information as strategic asset in business intelligence (BI)

9.17.4 Managing E-Retail Operations with Continuous Efficiency

Operations management for e-retailing is a critical issue. The diagram presents the touch points for e-retailing and encompasses all the functions required to handle the operating of e-retail business. We briefly highlight some of the functions undertaken in each of them:

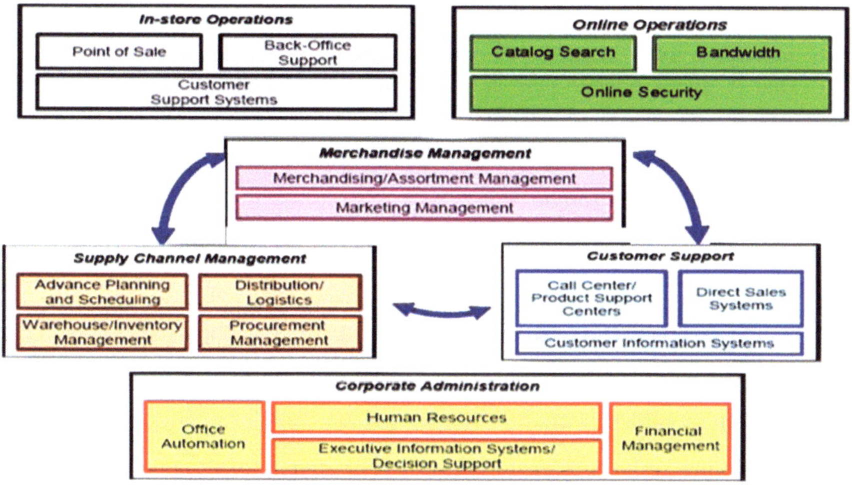

In-store operations—it will be for store purchase and would have functions like point of sale, back-office operations and customer support.
Online operations—operations like catalog search, high bandwidth and online security will be priority.
Merchandise management—will broadly deal with merchandise handling and marketing of product.
Supply chain—will encompass planning, scheduling, procurement, distribution, etc.
Customer support—This is the most important in terms of retaining customer. Product support and customer information system along with Business Intelligence will help in generating sales and growth.
Corporate administration—The corporate admin will have information flow from executive information system (ESS)/decision support system (DSS) to HR and finance for smooth operations and strategic decision making.

The success of existing e-retailers would increase competition and lead to aggressive price-cutting by those who will be struggling to survive. Continuously improving efficiency and passing on benefits to the consumers will be the mantra to survive and thrive. This efficiency will result from robust IT systems, competitive buying and merchandising, logistics and warehouses. Thus, attracting new customers and retaining old one will be a success recipe.

9.17.5 Use of E-Marketing Strategy

No retail business can survive without marketing. However, with the changing rules of the game (vis-à-vis traditional retailing), the need to develop an e-marketing strategy is more than important. Certain strategies that can be used are

- Deploy web analytics
  - Derive data with respect to seeker behavior in web pages and use it to improve activity in site
  - That is, check bounce rate on a web page (% of people who navigate away from a web page without doing any activity available in the web page)
  - Certain web analytics software: IRIS metrics, HitBox, Web trends
- Search engine optimization
  - Ranking well in the organic search results can provide better targeted traffic.
  - Try optimizing the site for highly specific keywords that would indicate readiness to buy or take some kind of desirable action.
  - Focusing on desirable traffic generates better quality sales leads, resulting in more sales.
- Web promotion plan
  - Use reciprocal links to enable visibility through affiliate marketing
  - Update web site content periodically
- Email/post card marketing
  - Targeting right customer segment
  - Updates through email newsletters, advertisements, ezines about offers, discounts, schemes available in web site

9.17.6 Employee Skill Training

Employee are the core strength for this organization and training them for certain skill set will be necessary for better customer experience and service 24 $\times$ 7. Improving employee skills will help in achieving the execution of business strategy—the satisfaction of customers achieving operational efficiency.

The benefits from this exercise will be

- Increased employee productivity
- Improved operational efficiency
- Increased consistency of knowledge across fulfillment network

Indian Information Technology Act - Compliance is necessary in order to safeguard the privacy and personal information of customers (e.g. The money laundering case of Citibank customers by some employees of the BPO company MSource which amounted to around $425,000) and also not indulge in any activities which may be socially unacceptable (e.g. The DPS MMS scandal which was openly sold on Bazee.com site). Complying with the Act would also mean that they cannot sell or auction any third party copyright data without prior permission of the concerned authority (e.g. The sale of Harry Potter books by Bazee.com without the prior permission of the author)

9.18 Internationalization Strategy

Futurebazaar.com will have to make huge FDI investments in order to enter newer geographies.

9.18.1 Need for Internationalization

9.18.1.1 Resource Seeking

- Tie up with suppliers to enhance its length and breadth of product line

9.18.1.2 Market Seeking

- Penetrate to newer market outside India

9.18.1.3 Efficiency Seeking

- Tap low cost suppliers abroad
- Achieve economies of scale
- Establish robust SCM
- Achieve greater synergy with sister retail outlets like Pantaloons, BigBazaar, @ ZONE, Central.

9.18.2 Increasing Internet Usage

The increase penetration of broadband and Internet across the globe has provided e-tailing a sustainable platform to operate and target newer geographies. Some of the fastest growing economies in terms of Internet usage can be the potential markets for the company.

WORLD INTERNET USAGE AND POPULATION STATISTICS					
World Regions	Population (2008 Est.)	Internet Usage (2008)	% Population Penetration	Usage % of World	Usage Growth (2000-2008)
Asia	3,776,181,949	578,538,257	15.30%	39.50%	406.10%
Europe	800,401,065	384,633,765	48.10%	26.30%	266.00%
North America	337,167,248	248,241,969	73.60%	17.00%	129.60%
Latin America/Caribbean	576,091,673	139,009,209	24.10%	9.50%	669.30%
Africa	955,206,348	51,065,630	5.30%	3.50%	1031.20%
Middle East	197,090,443	41,939,200	21.30%	2.90%	1176.80%
Oceania / Australia	33,981,562	20,204,331	59.50%	1.40%	165.10%
WORLD TOTAL	6,676,120,288	1,463,632,361	21.90%	100.00%	305.50%

9.18.3 Existing Player in Online Market

9.18.3.1 International Market

e-bay—World's largest Online marketplace with 89 million users spread over 39 countries. It can be described as a forum for the buyers and sellers. It sold goods worth $60 billion in the year 2007. However, it has a weakness wherein small size trader prevents to take advantage of economies of scale.

Amazon—With a revenue of $15 billion, this is probably the largest online book store with warehouses spread over US, Canada, UK, France, Germany, Japan, and China.

9.18.3.2 Domestic Market

Ebay.in (formerly Bazee.com)—Well established online market with highest penetration in Indian market.

Indiatimes shopping—has the loyalty and brand reputation of the Times Group.

9.18.4 Futurebazaar's Target Range of Products

- Apparel
  - Men
  - Women
  - Infant
  - Sports Wear
- Jewellery
  - Diamond
  - Gold
  - Gems
  - Precious Stones
- Home & Décor
  - Linen
  - Furnishings
  - Security & Safes
- Books
- Movies
- Kitchenware

- Electronics
  - Home Entertainment
  - Mobiles
  - Cameras
  - MP3 players
  - Memory & Storage Devices
  - Computers & Laptops
- Toys & Games
- Consumer Durables
  - Washing Machines
  - Air Conditioners
  - Vaccum Cleaners
- Kitchen Appliances
  - Microwave Owens
  - Food Processors
  - Juicer Mixer Grinder

9.18.5 Potential International Markets

9.18.5.1 Asia

- Japan has strong presence of Online stores and hence should not be targeted
- Absence of strong consolidated online stores though eBay has good presence in Asia
- China mostly used for sourcing and large consumer untapped market exists
- Rest of Asia has large unserved market

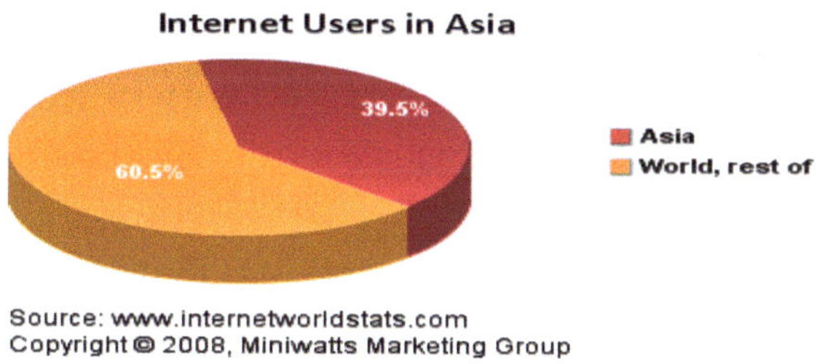

9.18.5.2 Latin America

- Amazon almost non existent in South America with no regional warehouse
- eBay has presence in Brazil and Mexico
- Strong markets exist in Brazil, Mexico and Argentina

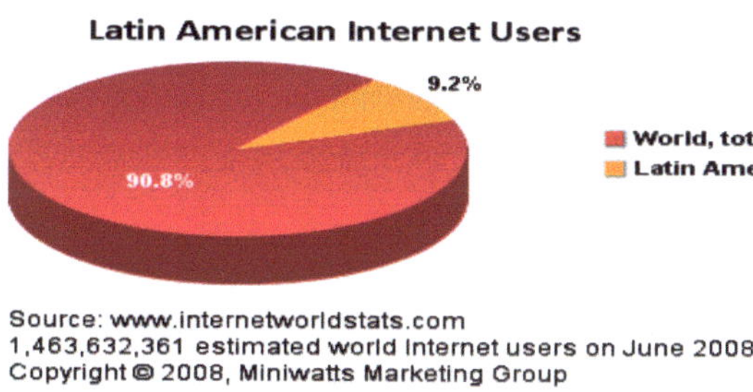

9.18.6 Road Map for Internationalization

The road map for internationalization will be based on the Uppsala model which suggests that instead of leapfrogging into any market, the company goes through certain well thought strategic decision moving a step at a time. For this we suggest

- Strengthening sourcing companies in economies like China with distribution network in India
- Consolidating presence in India
- Spreading distribution across SAARC and ASEAN region
- Opening Retail outlet across Asia
- Entry into South America

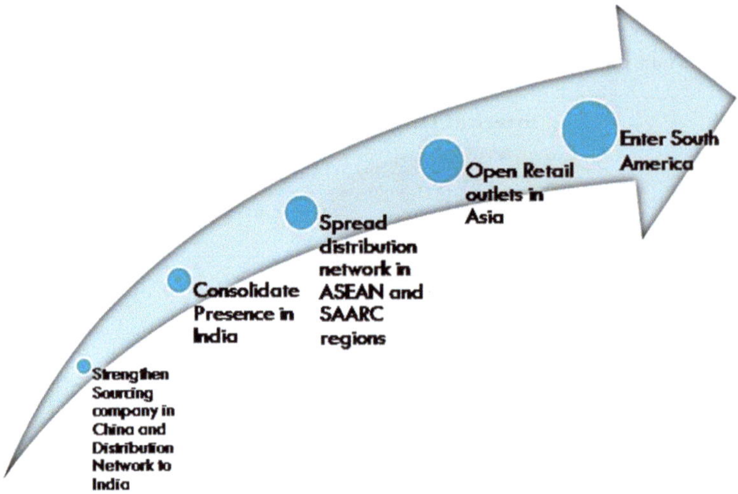

9.18.7 OLI Framework for Internationalization

We have used the ownership, localization and internalization (OLI) framework for suggesting the entry strategy.

9.18.7.1 Strategy for China

- Greenfield investment to establish sourcing company to procure products from Chinese suppliers
- Establish its B2B distribution network from Chinese suppliers to India and other countries
- Strategic alliances with logistics partners for B2C home delivery
- Buy majority stakes in suppliers and backward integrate
- Forward integrate by setting up retail stores like Pantaloons, Big Bazaar

9.18.7.2 Strategy for Rest of Asia and South America

- Strategic alliances with logistics partners for B2C home delivery
- Setting up retail stores

9.19 ROI Framework for Investment Evaluation

The basis of the ROI framework is to match the capital investment with the current rates. Herein high Internet and credit card penetration will lead to increase in number of online customers leading to high sales and revenue.

In terms of capital expenditure, higher IT investment can help increase the reach in a phased manner leading to extensive network and rationalization of capital expenditure.

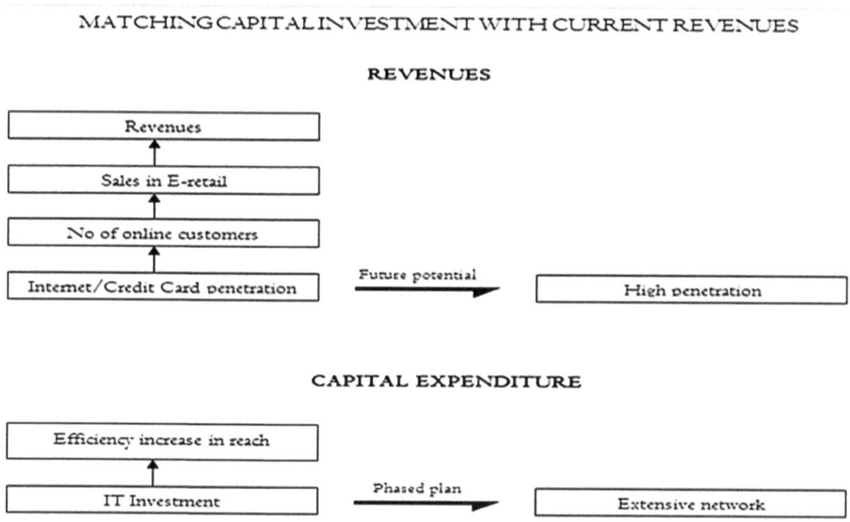

For futurebazzar.com, the revenues have been of the order of Rs. 20 crore in Feb–Mar2008 with 10 % of the revenue from catalog retailing with high use of equity funding.

The expected revenue is expected to cross Rs. 182 crore, with the e-tailing market aimed at $15 billion

9.20 Conclusion

In conclusion, it is apparent that e-tailing offers significant value addition by helping reduce operational costs, understanding consumer behavior and patterns, helping businesses develop effective campaigns, services and products, and identifying unique cross-sell and up-selling opportunities. It provides a platform for greater differentiation. However, e-tailing cannot flourish without adequate development in secure IT infrastructure, widespread Internet access through PC, mobiles or other devices, a backward integrated supply chain and logistics systems and adequate government commitment on cyber laws to protect consumer interests.

While our analysis in suggesting an IT strategy delved on the fact that a sustainable e-retailing model will be the need for the hour. We have suggested a proper use of supply chain, e-marketing methods, employee learning, and IT strategy to suggest growth opportunities for futurebazaar.com and then explained as to how it can leverage the IT infrastructure to go for internationalization with potential markets to target.

Review Questions:

1. Was there a business imperative to start future e-commerce?
2. What kind of automation benefits e-commerce can provide in retail industry?
3. Does e-commerce provide strategic advantage to future e-commerce? How can this advantage be made sustainable?

9.21 Summary

E-commerce portals initially were meant for providing support to online buying and selling transactions only. These portals only were meant for sales personnel without any strategic intent. Now, in the knowledge economy, e-commerce portals aspired to be enterprise wide solutions to a broad and diverse set of departmental problems. Initially, e-commerce portals only laid emphasis on technology, but of late, the emphasis is on providing solutions to business processes. The design approach initially was mostly based on features but now it has moved onto back-end integrations offered by portal vendors. Any implementation would require 6–12 months durations, leading to questionable economic return and unmet expectations. Hence, during design process, involvement of end-users and different stakeholders is necessary. The team drawn from different functions will set the priorities and provide solutions to the business model through e-commerce portal. To avoid failures, organizations should follow steps in defining a portal strategy that focuses on providing strategic advantage.

9.22 Review Questions

1. Why do we need to plan for e-commerce portal design?
2. What are the steps involved in e-commerce portal design?
3. How do you ensure that e-commerce portal design is aligned with business goals?
4. How cloud computing will impact e-commerce portal design?
5. What do you understand by road map? Explain with respect to a real estate construction.
6. What is the difference between As-Is and To-Be process?
7. What is the difference between traditional and recent (in knowledge economy) approach for e-commerce design?

References

http://www.pantaloon.com/E-tailing.htm
http://www.retailforward.com/retailintel/rfis_default.asp
http://www.futurebazaar.com/b2c_futurebazaar/b2c/init.do
E-retailing By Charles Dennis, Tino Fenech, Bill Merrilees
Calkins, J; Farello, M, Shi, CS (2000) From retailing to e-tailing. The McKinsey quarterly

Chapter 10
Future Trend: Social Commerce

10.1 Learning Objectives

The chapter will discuss the following concepts:

- What is social e-commerce;
- How do firms get benefits out of it;
- Value addition from social commerce;
- Strategy for social commerce;

10.2 Introduction

In the year 1999, there were too many entrepreneurs who had bloomed using dot-com portals. Many of them were offering products and services through e-commerce. The mood in the e-commerce circle was upbeat. These Indian entrepreneurs wanted to emulate models of Amazon.com. New ventures like Fabmart, Firstandsecond.com opened their offerings to the Indian consumers. Very soon, Sify.com, rediff.com joined the bandwagon and offered flowers, gifts, etc., to their customers. In a slight detour, Apnaloan, instead of selling traditional products, offered to sell loans through e-commerce portal. Another portal, Shaadi.com, started offering matchmaking through Internet. All these happened before the bubble burst for dot-com portals (NASDAQ crashed in April 2000). Investors (including venture capitalists and private equity contributors) lost their money.

After the crash, it took quite a while to bring the positive sentiments back to e-commerce business model. In the space of 6–8 months, the 'new' business model (e-commerce) had gone from termed as 'innovative, expansive' to 'immature, FAD' as many (as many as 500) business houses closed down. Still the spirit survived and many months later, e-commerce was revived. Today, we have

S. Mohapatra, *E-Commerce Strategy*, Springer Texts in Business and Economics, DOI: 10.1007/978-1-4614-4142-7_10,

new organizations that are offering products and services that were earlier offered through traditional channels. This trend seems to remain in India for ever as more and more customers have become tech savvy and are willing to spend time online being engaged in several activities.

A village near Hyderabad is the testimony to this change. It is around 45 min drive from main city and as you enter you find that the infrastructure hasn't changed yet. The roads still have potholes, there are loose wires everywhere and no new institution (such as hospital or school) has been constructed in last 5 years. But to one's astonishment, one will find satellite TVs (Direct to House—DTH) in almost every household. The customer makes 'pay per view' payments to watch the show or movie of his desire. What is more astonishing is that the villagers have purchased these without going to the market, through e-commerce. Almost all the products that have been ordered have arrived on the fourth or fifth day after ordering. The buyers have been able to get best of the rates, sometimes even cheaper than that of physical stores.

This could be the future of e-commerce with ever ubiquitous Internet changing behavioral pattern of the buyers. It is quite understandable if educated, urban population indulge in online shopping, but thinking about the spurt in purchase in semi urban and rural areas (through e-commerce) gives a different perspective that has become interwoven to Indian social life. The social commerce has brought in a complete change among Indians. This is true for the entire civilization today. Socio e-commerce has taken a big leap in customers' lives throughout the world.

10.3 Social Power and Civilization

The year 2011 saw the rise of social power as people used Facebook and Twitter to knock down dictators in Tunisia, Egypt and Libya. Syria also has gone to the polls (at the time of writing the manuscript) which were the result of public outcry using social networking sites such as Facebook, Twitter. Similar things are also happening at other places. Many ordinary people have used social networking sites to bring down mighty corridors of powers to their knees. By joining hands with Wikileaks, the ordinary denizens could bend the rules for Internet freedom (that the US State Department wanted to introduce). Using the same tactics, both customers and employees have started redefining the business models.

Marketers and firms have used social power to design products, market them, and use the feedback mechanisms to improve them further. The present age belongs to the age of empowered individuals, who use potent technologies and harness social media to organize the business strategies. The managers no longer dictate the communication threads; rather they fall in line of social power and reframe their policies and strategies accordingly. Salesforce.com used the concept of social commerce to become a number one in selling its customer relationship management (CRM) software products. As per Marc Benioff, CEO of Salesforce.com, "social commerce is about corporate spring". In this new world of business, companies and leaders will have to show authenticity, fairness, transparency, and good faith to its stakeholders. If they don't care about these aspects, then customers and employees may not continue with the loyalty that they had shown earlier.

Customers who don't like a product may quickly broadcast them which can have a disastrous effect. Potential buyers will find out about these unpleasant experiences of the customers and will think twice before purchasing these products. Traditional companies, who have never used this approach, will definitely find the route of social networking based business models as difficult propositions. These are so different than the traditional business models and hence the mindsets of the executives require a reorientation. But overall, these changes suggest a new trend for the business and society as well. The business is fast becoming more reflective and democratic of the will of customers. Social power can now make or break a product, service, and a business model. The customers can become the source of new, innovative ideas to move the company forward. In the same way, disgruntled customers can damage your reputation.

The change required for the business leaders to adapt to the social commerce is to be able to 'listen' to these comments, ideas over the net and bring about changes accordingly. The concept these business leaders should adopt is 'trust is built through transparency and showing openness to different criticisms'. The more the company exposes itself to the criticism and share the problems with the customers, the more acceptable the firm becomes. This will lead to success which can be sustainable. For example, Salesforce.com had reliability problems with one of their servers. Initially, the company was not talking about it and the customers were not happy, rather they were upset. It turned into a public relation (PR) problem. The management team then decided to have a web site that explained all the issues related to the server. Detailed information related to technical problems was mentioned before even the customers could complain about them.

10.4 Understanding Social Commerce

Social commerce is a concept where electronic commerce is used in conjunction with social networking sites. In a way it is a subset of electronic commerce but involves social networking sites (online). The concept supports social interaction and user contributions, to assist in the online buying and selling of products and services. The concept helps in increasing online transactions by taking inputs from social networking sites. The term social commerce was introduced to describe a set of online collaborative shopping tools such as shared pick lists, user ratings, reviews, suggestions, etc., that are generated by users of the social networking sites. These informations are on different products and services that have been experienced by these users.

The concept of social commerce denotes user-generated reviews, comments, and content that can act as 'free advertisements' for different products. Using these comments, prospective buyers can buy these products and services online through an e-commerce site. Usually, this e-commerce site is integrated with the social networking site and can be accessed from the social networking site itself. The buying process includes collaborative e-commerce tools that enable shoppers to get advice from trusted individuals, find goods and services, and then purchase them. The social networks that spread this advice have been found to increase the prospective customer's trust in the buying process.

With advancement of technology, the area of social commerce has been expanded to include more social media tools and techniques. Buying movie tickets depend on the reviews written by the movie goers who have seen the movie already. The contents used in the reviews, can be read by the users at their convenience and then they can use e-commerce sites to buy these movie tickets. In apparel industry, automobile industries, e-commerce sites have taken serious notes for the comments generated by the users. These comments are not only authenticated but also provide credibility of the e-commerce site. Sites such as carwale.com, cardekho.com have tracked each and every review comment of different models of the car manufacturer. Using these comments not only the manufacturers have tried to improve their product features but also have strived to improve service levels in their supply chain. Other techniques used by the sites are customer ratings and reviews, user recommendations and referrals, shopping tools, social forums and communities, social advertising. The difference between "social commerce" from "social shopping" is that social commerce is a collaborative networks of online participants (which include vendors, users, etc.), and social shopping as collaborative activity of online shoppers.

10.5 How has Social Commerce Evolved Over a Period of Time?

Social commerce, with roots in e-commerce has been branching out through social networking web sites like Facebook and the recently introduced social shopping web sites. Facebook commerce, also known as F-commerce is slowly gaining prominence amongst customers, suppliers, and retailers alike. Retailers are looking at having their own Facebook page and are developing applications on Facebook platform so that consumers can take buying decisions and purchase the product/service at the same place. To sum it up, this is the concept of buying at the same place and at the same time.

After its advent through social networking sites, social commerce has found its way into the virtual marketplace with social shopping web sites. An example of social shopping web site is Stylehive (http://www.stylehive.com), which is a combination of social networking and online shopping business models. Here, shoppers browse through various product offerings, compare prices, read user reviews, check best sellers list, interact with other buyers, and finally take purchase decisions.

Industry reports on Generation Y suggests around 60 % take the help of social media to engage with brands and businesses, and over 50 % feel that Facebook, blogs, and related online media affect their opinions about offerings (products/services), while web sites are as influential as brick-and-mortar stores in nurturing the sentiments of the Generation Y.

10.6 Social Commerce Important Dates

1971	First email was sent
1994	One of the World's first Social Networking web site—Geocities is founded
2000	The *.COM* bubble bursts—Stock Market crashes
2003	My Space is launched
2004	Facebook is launched
2006	Twitter is launched
2007	Virtual Gifts Sold on Facebook
2007	Apps Platform launches—Market Place opens on Facebook
2007	Facebook Pages for Brands launched
2008	Dell $1 million revenue—Twitter sales alerts
2009	Facebook's *first* retail transaction via *1800-Flowers*
2010	Disney launches group ticketing store of Facebook
2011	Google + enters social networking
2011	Facebook stops *Facebook Deals*

Features of Social Commerce

Ratings and reviews are consistently "in-demand" features by customers of social commerce stores. With the implementation of the "sophisticated recommendation technology", the consumers not only get access to the reviews that help them to make highly informed decisions but also switch to a brand offering the same product at a lower price. Customers get product recommendations based on their own interests, preferences, and actions on the web. A study conducted by Brand Reputation showed that "84 % of consumers were more likely to check online for reviews prior to making a purchase."

Most Social media networks have large numbers of individual members, who are potential content generators and a store house of information. The potential of networked users is utilized to generate new ideas, advertise, and create added value at virtually no cost, while increasing efficiency by understanding customer needs, identifying potential customers and building customer loyalty. Recently, in an effort to exploit the power of such sourcing, Volkswagen launched an ad campaign using YouTube, focusing on ecological concerns. The campaign encourages users to develop environmental solutions and share them. VW utilizes these ideas and incorporates it, in its own ad, and delivers a creation by customers to customers.

The above examples illustrate the value and importance of presence on Social Media. All the same, in order to effectively make up-to-date information available to the consumers, MIS (Information Systems) play a crucial role. Also, there are requirements for inputs from customers and users, in the form of Feedback (Subjective) and Ratings (Scale Objective). Thus, real-time capture of data is essential and key to the implementation. It is here that Information Systems take center stage and manifest their true irreplaceable requirement.

The Facebook 'Like' Button on the Product's Web Page

When users visit a web page of a particular brand, they can 'like' the brand's offerings. Hence, the brands can utilize hoppers to essentially 'promote' products. Hence, social networking sites like Facebook help e-Commerce sites in three ways:

1. Better Understanding of the Consumer's Behavior:
   By integrating the Facebook 'Like' button on product pages, companies can analyze the popularity of the products. The product having the most 'likes' would be more profitable when compared to the product having the least 'likes'. Hence, this ensures immediate understanding of the customer's preferences. The companies can also do an alpha or beta testing of products without actually having to produce the product. They can also gage the response their 'future' products may receive by the number of responses (likes) they get from the customers.
2. Instant Personalization of the User Experience:
   With the integration of the Facebook 'Like' button with tools such as "Facebook Instant Personalization pilot" program, the visitor's experience can be personalized by using their public Facebook information.
3. Brand Growth:
   By making use of the various social networking sites as platforms, the brands are able to reach out to a large section of the consumers in a cost effective manner. This is also helping them to garner visibility on many fronts. This enables the product's success and consequently brand growth.

10.7 Advantages of Social Commerce

It ensures a personalized shopping experience for the customer by having access to the customer's social graph and interests on social networking sites the retailers can develop promotional strategies and plans that suit to the customer's preferences and interests. The retailers can also position their offerings such that they can attract prospective customers. It also creates direct contact with 'Communities'. Social commerce not only offers the opportunity for consumers to engage with online retailers, but also enables them to have direct contact with other consumers.

Hence, the consumers can exchange reviews about the products they have purchased or intend to purchase.

Social commerce also creates a trusted environment. Trust is especially important where the goods and services can be researched extensively and can only be viewed online, i.e., which cannot be touched and felt. With technology providing immersive shopping environments and great usability it makes the experience seamless for a customer right from providing the content, product reviews, payment options to final purchase. The site also provides real-time feedback. Even though word of mouth publicity is the major influential factor for the retailers to improve their products/services and promotional strategies, with social commerce, retailers are now able to receive and manage consumer feedback in a matter of few minutes. With real-time and instant access to the consumer behavior at their fingertips, retail brands can react accordingly by ensuring that the products on offer are the most relevant for their consumer base and also analyze shortcomings of their products, hence providing better service to the consumer.

10.8 Pitfalls

Social commerce, backed by the right strategy, connects social media investment with new channels of revenue. The challenge is to recognize the appropriate techniques to make that connection and integrate them with suitable marketing, business, and communications strategies, which results in right creative user experience.

The following are some of the trends and the challenges of social commerce.

- Moving Away from the Traditional Media
  Social Media provides fascinating opportunities to businesses to not just listen to customers but also engage with them and thereby assist in strengthening relationships. However, to do that, companies need to adapt their culture to that existing in Social Media. Social Media is the mother of all communication tools, but it will not change one's business on its own. The biggest challenge remains the exploration of new innovative ways in which businesses could engage its customers.
- Offering a United Shopping Experience
  Social commerce translates social media into e-retail sites and complements it by providing the function of e-commerce. However, businesses often focus on and achieve just one of these two, but not both. An example of a business having both F-store integrated with its e-shop is Funkrush (Screen shot of the same has been pasted). In addition, businesses have also been on the look-out for new platforms, such as Tumblr and YouTube, to promote and market their offerings. Considering the fact that multichannel shoppers spend over 80 % extra for each transaction when compared to shoppers who merely shop in store, retailers face the task of achieving the same in such a limited customer's exposure—

something that could be done with the help of single logins, thus offering great customer service, speedy checkout and personalized payment.

- Privacy
  As much as social media offers exciting new things to consumers and public in general, it is a known fact that the constantly changing privacy rules and instant sharing have forced consumers and users to rethink their strategy of discussing their likes and dislikes as openly. Figures suggest that more than 71 % of social networking users (Age Group: 18–29 years) are relooking their privacy settings and are attempting to limit the content they share online. Adding to this, the latest hacking scandals involving businesses such as McDonald's and MasterCard, as well as the accidental "leakage" of credit card numbers have merely increased customers' concern over the safety of their personal data. Hence, gaining trust from customer, specifically involving personal data would be difficult and retention of the same would be even bigger a task. One way to overcome this challenge is to offer customers with a well written privacy policy that is easily understood by the customers, so they are aware of the content they share and the people they share it with.
- Customer Engagement
  As social networks continue to expand, it is imminent for brands and businesses to find ways to rise above the common chaos and ensure there exists a direct interaction with their customers. The rising number of social networking sites would not just confuse the customer, but also the e-retailer. Businesses must then carefully watch how social media platforms operate and thereby assign only those that best suit their purpose.
- Many social commerce sites integrate the payment gateway inside the Social Media networks and not in their web sites. Hence, the users who would want to make a purchase are redirected to the web site to complete the purchase.
- Facebook's security issue is another important issue. The buyers should be convinced about the payment security for social commerce to flourish. Hence, having a secure payment network is utmost important.
- Tools for social commerce change rapidly. Prior to Facebook, social sites like MySpace, Orkut, Friendster, and Bebo were in vogue. Hence being informed about the changes in customer interests is important.
- Unlike direct selling, there are a lot of hidden soft costs: it takes time to develop sustaining relationships with customers.
- Building a strong relationship with the customer may not be possible as there is no direct interaction. Therefore, retaining a customer is more difficult.
- If the customer feels they have not been treated appropriately, they have powerful tools or mediums (YouTube, Twitter, etc.) to express their disappointment and negatively impact a brand's reputation.
- Usability testing has become so sophisticated that webmasters can track a visitor's actions with precision. Data Analytics can provide the visitor information and the efficiency of the marketing programs and sales conversions.

- With social commerce, these statistics are nonexistent. While "Facebook Insights" provides data on user interaction and engagement, it does not offer details on user activity as in the case of data analytics as it only relates to grabbing customer behavior and sales conversions.
- Also, one cannot optimize their Facebook social commerce platform for the search engine. Facebook storefronts use iFrames and Flash which are considered to be not much efficient.

10.9 How to Address These Pitfalls?

These issues need to be addressed at strategic level. These challenges need to be remembered during design of the web sites. During design, the following steps need to be followed:

(1) Facilitation of planning and control;
(2) Minimization of information redundancy;
(3) Integration of processes;
(4) Efficient metrics;
(5) Personalization/Customization;
(6) Feedback.

By integrating various processes, a unified shopping experience can be provided to customers by combining social networking, online transactions, and virtual marketplace business models. Security measures are taken by using intrusion detection systems, firewalls, antivirus and antispyware software, encryption mechanisms, digital certificates and rigorous software testing and metrics. Social networking and social shopping web sites are equipped with various data privacy mechanisms which help users manage their privacy settings. Information systems (IS) used in these web sites have been programmed to provide flexibility in terms of availability of personal information, demographics, updates, and areas of interest. The benefit of customization through various processes in information systems helps social commerce web sites in reaching out to the right customers at the right time and place. Web sites like Facebook and Stylehive have customization processes in place for effective advertising. IS, thereby helps in chalking out a personalized marketing strategy for better customer engagement (Fig. 10.1).

10.10 What is the Future of Social Commerce?

Social commerce has immense potential in becoming one of the major sources for generating revenues in the coming future. As of now, social commerce platforms on web sites like Facebook are known to be effective only for impulse purchases. However, if a balance between data privacy policies and giving out the right

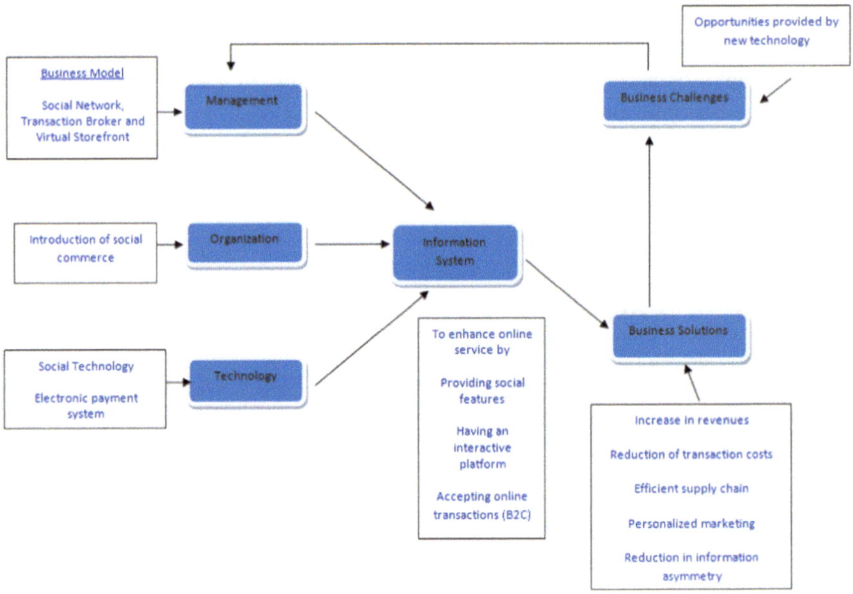

Fig. 10.1 Social commerce framework

information to advertisers is maintained, social commerce will be the next best thing in this era of digitalization.

Another gap seen in the social commerce platform is the absence of B2B transactions. Social networking and social shopping web sites are limited to B2C transactions, thereby providing immense scope for business to business dealings through social media and e-commerce.

10.11 Is India Ready for Social Commerce?

India is the second fastest growing economy in the world. In the last few years, Indian has developed radically. There has not only been economical development but the country has also become technologically advanced. In India, the year 1990 marked as the year of science and technological advancement in the country. In the last two decades, the country has come a long way. Computer and Internet have become available in almost every home. This has created a market for e-commerce in India. Also, the consumers have become quite smart and are looking for ways which prove they can make profitable purchase. India is not only ready for e-commerce; e-commerce has already become quite popular in India too.

There are many reasons which make India a suitable market for e-commerce. Here are some of the reasons:

With passage of time, the mindsets of consumer have changed. Unlike earlier days, the consumers have become tech savvy these days. Traditionally, consumers in India preferred going out and shopping in the markets. They wanted to have the 'feel' of the goods and then discuss among family members before making a purchase decision. However, e-commerce does not only provide one with convenience but also allows them to compare various kinds of offers. This helps the consumers to save time and money. Technology (3D effect) helps them to get the 'feel', while discussion forums allow them to have 'accurate discussion' among themselves. Thus, consumers have now started developing a penchant for e-commerce rather than traditional method of shopping in the markets.

Cyber policies in India have given direction to Foreign Investment in telecom sector. In India, people have become quite Internet friendly these days. The numbers of users have grown phenomenally over the years. The number of Internet connections has grown to 100 million in 2010. Availability of Internet has become cheaper; infrastructure investment in the sector has been good with long term vision in mind. New connections are being added every day. Since people are becoming quite Internet friendly these days, e-commerce is becoming a comfortable option for the people. It is believed that around 75 million household are ready for e-commerce in this nation.

After the retail sector has opened up, many global players have made plans for making entry into Indian market. With their entry, technology-based offerings have increased. These players have recreated the market of e-commerce in India. Thus, the consumers get the best of the options while sitting at home only. These big names are investing in the e-commerce market from a long term perspective rather than small term. Thus, the e-commerce market is to grow even more bigger and better in times to come. Apart from retail industry, some of the sectors like traveling and hotel industry have already proved to be quite successful in the field of e-commerce. These sites use users' feedback to generate trust among perspective buyers. These sectors have increased their market potential through social commercial portals. The success of these sectors has incited other sectors to enter the market of social commerce. Using already existing social networking sites, firms have integrated their offerings and this is precisely the reason why the social commerce market has expanded so quickly in India.

Above mentioned are some of the reasons which make India a suitable market for social commerce. However, for a section of Indians, there is still a slight bit of hesitance for social commerce. There is an element of mistrust among these consumers who feel that the comments in the site might have been doctored to increase online purchase. Eventually this hesitation and reluctance will go with peer pressure and social interactions. Since the Indians are more social than the western counterparts, there are strong reasons for believing that the market for social commerce will only grow in India in times to come. According to a survey, it is believed that the number of social commerce consumers will grow to 460 million individuals by 2024–2025.

Flipkart, Superbazaar.com, Olx. Com, Flickr.com are some of the social commerce of online shopping web sites that have already made it big in the Indian e-commerce market. With bigger and better online shopping sites like Amazon to enter the Indian e-commerce market in the near future, it would be right to say that the future of e-commerce is quite bright in India.

10.12 Case: Halfmantr

About Halfmantr

Halfmantr is an info-social web portal owned by Grey Applez India Service (P) Ltd. The company was incorporated in January 2012 and the following are the core values that company envisions:

Vision

At Halfmantr, we aspire to enrich and augment the competency and knowledge of the most precious resource on the planet—"Human Resource".

We envisage being a knowledge–powerhouse born out of new production paradigms based on knowledge and its application.

Mission

We aim to be a student/aspirant centric portal strives to ensure delivery of comprehensive tailor-made and knowledge-based support for various prestigious competitive examinations. We are committed to the core values of "quality and equity" and endeavor to meet them by providing the most authentic, relevant and swift information which is accessible and available to all.

We envision mitigating the information asymmetry in the country's hinterland and enabling the potential human resource in these areas to be employable in diverse sectors.

Changing paradigm: From "social" to "info-social" media
The social media and its availability and accessibility to a bulk of population that too at low costs is no less than a revolution. This has given more "choices" to the Internet users. Thus, social media has not only strengthened the civic involvement

but has also carved in new identities and aspirations. Gradually, the demand for customized information and its cocreation is increasing on the Internet. With plethora of information now available at just one click, there is a demand for the customized information.

Halfmantr has incorporated these two features into its offering, i.e., social media and customized information. Halfmantr provides an interactive platform where both horizontal and vertical communication (customized) can take place. Initially, the information as per the customized needs of the users would be delivered with the some time lag; however as per the expansion plan in next few quarters it will happen on real-time basis.

The social networking connects the users across the geographies, the info-social networking apart from providing the connectivity mitigates the information asymmetry as well. As stated above, there are two kinds of communications that take place in info-social networking of Halfmantr:

1. *Horizontal Communication*: It refers to the communication between the peer groups. This is the heart and soul of any social networking site. In this kind of communication, the exchange of information takes place between the peer groups. "Twitting" on Twitter, uploading a video or picture on Facebook, posting a "Scrap" on Orkut, etc., are the example of this kind of communication.
2. *Vertical Communication*: This kind of communication refers to the information sharing from an expert or a team of experts on a particular topic. This category of communication is an additional feature of the info-social networking. Moreover, this kind of communication is user driven on Halfmantr unlike Blogs which are predominantly written as per the writer's discretion.

Halfmantr: "Free Lunch" is Possible!

The cliché "There is no free lunch" has become anachronic with the new web-based business models. It's now viable to deliver goods and services at free of cost or at the cost below the conventional market prices. The disintermediation and reintermediation by web-based business models has altered the traditional distribution models and value chains.

Apart from this, the "customized information" can be delivered absolutely free of cost if a threshold number of users (also called traffic) visit a web site. The traffic can be leveraged for the revenues. This is because of the facts that as the traffic and the eye balls on the web site increase the advertisements and endorsements to be placed on the web site become the sources of revenue. If this revenue can compensate for the cost incurred in acquiring the information, marketing, and delivering it on the Internet with some profit, a viable business model can be prepared out of this. Halfmantr is based on this concept.

Only Quality Matters

Since there is no direct transaction of money involved in the delivery of information, the legitimate consumer rights are not available to the users. Likewise, there is no legal or moral binding on the publishers of web site to provide quality information. Thus, the pertinent question which arises at this point of time is that what are the factors that would be instrumental in ensuring the proper quality of the information which is delivered without any quid-pro-quo?

The answer to these complex questions is simple, i.e., invisible hands of the markets. Since the revenue earned in such model is directly proportional to the number of visitors, only the quality information could cater the purpose of acquiring the eye balls and retaining them in long run. Thus, the visitors on the web site have to be essentially treated like clients (even if they are not paying anything) and the quality has to be the hallmark of the entire business model.

Business Model of Halfmantr: Entirely Internet Driven

The business model of Halfmantr is entirely driven by Internet. Internet has made it possible for Halfmantr to acquire the high quality customized content, deliver and market it at low costs. Thus, all the stages in the business model of Halfmantr are driven by Internet. The following diagram represent Halfmantr's business model:

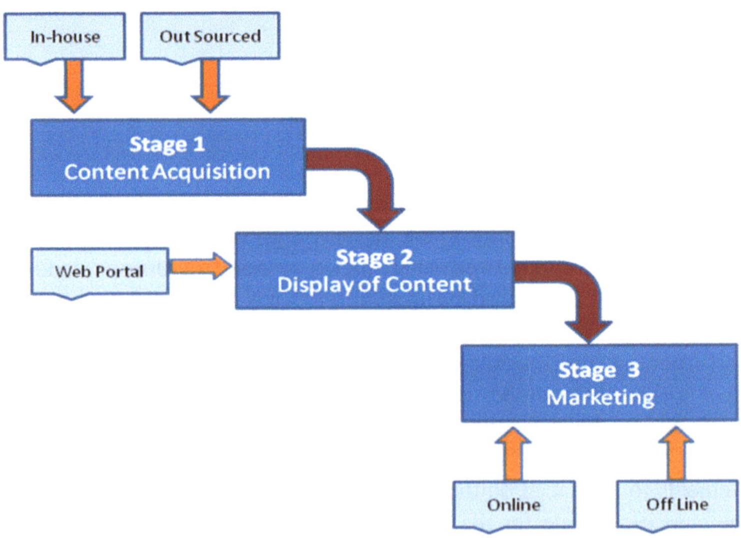

In all the three stages of the business model, Internet is playing a pivotal role to minimize the cost and to make the offering effective. The role of Internet in the three stages is as follows:

1. Stage 1—Content Acquisition
   In this stage, Internet has played a major role in cost curtailment in the following ways:

   - Internet has made it possible to acquire the content from the sources where the high quality is available at low costs. As a result the content is acquired from multiple sources across the country.
   - The content writers use Internet for research and literature analysis to improve the quality of work.
   - The job work like typing, formatting, proof reading, etc., is outsourced to the sources where the cost is low irrespective of the location; this has been possible only due to Internet connectivity.

2. Stage 2—Display of Content
   This stage involves the displaying and managing of content on the web portal as well providing an interactive platform for the info-social networking. This stage is completely technology driven. The Internet is helping in this stage in the following manner:

   - The web portal of Halfmantr is designed using "Open Sources" of technology which are available free of cost on the Internet;
   - The company has to incur the cost only in customization of the software, however since the Open Sources are used, the cost to acquire the software is very minimal.

3. Stage 3—Marketing

   In this stage, the Internet is being used in following manner:

- By Promoting Halfmantr on social networks like Facebook, Orkut, Twitter, etc.;
- Search Engine Optimization of the web pages;
- Promoting web site through blogs and backlinks;
- Using Pay Per Click campaigns.

The Target Market (1st Phase)

Halfmantr in its first phase has planned to target the most prestigious exam of the country, i.e., Civil Services Exam. The exam takes place in three stages and as per the need of the exam the customized products and services would be available for the aspirants. The following are the reasons for initially choosing this exam:

1. Unlike for the GRE, GMAT, and MBA entrance examination, there is relatively very less competition in the online segment for Civil Services;

2. The market is very big and scattered all over the country. On an average, about 2.5 lakhs candidates appear every year for the exam and about equal number of aspirants have an eye on the exam;
3. The exam includes sections like current affairs etc., which require constant updating, this can retain the aspirants on the web site for long time;
4. The Civil services examination is on a crossroad off late. In recent past, the examination pattern has drastically changed. The age old strategies and sources have become anachronic and the predictability of exam has become a myth in last couple of years. As a result, every teacher in the coaching is advising the students to not just rely on the conventional magazines/newspapers but also to spend time on Internet;
5. In 2014, major changes are going to happen in the examination pattern. As a result, all new and old sources would come on a level playing field. The newer methods of knowledge like Internet and e-learning would play a major role as informational tools.

Expansion Plans

The following are the expansion plans for the business for next three quarters:

1. *Bank P.O. Entrance Exams*: The process of targeting this segment has started; the content is in the developmental stage;
2. *GD/PI section for MBA*: This stage of the MBA entrance requires knowledge about current events at national and international level along with some public speaking tips. The former one is already in process as it is a regular section of the Civil Services exam. The team is working on the latter aspect of this exam.

Social Relevance

Like the other developing countries, India too is marred by inequalities and asymmetries. The current entrance examination pattern of the country which although is based on merit, does not take into account the contextual variables of the candidates like their socio-economic condition, place of residence, medium of instruction, etc.,

In such scenario, it is a natural corollary that the sections of society which economically affluent and have better access to the resources would perform relatively better than the others. An open source of information like Halfmantr would try to mitigate this by providing the quality study material which is available and accessible to all.

10.13 Case Study: Travel Through Socio-Commerce Route

Travel Sector start-up: TravelTriangle, Get Best Agents to Plan Your Trip Online (written by Sankal Agarwal, CEO of TravelTriangle).

India is the world's second fastest growing economy among the major economies and along with it, the wallet of the average Indian is growing fatter. He has started to spend more and travel more. Vacations are an absolute must with the kind of lifestyles people lead today. With this need, arises the Travel Sector. In this rapidly growing industry, traveltriangle.com is a web-based start-up founded by Sankalp Agarwal and Sanchit Garg. Traveltriangle.com is a one-stop solution for the travel plans of the customers. Based in Noida, traveltriangle.com has some interesting features up its sleeve.

What is Traveltriangle and How is it Different from the Traditional Method of Booking Holiday Packages?

Traveltriangle.com is a platform which brings together agents with best deals as per the customers travel needs. Each request of traveler is worked upon by more than three travel agents (local to the destination), who compete to provide the best experience and price to the traveler. This facilitates the traveler to compare and book the best deal online without any hassles. If not with traveltriangle.com, the traveler has to call each agent individually and negotiate, and then decide upon one without knowing the reason for his quote. Later, the user may discover a better deal. This would not happen with TravelTriangle.

The other unique proposition is that only those travel agents who operate from traveler's destination are able to provide quote on traveler's request. In return, traveler gets expert guidance and customization based on his personal preferences. Who would know a destination better than agent local to the destination!

We also provide 'agent reliability guarantee' so that travelers' purchases from our platform are safe. Further it is all free for travelers!

All in all, traveler gets to save time and money, meets trusted agents online, and adds local attractions to his trip successfully.

Tell us About the Background of the Owners and the Team

I, Sankalp Agarwal (26) and Sanchit Garg (26), my school friend started traveltriangle.com after quitting jobs in the middle of 2010. Prior to this we worked at Adobe and Yahoo respectively. Both of us are Computer Science graduates, myself from IIT Kharagpur 2008 batch and Sanchit from IIT Bombay 2008 batch. Our team includes our friend Prabhat Gupta (IIT Guwahati) as core development member. With the kind of chemistry we share, the mood is high at TravelTriangle and we're aiming to revolutionize the way people decide about their travel trips.

Why the Name Traveltriangle?

We have all been through the cumbersome process of planning a trip. Look for agents, compare a few of them and then make a choice based on good faith. The idea here is to bring the best dealers at the same platform coupled with reviews and trip itinerary. The name TravelTriangle excited us and at the same time is meaningful as we are connecting three entities: travelers, travel agents, and an efficient marketplace.

What are Your Expansion Plans?

Right now we are focused on providing a 'wow experience' to travelers while booking their trips. Our challenge is to reach out to a larger set of people while stabilizing the platform. The back-end operations also need to be scaled accordingly. We are looking forward to angel/seed funding in the next 3 months for this scale up. Once we are established with a big customer base, we may look at the possibilities of offering other products.

How do you Aim to Generate Revenue? What is Your Revenue Model?

Our services are free for travelers. They get quotes from multiple agents. Agents subscribe and pay to us for number of conversions done. Right now agents provide quite hefty commissions to B2B partners who bring them customers. We are trying to structure this process and bring down commissions by connecting travelers directly to tour providers. Finally, it is the traveler who benefits in terms of saving the money.

Who are Your Competitors and How are You Different?

Our main competitor is Zicasso but currently it is not a full-fledged company and is not at all present in India. Traveltriangle is *not* a travel agent. Traveltriangle.com is the 'marketplace' where one can search trips from leading travel agents. With this, we save the customer from doing all the research and comparing plans from multiple travel agents. Our unique usage of technology provides a traveler with virtual tours and 3D panoramas of their destinations. The goal is to help traveler find the most suited trip without any hassle.

Other details can be worked out from here:

Prop for traveler	Online travel agent	Meta travel agent	Traveltriangle.com
Customization	Few inclusions over fixed tour package (negligible)	0	Complete customization of tour package
	Done by call center professionals	Done by agent in an unorganized manner	Done by 3–4 trusted agents local to the destination
Best Deals and Prices	Maybe	Maybe	Yes
Number of quotes	Single	Multiple	Multiple
Quote comparison	Done by Traveler	Done by Traveler	Automatic by platform
Traveler Experience	Focus on sale of fixed package to customer	Lot of phone calls, Unknown agents, No trusted payment	Focus on creating best experience for traveler

Tell us Something About Your Affiliations

We currently have around 50 travel agents on board with us. We would be closing around 100 more by mid-march. We have personally met with each of them and have done background check before we bring them on board. These agents are distributed throughout India and abroad. Most of them are pretty big who have multiple branches in the country. These agents use our portals to target travelers for their business.

Are you Looking at Hiring?

Yes, we are looking for enterprising folks who can assist us in sales and marketing in an energetic and vibrant environment.

What are Your Expectations From our Readers?

While we promise of providing best services to each of our customers, we would need their support to make this one stop solution for travel. Our request to them is to come on our portal (http://traveltriangle.com) and try out our services for their next bookings; we assure them that they'd get the best deal available for their trip. The best way to follow our deals and updates is via Facebook (http://facebook.com/traveltriangle)

Here's the gateway to your next trip: www.traveltriangle.com

10.14 Case Study: LensKart in India, Know Your Lenses

Working, for 11 months, as a program manager at Microsoft in the US was enough to convince Peyush Bansal that he wanted to be his own boss. Though the money was good, he wanted to come back to India and be an entrepreneur. He wanted to make a difference through online portals. His business model was based on social commerce and he wanted to use word of mouth, consumer feedback and user forums for his marketing strategy.

By the end of 2007, he was in India looking for business opportunities. He found business potentials in e-commerce portals. He also knew that he would succeed only if users gave good feedback about the services offered through the site. Thus, the idea of social commerce was born. He looked at the student market in India and saw numerous opportunities—one of them being providing student accommodation. He started www.searchmycampus.com, for providing accommodation to students in Delhi. He was honest and upright in providing transparent information. He also encouraged students to provide feedback for the quality of services and these comments were made available online. As a result, this classifieds site soon went beyond providing information for accommodation to provide information on books, part-time jobs, carpool facilities and internship opportunities. The student database that was created through this portal had lot of market potential. A lot of educational institutions were interested in this database since this was their target audience. The revenue model was based on number of enquiries that each college received through this portal.

However, Peyush wanted to go big and was sure that he wanted to grow out of this business. He wanted to sell products as he felt it would be difficult to scale up services. He thought of selling products through web site.

He started with an initial funding of Rs. 25 lakh. The money was used to hire people, such as a web site developer and content managers, and to buy office equipment. The first office was set up in the basement of his parents' house at Greater Kailash in Delhi. In the next few months, he hired more people and, by June 2008, he had 20 employees. He registered his company as 'Valyoo Technologies'. Initially, they started working with small retail setups in the US—selling jewelery, cosmetics, eyewear, etc. The web portal served a base to retailers in the US for expanding their operations in India. By collaborating with these US-based companies, the web portal got its revenue from the commission on each sale made in India.

Slowly Peyush started focusing on selling spectacles, sunglasses, and contact lenses through web site. He was surprised at the response that the site generated.

By mid-2010, the site was able to earn revenue of $100,000 a month. He then started Lenskart.com toward the end of 2010 and started by selling contact lenses. By February 2011, he had expanded the inventory to spectacles and sunglasses. However, there were many challenges that he faced. Delivery of products at promised time was a big bottleneck. He understood that to be successful in e-commerce, he needs to control the logistics. He used a two-pronged approach to instill confidence in customers. One, he set up a chat line, which clients could use to clarify queries, and two, he offered a 14 day, no-questions-asked return policy.

Internationally, e-commerce business has been huge and although India has a larger population, the growth has only started in 2010. Some of the verticals like jobs and travel verticals had already been there. Other retail verticals have also started to come online. It is a very positive thing. The response for the market is good enough for one to say that the business will grow. It also shows that it is not going to be a bubble this time. There are buyers and people are willing to spend their money, and they are getting their value for money. So Peyush pushed further and went ahead with providing comments and feedback from users of the site.

Procurement in E-Commerce

As far as storing stocks is concerned, there is a need to have a strong supply chain. Overdependence on channel partners can be risky. These are common problems. Having a healthy stock is important and LensKart as a company believed in stocking products and selling them. The company believed in keeping it simple. However, those who want to scale up, should have strong logistic support. There is enough room for people to play around the model. People have also been trying innovative ways to ensure procurement. People are thinking of ways wherein they do not have to stock products but we are keeping it simple and stocking products. With FDI in retail business not far, socio-commerce is going to be the mantra for future.

10.15 Summary

Socio-commerce is the way to make e-commerce a sustainable model. The ultimate beneficiary of this movement will be customers who will enjoy discounts, free shipping, cash-on-delivery, and experience of a product without even buying it. The socio part of e-commerce has taken the corporate world by storm and could be the key factor in sustainability of a business model. No wonder, many Venture Capitalists, including Tiger Global, has been increasing their investment exposure in Internet business. It has invested in Facebook and Linkedin in US, Youko.com and Dang Dang in China, Digital Sky Technologies in Russia. In India, it has invested $82 million in e-commerce ventures. This amount of investment clearly indicates the faith that the investors have in e-commerce ventures particularly those with socio commercial approach and these models are going to remain for the long term.

Social networking sites can be valuable sales and marketing tools, as well as fun diversions. Inherent in these applications are security risks that can put the individual or a company in a compromising position or at serious risk. Aside from not using these sites at all, end user education, alongside documented policies and procedures, is the most fundamental protection that exists. A well-informed user will not only help to maintain security, but will also educate others on these issues and establish best practices which can be standardized and updated as applications mature or as new applications come along.

10.16 Review Questions

1. What is the concept behind socio-commerce? How is it different from vanilla e-commerce business model?
2. What are the benefits to different stakeholders in socio-commerce?
3. How has Social Commerce evolved over time? What are its advantages and pitfalls?
4. What are precautions that a marketer should take while using socio-commerce channel?

Chapter 11
Drivers of Online-Selling Diffusion: A Look at Organizational and Environmental Factors Through Time

11.1 Introduction

Since the Internet began to be used in the business arena, it has been of interest to identify the factors driving online-selling diffusion, and to understand how these factors affect online-selling development or the extent of its use. Currently, the study of the online-selling phenomenon is relevant, since it is continuously evolving (Cagliano et al. 2003) and even now generalizable evidence is lacking.

As a whole, the empirical research undertaken has identified many and varied drivers of online-selling diffusion (factors to do with the competitive environment and organizational factors), which has led some authors (such as Fillis et al. 2004; Kim and Galliers 2004) to study them. However, more empirical research is needed to validate the effective influence of these drivers.

Furthermore, the identification and analysis of the determinants of B2C online-selling should take into account the particular features of this marketing format within end-consumer markets. Although the potential for development of B2C online-selling is extraordinary—especially when consumers has substantial purchasing power and possess the technological equipment necessary to connect to the Internet—limitations still exist, and these require to be identified and analyzed. At the same time, research should be longitudinal—contemplating the temporal evolution of the phenomenon—and not only cross-sectional.

Adapted from an article originally published in the *Journal of Theoretical and Applied Electronic Commerce Research* by Inma Rodríguez-Ardura, Antoni Meseguer-Artola and Jordi Vilaseca-Requna, VOL 3/ISSUE 2/AUGUST 2008/18-29 © 2008 Universidad de Talca—Chile.

S. Mohapatra, *E-Commerce Strategy*, Springer Texts in Business and Economics,
DOI: 10.1007/978-1-4614-4142-7_11,

11.2 Driving Factors of B2C Online-Selling

Few innovations introduced in the field of distribution in the past few decades have as many advantages for both consumers and firms as B2C online-selling, a marketing format enabling the sale of information, goods, and services through the Internet. Moreover, the benefits of B2C online-selling are relevant: it is global, it is capable of interconnecting and interrelating millions of consumers and firms, it enables marketing communications to become interactive, the business opportunities deriving from its use are very varied, and so on.

Nevertheless, and despite these advantages, online-selling still remains an emerging marketing format, particularly with regard to firms' electronic exchanges with end-consumers (B2C). Unlike electronic exchanges between firms (B2B), B2C online-selling is more dependent on elements from the end demand, which are often beyond firms' control.

11.3 The Internet Community

Analyses of online-selling do not always consider factors relating to the end-consumers, despite their importance. This may be justifiable in the case of B2B online-selling, but even many studies of B2C online-selling ignore such type of factors (e.g., Arnott and Bridgewater 2002; To and Ngai 2006). Among the aspects relating to the consumers worth considering, the size of the potential market is particularly important (Javalgi and Ramsey 2001; Meseguer et al. 2003; Rodríguez-Ardura et al. 1999). Indeed, reaching a critical mass of potential customers who are habitual users of the Internet may turn this group of users into a large enough market to become profitable and consequently attractive to firms (O'Keefe et al. 1998; Kau et al. 2003).

11.4 The Technological and Legal Framework

As well as being conditioned by the potential market, the development of online-selling may also be influenced by other factors imposed by the competitive environment (Kim and Galliers 2004), among which we could highlight those to do with the technological infrastructure, and factors relating to the legal framework within which marketing activity on the Internet takes place (Javalgi and Ramsey 2001).

As an application of the Internet, online-selling depends on information infrastructures and telecommunications for its development. Specifically, Stewart et al. (2002) point to the broadband penetration rate as one of the factors best explaining the different levels of online-selling diffusion observed in countries such as the United States, Canada, the United Kingdom, and Australia, where the conventional Internet access infrastructure is widely available (Dutta 1997). Indeed, the penetration of low-cost broadband in the population allows firms to provide a better service to their customers, since it allows them to develop web sites with personalization mechanisms (Ansari and Mela 2003) and personal interaction with the customer services area, or other personnel from the organization (McGowan and Durkin 2002), and to incorporate various differentiating multimedia elements (Porter 2001). Thus, many authors have found evidence of the positive effect of advanced designs that are suited to the audience on the results of online-selling activities (Dholakia and Rego 1998; Lohse and Spiller 1999; Mandel and Johnson 2002; Eid and Trueman 2004; among others).

On the other hand, the diffusion of online-selling also depends on the degree of involvement of the public authorities in developing a legal framework and a set of policies that favor its development (Javalgi and Ramsey 2001; Fillis et al. 2004; Fisher and Harindranath 2004). Among the various areas where the public authorities can intervene—legal, fiscal, market access (White House 1997)—consumer protection is of particular importance, and within this area, privacy stands out (Hoffman and Novak 2000; Javalgi and Ramsey 2001). In fact, there is some evidence of the positive effect of a political–legal framework for privacy on the development of business activity on the Internet (Phelps et al. 2000; Sheehan and Hoy 2000; Graeff and Harmon 2002; among others). This is because the Internet offers unprecedented opportunities for the invasion of privacy: it is easier to obtain information about individuals, combine it and integrate it with information obtained from conventional physical channels. Although it is possible to find out much more about consumers from traditional channels, access to this information can become too costly, can take too long or be too difficult to gather. Conscious of this, users value their privacy on the Internet very highly, and the control of the information obtained about them (Hoffman et al. 1999), and they are more liable to provide personal data and indeed to make purchases when there are mechanisms in place that control the personal information collected and what use is made of it (Hoffman et al. 1999; Swaminathan et al. 1999). And since there is a positive relation between future purchase intentions on the Internet and the probability of an effective purchase online (Brown et al. 2003), we can plausibly expect that having a legal framework regulating privacy on the Internet will favor Internet transactions.

11.5 The Business Strategy

Apart from considering factors relating to the firm's competitive environment, it is also necessary to take into account factors relating to the firm's internal environment. Including this second group of factors is habitual in holistic or integrative analyses of the diffusion process of innovations such as online-selling (Gibbs and Kraemer 2004; Kim and Galliers 2004), and helps explain why some firms opt to adopt online-selling activities while others prefer to stick to conventional marketing formats.

One aspect relating to the firm's internal environment that authors have considered to be particularly important in the decision to adopt online-selling is their marketing or business strategy. Indeed, the literature on online-selling provides some evidence about the influence of the firm's strategy on the diffusion of this marketing channel (Vilaseca et al. 2007). However, the particular characteristics of the Internet raise the question of whether the company strategies advocated in the past few decades (differentiation of the value proposition, satisfying the customer by giving greater value, orientation toward the relationship, etc.) are appropriate on the Internet, and consequently whether such strategies favor the development of online-selling or not. These doubts about the use of such strategies on the Internet are due to the fact that online consumers have greater access to information about the commercial offer (Bakos 1997) and increased capacity to intervene directly in the shaping of a value proposition adapted to their specific preferences (Pires et al. 2006).

Some studies in the field of consumer behavior (e.g., Harrison et al. 2006; Pitt et al. 2002; Rezabakhsh et al. 2006) have stressed the Internet's potential to enhance consumer empowerment. Moreover, a number of renowned authors (e.g., Alba et al. 1997) have related online consumers' greater empowerment with a supposed greater efficiency of electronic markets. The explanation for this would be that online consumers, who have a greater capacity for communicating with firms and other consumers, for identifying the best products to satisfy their needs, for evaluating their different purchase options, and for intervening in the design of the value proposition, would be more capable to adopt efficient purchase decisions (i.e., acquiring the desired product more cheaply) (Rodríguez-Ardura and Martínez-López 2008). This way of behaving would provoke an intense competition among firms, fundamentally on the basis of price (Bakos 1997; Brynjolfsson and Smith 2000).

Unlike in conventional channels, on the Internet there are intermediaries or shopbots that provide access to information about the prices and products of a relatively large number of competing retailers, meaning that the cost of searching for products is lower than is usual in traditional shopping (Brynjolfsson and Smith 2000; Smith 2002). Information asymmetries between buyers and vendors conceivably decline with these purchasing agents, so that consumers seize more power in the exchange process.

All these have led to the prediction that as consumers become more skilled in the search for product information and use the Internet to enhance their empowerment, marketing communications, product differentiation, and brand image, among other marketing tools, will lose their importance in the creation of signals of product characteristics, quality, or suitability (Ward and Lee 2000). According to this reasoning, brands would lose their importance as guarantees of product quality, being replaced by information about the product, and the consumers would be able to identify which vendors provide the lowest prices for products of similar characteristics. Ultimately, greater price competition between companies could be expected, leading to a situation of perfect competition (Alba et al. 1997; Bakos 1998).

However, the empirical studies carried out have not provided definitive evidence about online price levels, partly due to the difficulty of generalizing from small samples (Smith et al. 2000). Some research has found that the prices of certain products are higher on the Internet (e.g., Bailey 1998; Clay et al. 2002; Xing et al. 2004), but other studies has found the reverse (Brynjolfsson and Smith 2000; Clemons et al. 2002; Lee and Gosain 2002; Zettelmeyer 2006). In contrast, there does appear to be some agreement that price dispersion on the Internet is very high (Bailey 1998; Baye et al. 2004; Clay et al. 2002; Clemons et al. 2002; Iyer and Pazgal 2003; Lee and Gosain 2002), and even equivalent to that found in conventional channels, and also that there is a strong concentration of the supply, which means for example that retailers with the lowest prices do not obtain the highest sales (Brynjolfsson and Smith 2000). We should consider a number of arguments that question the idea that online-selling development is related to a greater emphasis on marketing and business strategies that involve price reductions:

a. Shopbots do not always provide precise enough information about prices. In order to make accurate comparisons, consumers not only need to know the sales price of the product, which shopbots usually provide, but also the transport charges, taxes, and other costs involved in online purchasing (Kung et al. 2002).
b. The information about product characteristics provided by the shopbots could be excessive. As the number of online businesses grows, so does the information these shopbots provide in their search results. Faced by such an excess of information, consumers tend to take "shortcuts" or make heuristic evaluations (Suri et al. 2003). These shortcuts take the form of purchasing in known and trusted sites, even if their prices are higher.
c. The diffusion of shopbots for product search and comparison is limited. Some consumers do not use these intermediaries to find and compare products, either because there are no shopbots available for the product-market they are interested in, or because they are relatively inexperienced users of the Internet (so they do not know that these systems exist, or how they work), or because they wish to invest the least time possible in their online purchases (Ward and Lee 2000).
d. Some firms prevent their products and prices from being considered by shopbots (Iyer and Pazgal 2003; Smith 2002).
e. Some firms use shopbots to reduce the effectiveness of consumer searches. They diffuse exceptionally low prices for a small number of their products to these intermediaries to encourage traffic to their virtual store, where the majority of their products are relatively more expensive (Smith 2002).

Although shopbots put significant pressure on firms' margins (Smith 2002), firms will conceivably keep developing strategies to mitigate the competitive pressure. These will include product differentiation, brand awareness and reputation (Pan et al. 2002; Smith and Brynjolfsson 2001; Xing et al. 2006), segmentation practices and price discrimination (Clemons et al. 2002), and so on.

Although the price is an important element in the design of the value proposition, other elements may also be important for online firms (Degeratu et al. 2000; Lee-Kelley et al. 2003; Lynch and Ariely 2000; Swaminathan et al. 1999): product information, web site design, customer service, reliability and speed of delivery, brand image, facilities for making orders, loyalty programs, personalization of the communication, switching costs, and so on. Researchers have found some evidence that an important segment of online consumers do not search actively in competing sites before making their purchase decisions (e.g., Deck and Wilson 2006), and that consumers are no more sensitive to prices online than they are in conventional channels (e.g., Degeratu et al. 2000; Jensen et al. 2003; Sotgiu and Ancarani 2005). Moreover, convenience has been identified as one of the most important benefits sought by online consumers (Chiang and Dholakia 2003). Online businesses that can exploit the benefits of convenience provide more satisfaction to consumers seeking to save time and effort in their purchases, or those who tend to purchase in reputed retailers and acquire recognized brands.

Thus, it seems plausible to expect that firms will define online strategies to prevent prices from being pushed downward and the market from heading toward perfect competition. Furthermore, this situation could be heightened as the sales attributable to online-selling grow. This is because while online-selling has a limited market, firms that adopt differentiation strategies in conventional channels would probably be more ready to sell their products on the Internet more cheaply, in the expectation that they will eventually be reaching a sufficiently attractive number of customers (Porter 2001). But as online-selling expands, companies will probably opt for the same competitive strategy on the Internet as they adopt in conventional channels (Porter 2001; Zettelmeyer 2000).

11.6 The Design of a Secure Value Proposition

Finally, we should consider that firms' adoption of systems making communications and transactions on the Internet more secure may significantly influence the results of their marketing activity in this channel. This is because in spite of advances in security mechanisms (cryptography, authentication), consumers may be reluctant to use the Internet to carry out secure transactions. Negative perceptions about security may still represent an important break on online purchases (Bhatnagar et al. 2000; Liebermann and Stashevsky 2002; McKnight et al. 2002; Swaminathan et al. 1999).

It seems that winning the consumer's confidence is an important objective for companies operating on the Internet, since online-selling purchases not only involve the traditional risks of direct sales (examination of goods before purchase, deferred delivery, returns, etc.), but additional risks as well, such as the fraudulent use of credit cards (Kau et al. 2003), which are only partially solved by means of bricks-and-mortar strategies (Huizingh 2002). Thus, incorporating various technological components into the process (security protocols, guarantee seals from brands such as Visa or VeriSign, high-quality web site design technology, etc.) may help generate confidence in Internet retailers (Reynolds 2000), which ultimately favor online-selling sales.

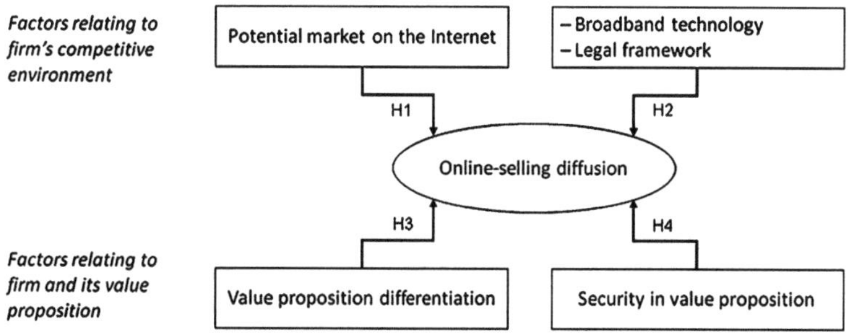

Fig. 11.1 Environmental and organizational drivers of online-selling diffusion

This leads us to formulate the following hypothesis:

H1: The size of the potential market on the Internet positively influences online-selling diffusion.
H2: The diffusion of broadband Internet connection technologies in the market and the establishment of a legal framework for online consumer protection positively influence the development of online-selling.
H3: An emphasis on marketing elements that differentiate the value proposition and provide the consumer with greater value (to the detriment of price-related strategies), positively influences online-selling diffusion.
H4: Designing an online value proposition perceived as "secure" positively influences online-selling diffusion (Fig. 11.1).

11.7 Empirical Study

The data used refer to a specific geographical area: the Spanish market. Whatever the market, collecting data about the online-selling phenomenon is not without its difficulties. There are few measurements made, and the ones that are often focus more on access and connectivity than on the use that is made of the Internet in the marketing and business arena (Vilaseca et al. 2004). This obliged us, as we describe below, to resort to various sources that employ different methodologies to obtain the data for the variables considered in the model.

We used the sales turnover from B2C online-selling in Spain (expressed in millions of euros) as indicator of the online-selling diffusion. Following OECD recommendations, this indicator represents the sum of Spanish consumers' purchases on the Internet, regardless of the channel employed subsequently for the physical distribution and payment of the products purchased. The data on this indicator were obtained from the *Study of B2C e-commerce*, a representative survey of the Spanish population over 14 years of age elaborated annually from

1996 by the AECEM (the Spanish Association of e-Commerce) and the Red.es Observatory (the public firm of the Spanish Government that promotes the development of the Information Society). The survey is based on computer-aided telephone interviews (Bellview-CATI system) of a sample of the population selected at random from telephone lists.

To measure the size of the potential market represented by the Internet we used the number of Internet users in Spain (in thousands of users), with data from 1996 to 2008. An Internet user is understood to be a person over 14 years of age who accesses the medium at least once a month. The data were obtained from the *General Framework of the Media* in Spain, elaborated by the Spanish Association for Research into the Communications Media (AIMC) on the basis of the *General Media Study* (*EGM*). The *EGM* is a representative survey of the Spanish population over 14 years of age enquiring about the general audience of the communications media. It is carried out three times a year, and the complete survey is based on approximately 43,000 personal interviews.

To measure the technological factor (diffusion of broadband) and legal factor (legal framework of consumer protection on the Internet) of the competitive environment of online-selling, we used a dichotomous variable that equals 0 for the period between 1996 and 2001, and 1 from 2002 onwards. These values can be expected to capture the structural change occurring from 2002 caused by the takeoff of ADSL among private users—after the Spanish Telecommunications Market Commission authorized the dominant operator to begin operating as a direct service provider—and the diffusion of the draft of the first law designed to regulate commercial activities on the Internet, Law 34/2002, 11th July, known as the Law of Information Society Services and Electronic Commerce.

As indicator of the relative importance of differentiation strategies and consumer relationships compared to price leadership strategies, we used the price of one of the best-selling products on the Internet: the computer. For this, we took data provided annually by the European Information Technology Observatory on the prices (in Euros) of the best performing computer on the market at any given time in Europe.

Finally, for the security factor in firms' value proposition on the Internet, we took as indicator the number of servers with the ".es" domain (the country code for Spain) that use security protocols per 1,000 users. To measure this, we used the monthly data obtained for Spain by the firm Netcraft.

11.8 Interpolation Process and Trend Analysis

When analyzing the evolution in the online sales volume from 1996 to 2008, we find a clear acceleration in its growth from the year 2001 onwards (see Fig. 11.2). A number of important events occurred from 2001, which may have had an effect on this (e.g., the development of broadband and the preparation of the Law of Information Society Services and Electronic Commerce).

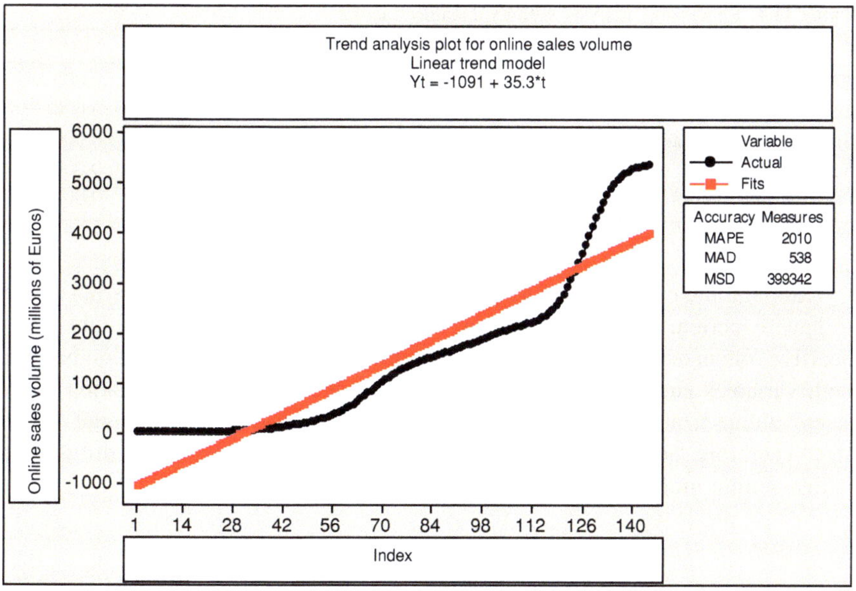

Fig. 11.2 Evolution of online sales volume and analysis of trend

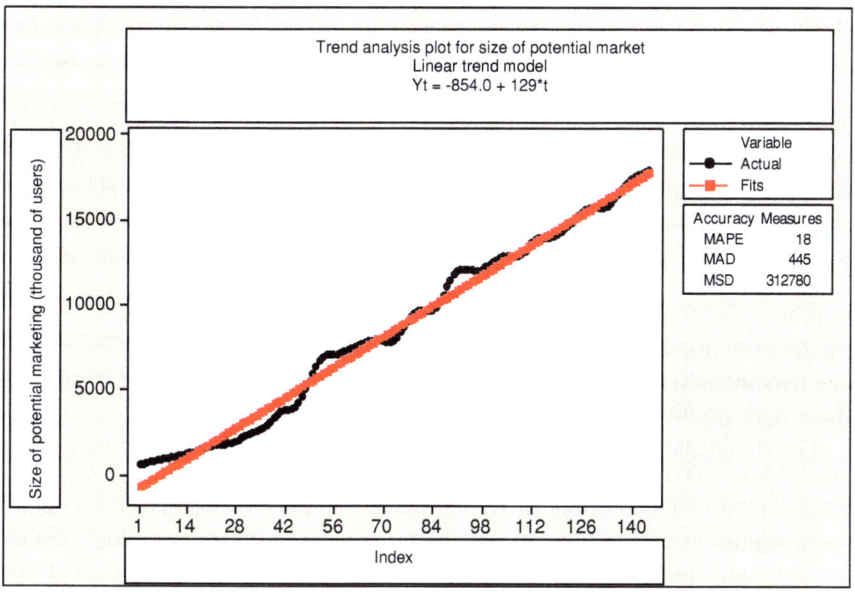

Fig. 11.3 Evolution of internet users and analysis of trend

Table 11.1 Regression analysis with explanatory factors

Predictor	Coefficients	Standard coefficients	T	Significance
Constant	−423.1	106.8	−3.96	0.000
Technological/legal framework	424.50	48.67	8.72	0.000
Size of potential market	0.09871	0.01203	8.21	0.000
Secure servers	41.9531	0.8521	49.24	0.000
Price of computers	0.14472	0.04062	3.56	0.001

Although the evolution of the potential market on the Internet does not appear to have experienced significant changes of trend (see Fig. 11.3), it might play a decisive role in explaining online-selling diffusion. In fact, the correlation between both variables equals 0.717. However, there is a 28.3 % of the variation of the sales volume from online-selling which is not explained by the potential market size. Therefore, additional factors must be considered to explain the diffusion of online-selling more precisely.

11.9 Results

By considering the determinants identified in the literature review, we ran a multiple regression analysis (see Table 11.1). The explanation of the total variability of the online sales volume is very high with the variables into the model (R^2 is 99.5 %). The model is significant as a whole (the F-value of the analysis of variance is 6523.13, with a p-value equal to zero), and the variables considered have coefficients significantly different from zero (with p-values lower that 0.05), therefore their presence is statistically justified in the explanatory model. With this analysis, we confirm the validity of the hypotheses H1, H2, H3, and H4.

The coefficient accompanying the variable Internet users is significantly different from zero ($p = 0.000$) and positive in sign, so we can consider the first hypothesis (H1) confirmed. Likewise, we note the presence of a structural change from the year 2001, since the coefficient corresponding to the dummy variable is significantly different from zero ($p = 0.000$). Thus, we can also confirm the second hypothesis (H2). As a whole, the development of the technological and legal framework positively influences the growth of e-commerce.

The significance of the coefficient associated with the variable price of computers ($p = 0.001$) and its positive sign allows us to validate H3. This positive effect on the evolution of online-selling shows that the possession of computers is not a significant barrier to accessing the Internet, in contrast to previous findings for the same market (Meseguer et al. 2002; Rodríguez-Ardura et al. 1999). The positive relation between the price of this product (one of the most exchanged on the Internet) and the sales turnover attributable to online-selling appears to be indicating that demand on the Internet is inelastic, and that other marketing tools (brand image, quality, customer service, etc.) may be more important to the consumers accessing this medium.

Finally, we find that the variable secure servers is significant in the model (the regression coefficient associated with this variable is significantly different from zero, with $p = 0.000$). Its effect on the evolution of online-selling has, moreover, a positive sign, since its growth positively affects the online sales volume.

11.10 Conclusions

This chapter defines a theoretical model to explain the evolution in B2C online-selling diffusion, which considers different types of drivers of this phenomenon. We also evaluate the validity of the model obtained for a particular economy—the Spanish one—using a database from varying sources (public and private) that are representative of the Spanish economy during the period 1996–2008.

The first of the drivers considered—the potential market on the Internet—reflects the influence of a marketing factor from the Internet firms' competitive environment. According to the results obtained, this driver has a decisive importance in the diffusion of online-selling, far exceeding that of the remaining drivers examined. We appear to have reached a critical mass of users, making up a market with a sufficiently attractive size to firms, thereby ensuring their increasing interest in online-selling.

However, the size of the potential market is not the only type of driver influencing online-selling diffusion. Also relevant are other drivers concerning the companies' technological–legal environment, their value proposition, and the technological infrastructure they have available for Internet services. Two elements, coming from the technological and legal environment, condition online-selling diffusion: the adoption of broadband technology and the definition of a legal framework of consumer protection on the Internet. From our findings we can deduce that in countries such as Spain, in which Internet penetration rates among the population are beginning to be high (over 50 % of the population), the diffusion of broadband plays a relevant role. This type of technology facilitates users' access to advanced systems of marketing communication, personalized attention, and so on, making the Internet a more attractive environment for shopping. Its importance is in line with the initiatives of various governments, such as those of the European Union, which are promoting the diffusion of broadband in order to improve the competitiveness and dynamism of their economies (European Commission 2002). Equally, the establishment of a legal framework on the question of privacy, although it cannot provide complete protection for consumers on the Internet, is shown to be necessary for the development of online-selling.

The next driver contemplated (differentiation strategy *versus* price leadership strategy) reflects the characteristics of the business strategies on the Internet. The fact that the price of computers (one of the most sold product categories on the Internet) has a significantly positive effect when explaining online-selling diffusion, according to the analytical model obtained, leads us to deduce, on the one hand, that the computer is no longer an indicator of the barriers to access to the Internet, at least in markets that have achieved a critical mass of users. On the other hand, the positive relation between the price levels on the Internet and the online sales volume shows that electronic markets do not lead to a generalized reduction in prices. Instead, this positive relation indicates the importance of traditional elements in the definition of a differentiated marketing strategy—providing greater value to the consumers, and contributing to building closer relationships with them.

The last driver considered (security in the offer on the Internet), relating to technological aspects of the value proposition, has also been shown to be significant in explaining online-selling. Once again, consumers' confidence in the security of the communications and commercial exchange mechanisms provided by firms is shown to encourage purchasing on the Internet.

As the online-selling diffusion is a dynamic phenomenon that is still in a relatively immature situation, the drivers identified here and their effects might change in the future. With the growing adoption of online-selling by new strata in the population not corresponding to the profile of the early Internet users (urban population, with a university education, income levels above the population average, and with computer equipment in the home) (Rodríguez-Ardura 2010), some of the behaviors observed (such as the lower price sensitivity, for example) might change. Therefore, it is important to continue testing the model with data from later time periods, either to confirm its validity or to refine it.

11.11 Summary

This chapter proposes and examines both external environmental drivers and internal organizational drivers, which can influence the diffusion of online-selling among firms through time. The validation of this model, which concerns the Spanish economy over a period of 13 years, shows the contribution of these drivers on consumer purchases to firms that undertake online-selling activities.

11.12 Review Questions

1. What are the external drivers for e-commerce?
2. Differentiate the external drivers from internal drivers for e-commerce.
3. What are the factors that affect online-selling?
4. How can online-selling be made a sustainable strategy by marketers?

References

Bhatnagar A, Misra S, Rao HR (2000) On risk, convenience, and Internet shopping behaviour. Commun ACM 43(11):98–105

Degeratu A, Rangaswamy A, Wu J (2000) Consumer choice behavior in online and traditional supermarkets: the effects of brand name, price and other search attributes marketing science and the Internet. Int J Res Mark 17(1):55–78

Dutta A (1997) The physical infrastructure for electronic commerce in developing nations: historical trends and the impact of privatization. Int J Electron Comm 2(1):61–83

Kau AK, Tang YE, Ghose S (2003) Typology of online shoppers. J Consum Mark 20(2):139–156

Meseguer A, Rodríguez-Ardura I, Vilaseca J (2003) Situación y perspectivas del comercio electrónico en España: un análisis a través del volumen del negocio electrónico. Esic Market 114:77–107

Molla A, Licker PS (2005) eCommerce adoption in developing countries: a model and instrument. Inform Manage 42(6):877–899

Stewart A, Mulye R, Deans KR, Palihawadana D (2002) e-Marketing in perspective: a three country comparison of business use of the Internet. Mark Intell Plan 20(4):243–251

Adams DA, Nelson RR, Todd PA (1992) Perceived usefulness, case of use, and usage of information technology: a replication. MIS Q pp 227–247

Agarwal R (2000) Individual acceptance of information technologies. In: Zmud RW (ed) Framing the domains of IT management, Pinnaflex Education Resources, pp 85–104

Ajzen I (1991) The theory of planned behavior. Organ Behav Hum Dec Process 50:179–211

Lederer Albert L, Maupin Donna J, Sena Mark P, Zhuang Youlong (2000) The technology acceptance model and the World Wide Web. Decis Support Syst 29(3):269–282

Amit R, Zott C (2001) Value creation in e-business. Strateg Manag J 22:493–520

Ansari A, Mela CF (2003) e-Customization. J Mark Res 40(2):131–145

Rezabakhsh B, Bornemann D, Hansen U, Schrader U (2006) Consumer power: a comparison of the old economy and the Internet economy. J Consum Policy 29(1):3–36

Ballantine J, Levy M, Powel P (1998) Evaluating information systems in small and mediiun-sized enterprises: issues and evidence. Eur J Inform Syst 7:241–251

Barua A (1995) C.H.kriebel, T. Mukhopadhyay, Information technology and business value: an analysis and empirical investigation. Inform Syst Res 6(1):3–23

Beatty RC, Shim JP, Jones MC (2001) factors influencing corporate web site adoption a time-based assessment. Inform Manag 38:337–354

Brynjolfsson E, Hitt LM (2000) Beyond computation: information technology, organizational transformation and business performance. J Econ Perspect 14(4):23–48

S. Mohapatra, *E-Commerce Strategy*, Springer Texts in Business and Economics, DOI: 10.1007/978-1-4614-4142-7,

Byrd TA, Turner DE (2001) An exploratory examination of the relationship between flexible IT Infrastructure and competitive advantage. Inform Manag 39:41–52

Deck CA, Wilson BJ (2006) Tracking customer search to price discriminate. Econ Inq 44(2):280–295

Kim C, Galliers RD (2004) Toward a diffusion model for Internet systems. Internet Res 14(2):155–166

Chang MK, Cheung W (2001) Determinants of the intention to use Internet/WWW at work: a confirmatory study. Inform Manage 39(1):1–14

Charalambos LL, Benbasat I, Albert SD (1995) Electronic data interchange and small organizations: adoption and impact of technology, MIS Q 19(4):465–485

Chau PYK (1996) An empirical assessment of a modified technology acceptance model. J Manag Inform Syst 13(2):185–204

Chaudhury A, Kuilboer JP (2002) E-Business and E-Commerce Infrastructure. McGraw-Hill, Boston, MA

Cragg P, Zinatelli N (1995) The evolution of information systems in small firms. Inform Manag 29:1–8

Arnott DC, Bridgewater S (2002) Internet, interaction and implications for marketing. Mark Intell Plan 20(2):86–95

McKnight DH, Choudhury V, Kacmar C (2002) The impact of initial consumer trust on intentions to transact with a web site: a trust-building model. J Strateg Inform Syst 11(3–4):297–323

Hoffman DL, Novak TP (2000) Advertising and pricing models for the web. In: D. Hurley, B. Kahin and Varian H (eds.) Internet publishing and beyond: the economics of digital information and intellectual property. MIT Press, Cambridge pp 45–61

Hoffman DL, Novak TP, Peralta M (1999) Information privacy in the marketspace: implications for the commercial uses of anonymity on the Web. Inform Soc 15(2):129–139

Davis FD (1989) Perceived usefulness, perceived ease of use, and user acceptance of information technology. MIS Q 13(3):319–339

Brynjolfsson E, Smith MD (2000) Frictionless commerce? A comparison on Internet and conventional retailers. Manag Sci 46(4):563–585

Clemons EK, Hann IH, Hitt LM (2002) Price dispersion and differentiation in online travel: an empirical investigation. Manage Sci 48(4):534–549

Huizingh EKRE (2002) Towards successful e-business strategies: a hierarchy of three management models. J Mark Manag 18(7–8):721–747

Mohamad E, Atif A, Saddik AEI (2002) classification of the state-of-the-art dynamic web services composition techniques. Int J Web Grid Serv 2(2):148–166

European Commission (2002) eEurope 2005: an information society for all

Sotgiu F, Ancarani F (2005) The drivers of e-tailers' price levels international review of retail. Distrib Consum Res 15(1):75–89

Zettelmeyer F (2000) Expanding to the Internet: pricing and communications strategies when firms compete on multiple channels. J Mark Res 37(3):292–308

Zettelmeyer F, Morton FS, Silva-Risso J (2006) How the Internet lowers prices: evidence from matched survey and automobile transaction data. J Mark Res 43(2):168–181

Pires GD, Stanton J, Rita P (2006) The Internet, consumer empowerment and marketing strategies. Eur J Mark 40(9–10):936–949

Dahlquist G, Björk A (1974) Numerical methods. Prentice-Hall, Englewood Cliffs, New Jersey

Iyer G, Pazgal A (2003) Internet shopping agents: virtual co-location and competition. Mark Sci 22(1):85–106

Lohse GL, Spiller P (1999) Internet retail store design: how the user interface influences traffic and sales. J Comput Mediat Commun 5 (2):0 doi: 10.1111/j.1083-6101.1999.tb00339.x

Girish HS, John TN (1992) Perceived strategic value of information systems: measurement, determinants, and effects. In: Proceedings of the thirteenth international conference on Information systems, pp 266–267

Harrison DA, Mykytyn PP, Riemenschneider CK (1997) Executive decisions about adoption of information technology in small business theory and empirical tests. Inform Syst Res 8(2):171–195
Fillis I, Johannson U, Wagner B (2004) Factors impacting on e-business adoption and development in the smaller firm. Int J Entrepreneurial Behav Res 10(3):178–191
Rodríguez-Ardura I, Martínez-López FJ (2008) Playing cat and mouse: consumer empowerment and marketing interaction on the Internet. Int J Bus Environ 2(2):201–214
Rodríguez-Ardura I, Meseguer A, Vilaseca J (2008a) El comercio electrónico en perspectiva: dinámica y desencadenantes. Investigaciones Europeas de Dirección y Economía de la Empresa 14(3):55–66
Rodríguez-Ardura I, Meseguer A, Vilaseca J (2008b) Factors influencing the evolution of e-commerce: an empirical analysis in a developed market economy. J Theor Appl Electron Commer Res 3(2):18–29
Rodríguez-Ardura I, Meseguer A, Hormigo E, Ryan G (1999) El futuro de la venta telemática en España a través de la World Wide Web: un modelo estructural. In: Proceedings XI (ed) Profesores Universitarios de Marketing. ESIC Editorial, Madrid, pp 315–331
Rodríguez-Ardura I (2010) Antoni Meseguer, Towards a longitudinal model of e-commerce: environmental, technological and organisational drivers of B2C adoption. Inform Soc 26(3):209–227
Rodríguez-Ardura I (2010) Marketing.com y comercio electrónico en la sociedad de la información, 3rd edn. Madrid: Pirámide and ESIC
Igbaria M, Guimaraes T, Davis GB (1995) Testing the determinants of microcomputer usage via a structural equation model. J Manag Inform Syst 11(4):87–114
Alba J, Lynch J, Weitz B, Janiszewski C, Lutz R, Sawyer A, Wood S (1997) Interactive home shopping: consumer, retailer, and manufacturer incentives to participate in electronic marketplaces. J Mark 61(3):38–53
Fisher J, Harindranath G (2004) Regulation as a barrier to electronic commerce in Europe: the case of the European fund management industry. Eur J Inform Syst 13(4):260–272
Lynch JG, Ariely D (2000) Wine online: search costs affect competition on price, quality, and distribution. Mark Sci 19(1):83–103
Gibbs JL, Kraemer KL (2004) A cross-country investigation of the determinants of scope of e-commerce use: an institutional approach. Electron Mark 14(2):124–137
Bailey JP (1998) Electronic commerce: prices and consumer issues for three products: books, compact discs and software. OECD, Technical Report OECD/GD 98:4
Phelps J, Nowak G, Ferrell E (2000) Privacy concerns and consumer willingness to provide personal information. J Public Pol Mark 19(1):27–41
Reynolds J (2000) eCommerce: a critical review. Int J Ret Distrib Manag 28(10):417–444
Vilaseca J, Torrent J, Meseguer A, Rodríguez-Ardura I (2007) An integrated model of adoption and development of e-commerce in companies. Int Adv Econ Res 13(2):222–241
Vilaseca J, Torrent J, Cabañero C, Castillo D, Colomé R, Díaz Á, Ficapal P, Jiménez AI, Lladós J, Martínez MJ, Meseguer A, Plana D, Rodríguez-Ardura I (2004) ICTs and transformations in Catalan companies. Universitat Oberta de Catalunya and Generalitat de Catalunya, Barcelona
Bakos JY (1997) Reducing buyer search costs: implications for electronic marketplaces. Manage Sci 43(12):1676–1692
Joesph PT SJ Ltd (2009) Ecommerce, PHI Learning, New Delhi
Sheehan KB, Hoy MG (2000) Dimensions of privacy concern among online consumers. J Public Pol Mark 19(1):62–73
Clay K, Krishnan R, Wolff E, Fernandes D (2002) Retail strategies on the web: price and non-price competition in the online book industry. J Ind Econ 50(3):351–367
Chiang K-P, Dholakia RR (2003) Factors driving consumer intention to shop online: an empirical investigation. J Consum Psychol 13(1–2):177–183
Kagan A, Lau K, Nusgart K (1990) Information system usage within small business firms. Entrepreneurship theory and practice. Spring, New Orleans, pp 25–37

Pitt LF, Berthon PR, Watson TR, Zinkhan G (2002) The Internet and the birth of real consumer power. Bus Horizons 45(6):7–14
Lee-Kelley L, Gilbert D, Mannicom R (2003) How e-CRM can enhance customer loyalty. Mark Intell Plan 21(4):239–248
Lee CS (2001) Modeling the business value of information technology. Inform Manag 39:191–210
Li M, Ye LR (1999) Information technology and firm performance: linking with environmental, strategic and managerial contexts. Inform Manag 35:43–51
Porter MA (2001) Strategy and the Internet. Harvard Bus Rev 79(3):62–78
Brown M, Pope N, Voges K (2003) Buying or browsing? An exploration of shopping orientations and online purchase intention. Eur J Mark 37(11–12):1.666–1.684
Smith MD, Brynjolfsson E (2001) Consumer decision-making at an Internet shopbot: brand still matters. J Ind Econ 49(4):541–558
Smith MD, Bailey JP, Brynjolfsson E (2000) Understanding digital markets: review and assessment, In: Brynjolfssony E, Kahin B (eds.). Understanding the digital economy: data, tools, and research. MIT Press, Cambridge pp 99–136
Smith MD (2002) The impact of shopbots on electronic markets. J Acad Mark Sci 30(4):446–454
Kung M, Monroe KB, Cosx JL (2002) Pricing on the Internet. J Prod Brand Manag 11(5):274–287
To ML, Ngai EWT (2006) Predicting the organisational adoption of B2C e-commerce: an empirical study. Ind Manag Data Syst 106(8):1133–1147
Baye MR, Morgan J, Scholten P (2004) Price dispersion in the small and in the large: evidence from an Internet price comparison site. J Ind Econ 52(4):463–496
Ward MR, Lee MJ (2000) Internet shopping, consumer search and product branding. J Prod Brand Manag 9(1):6–20
Malone SC (1985) Computerizing small business information systems, J Small Bus Manag pp 10–16
Mehrtens J, Cragg PB, Mills AM (2001) A model of Internet adoption by SMEs. Inform Manag 39(3):165–176
Mirchandani AA, Motwani J (2001) Understanding small business electronic commerce adoption: an empirical analysis. J Comp Inform Syst 70–73
Mandel N, Johnson EJ (2002) When web pages influence choice: effects of visual primes on experts and novices. J Consum Res 29(2):235–245
Napier HA (2001) Creating a Winning E-Business. Course technology, Boston
McGowan P, Durkin MG (2002) Toward an understanding of internet adoption at the marketing/entrepreneurship interface. J Mark Manag 18(3–4):361–377
Tallon Paul P, Kraemer Kenneth L (2003) Investigating the relationship between strategic alignment and IT business value: the discovery of a paradox. IGI Publishing, Hershey
Premkumar G, Margaret R (1999) Adoption of new information technologies in rural small businesses. Omega 27(4):467–484
Cagliano R, Caniato F, Spina G (2003) E-business strategy, How companies are shaping their supply chain through the Internet. Int J Oper Prod Manag 23(10):1142–1162
Javalgi R, Ramsey R (2001) Strategic issues of e-commerce as an alternative global distributions system. Int Mark Rev 18(4):376–391
O'Keefe RM, O'Connor G, Hsiang-Jui K (1998) Early adopters of the web as a retail medium: small company winners and losers. Eur J Mark 32(7–8):629–643
Suri R, Long M, Monroe KB (2003) The impact of the Internet and consumer motivation on evaluation of prices. J Bus Res 56(5):379–390
Riemenschneider CK, McKinney VR (1999) Assessing the adoption of Webbased E-Commerce for businesses. Electron Mark 9(1):9–13
Harrison T, Waite K, Hunter GL (2006) The Internet, information and empowerment. Eur J Mark 40(9–10):972–993

Jensen T, Kees J, Burton S, Turnipseed FL (2003) Advertised reference prices in an Internet environment: effects on consumer price perceptions and channel search intentions. J Interact Mark 17(2):20–33

Graeff TR, Harmon S (2002) Collecting and using personal data: consumers' awareness and concerns. J Consum Mark 19(4):302–318

The White House (1997) A framework for global electronic commerce, Washington DC, July

Dholakia UM, Rego LL (1998) What makes commercial Web pages popular? An empirical investigation of Web page effectiveness. Eur J Mark 32(7–8):724–736

Swaminathan V, Lepkowska-White E, Rao BP (1999) Browser or buyers in cyberspace? An investigation of factors influencing electronic exchange. J Comput Mediat Commun 5(2)

Pan X, Ratchford BT, Shankar V (2002) Can price dispersion in online markets be explained by differences in e-tailer service quality? J Acad Mark Sci 30(4):433–445

Xing X, Tang F-F, Yang ZL (2004) Pricing dynamics in the online consumer electronics market. J Prod Brand Manag 13(6):429–441

Xing X, Yang Z, Tang F-F (2006) A comparison of time-varying online price and price dispersion between multichannel and dotcom DVD retailers. J Interact Mark 20(2):3–20

Bakos YJ (1998) The emerging role of electronic marketplaces on the internet. Commun ACM 41(8):35–42

Liebermann Y, Stashevsky S (2002) Perceived risks as barriers to internet and e-commerce usage. Qualit Mark Res 5(2):291–300

Lee Z, Gosain S (2002) A longitudinal price comparison for music CDs in electronic and brick-and-mortar markets: pricing strategies in emergent electronic commerce. J Bus Strateg 19(1):55–71

Index

S. Mohapatra, *E-Commerce Strategy*, Springer Texts in Business and Economics, DOI: 10.1007/978-1-4614-4142-7,

MIX
Papier aus verantwortungsvollen Quellen
Paper from responsible sources
FSC® C105338

If you have any concerns about our products,
you can contact us on
ProductSafety@springernature.com

In case Publisher is established outside the EU,
the EU authorized representative is:
Springer Nature Customer Service Center GmbH
Europaplatz 3, 69115 Heidelberg, Germany

Printed by Libri Plureos GmbH
in Hamburg, Germany